D1560239

Army and Revolution

Army and Revolution

France 1815–1848

Douglas Porch

Department of History
University College of Wales, Aberystwyth

Routledge & Kegan Paul

London and Boston

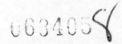

First published in 1974
by Routledge & Kegan Paul Ltd
Broadway House, 68–74 Carter Lane,
London EC4V 5EL and
9 Park Street,
Boston, Mass. 02108, U.S.A.

Printed in Great Britain by
The Camelot Press Ltd, London and Southampton

ISBN 0 7100 7460 3

Library of Congress Catalog Card Number 73-87317

To my parents

Contents

Preface and acknowledgments		ix
Abbreviations		x
Introduction		1
Chapter 1	The 1823 reserve mobilization and the 1824 law	9
2	The Restoration army, 1824–30	17
3	1830	34
4	Casimir Périer and the politics of stability	47
5	The Soult law	61
6	L'Arme Savante: Republicanism in the artillery	79
7	The Droits de l'Homme	93
8	Lunéville, 1834	100
9	Professional revolutionaries and secret societies, 1835–7	118
10	Strasbourg, 1836	127
11	Conclusion	138
Appendix I	Ministers of War, 1815–48	140
II	Regiments reported for republican activity, 1830–44	141
III	Garrisons and garrison towns	149

vii

Contents

IV Soldiers and NCOs arrested for republican activity,
1830–48   154

V   Officers reported to the War Minister for republican
activity, 1830–48   157

VI By-laws of the Société Philanthropique des Francs
Amis   160

Maps 1 Conscript literacy, 1827–9   161
2 Distribution of Protestants in France, 1824   162
3 Republican activity in the army, 1830–40   163

Notes   164

Bibliography   174

Index   181

Preface and acknowledgments

This book is a study of politics in the metropolitan French army between 1815 and 1848. It is concerned both with grass-roots political dissent and with day-to-day problems confronting soldiers of all ranks. I have tried to place political militancy in the army in the broader historical context of post-1815 France and to examine the military reforms instituted in reaction to it.

The Algerian army is not considered in this work because the catalysts for political activity in France – namely civilian republican agents – were not present in Africa. Consequently, Algeria was virtually free of political activity. In the only two military mutinies there, both in the same regiment, the soldiers demanded no political solution beyond the immediate redress of their grievance: freedom for a comrade accused of insulting an Arab noblewoman in 1833 and restoration of an extra pay allowance in 1834.[1]

I owe my thanks to the Master and Fellows of Corpus Christi College, Cambridge, for research grants which enabled me to complete my work. I should also like to thank those in England and France who have given me advice and encouragement over the last three years: especially the late Dr David Thomson, Mr J. P. T. Bury, Professor Louis Girard, Dr Christopher Andrew, Professor Douglas Johnson, and Gillian Flint.

Abbreviations

AEP   Archives de l'Ecole Polytechnique

AHG   Archives Historiques de la Guerre, Château de Vincennes

AN   Archives Nationales

AP   Archives Parlementaires

Introduction

'The Restoration and the army were inherently opposed right from the start.'[1] Seventy-five years later, Guillon's conclusion needs substantial reconsideration. Political opponents of a Bourbon Restoration undoubtedly existed in the army, which was still dazed by its Waterloo defeat. But military opposition to the Bourbons cannot be attributed only to the traditional political enmity of the Empire for the *ancien régime*.

The Restoration, it is true, declared war on an army that had deserted it in the hundred days. An ordinance of 16 July 1815 disbanded the Imperial army which, under Davout, had retired beyond the Loire as the allies approached Paris. Only the 16,000-man Strasbourg garrison disobeyed, demanding back-pay. The army dispersed, the government ignored earlier promises and accused nineteen officers who had rallied to Napoleon in the hundred days of treason. Colonel La Bedoyère, the first to lead his regiment into revolt, was executed on 19 August. Marshal Ney, 'the bravest of the brave', fell before a firing squad in Paris, while General Mouton-Duvernet was executed in Lyon and General Chartran at Lille. Several generals, including Belliard, Berton, Cambronne, Debelle, Decaen, Drouot, Dufour and Orano, were jailed and others exiled.

General Marmont, who had followed Louis XVIII to Ghent during the hundred days, protested against these harsh reprisals: 'Unjust, deadly and absurd consequences will surely be the result.'[2] Baron Pasquier echoed Marmot: 'These examples . . . far from producing the desired effect, put a large number of soldiers in a vengeful mood and resulted in a number of conspiracies.'[3]

In the south white terrorists attacked returning veterans; Marshal Brune was shot at Avignon and General Ramel at Toulouse, while soldiers of the 13th Infantry Regiment were massacred at Nîmes. Others were beaten or jailed.[4] Major Barrès, sailing from Brest to Bordeaux to avoid the terrorists, noted that veterans met only hostility in the south.[5]

In Paris a commission convened in October 1815 to examine

1

the conduct of officers during the brief return of the 'usurper', and Marshal Clarke zealously scaled down the mammoth Napoleonic armies to a size acceptable both to the allies and to the Bourbons. More than 15,000 officers had been dismissed and in part replaced by émigrés of limited experience and ability when the ex-Napoleonic Marshal Gouvion-Saint-Cyr took over the War Ministry in 1817.[6]

The new War Minister and the moderate Richelieu government promised a new era for the army. Saint-Cyr quietly retired many of the 387 ex-émigré generals[7] and reorganized the army on a new legal foundation. His 1818 law was immediately hailed as an attempt to reconcile legitimist and 'grognard'. Limited conscription was legislated, promotion regulations were fixed to prevent favouritism and, most important, a trained reserve was established incorporating Napoleonic veterans not employed in the new army.

Though opposed by conservatives, the law was welcomed by moderates, liberals and Napoleonic 'débris'. Armand Carrel, the future editor of the liberal *National* and a graduate of Saint-Cyr, praised 'la charte de l'armée', while the violently anti-Bourbon General Lamarque welcomed the law's democratic provisions: 'Through his law, Marshal Saint-Cyr hoped to eliminate these abuses of power and to open the door to lower-class officers who were in danger of losing all their rights. He was well acquainted with the court's attitudes and with the gluttony of an encroaching aristocracy.'[8]

Unlike the Bourbons, who sought to separate the army from the nation, Saint-Cyr believed the army should be drawn from the nation and that, as a national institution, it should reflect the values and aspirations as well as the social make-up of society. Guizot, who also supported the bill, pointed out that Saint-Cyr saw the army as a microcosm of the state:[9]

An army in his [Saint Cyr's] estimate was a small nation springing from a large one, strongly organized . . . having defined rights and duties and well trained . . . to serve its country effectively when called upon. Upon this idea of an army . . . the principles of the bill were naturally framed. Every class in the state was required to assist in the formation of this army. Those who were ambitious . . . were compelled in the first instance to pass examinations and then to acquire by close study the particular knowledge that is necessary to their position. The term of service, active and in reserve, was long and made military life, in reality, a career. The obligations imposed, the privileges promised, and the rights recognized for all, were guaranteed by the bill. Besides these general principles, the bill had an immediate result which Saint-Cyr ardently desired. It enrolled again in the new army, under the head of veteran and reserve, the remains of the old discharged legions . . . a special charter, it secured their future.

Saint-Cyr's law was based on Revolutionary principle and Imperial experience. He resurrected conscription, circumspectly renamed 'l'appel', in an effort to lift the army back to fighting strength. The Bourbons did not succeed in attracting more than 3,500 volunteers into the army in any one year, and in 1816 directed that all volunteers enter the Royal Guard. Although article 12 of the 1814 charter stated that 'conscription is abolished', article 1 of the law legalized the draft: 'The army relies entirely on volunteers but resorts to the following rules when understaffed.'

Conscription and the system of paid replacements were products of the Revolution and were therefore opposed by the Ultras. The royalist Chateaubriand denounced 'the republican principle of conscription' and claimed that national conscription was incompatible with the monarchy: 'How can we permit under a monarchy a recruitment system whose equalitarian principles smack of democracy?'[10] Through eloquent persuasion, however, Saint-Cyr managed to convince the majority of the Chamber of the importance of conscription. 'Large standing armies, however they are made up, drive nations into wars of aggression. We cannot completely avoid this as it is the case throughout Europe. But we have done all in our power to limit the danger by making our regular army as small as possible.' He continued in a more liberal vein, however, that conscription was a 'fundamental principle inherent in every political society, a principle indispensable to its existence'.[11]

Saint-Cyr's next consideration was a reserve. The term of service was set at six years, which in practice often worked out at four years, with a six-year reserve obligation for veterans written into article 23: 'NCOs and soldiers returning home after completion of service will, in the event of war, be called upon for six years' territorial service as veterans. These veterans may marry and take up a trade.' This provision theoretically satisfied the need for a flexible defence force, swelled and strengthened by the 'demi-soldes' – ex-Napoleonic soldiers living on half-pay.

On 26 January 1818 Saint-Cyr complained to the Chamber that opponents of a reserve in reality distrusted the old Bonapartist soldiers who would make it up:[12]

We must be candid, for the question of the army is a national question. We must ask whether we have two armies and two nations, one of which is cursed and considered unworthy to

3

serve king and country. And to return to a question close to my heart, we must ask if we will again call on those soldiers who made France great, or if we will condemn them as a threat to our security.

Saint-Cyr's reserve embodied the Revolutionary ideal of the citizen soldier, living as a civilian but ready to defend the nation in time of danger. This reserve was always suspect in the eyes of the Ultras, both for its complement of Napoleonic soldiers and its negation of the principle of a small, professional royal army.

But the liberal spirit of the 1818 law was contravened by General Latour-Maubourg, who succeeded Saint-Cyr in November 1819. In the atmosphere of political reaction following the 1820 assassination of the Duc de Berry promotional favouritism continued despite the guarantees of 1818, while reserve organization and training were neglected. Consequently, tension rode high in the army, as many officers testified. Royal Guard Colonel Fantin des Odoards noted royalist distrust of ex-Napoleonic officers in his regiment;[13] Lieutenant Saint-Chamans reported that royalist 'gentilshommes' and ex-Napoleonic 'vilains' in his regiment dined and worshipped separately,[14] and Major Barrès, a Napoleonic veteran, narrowly escaped dismissal in 1820 for failing to toast the king with suitable enthusiasm.[15]

The French Left was ill prepared to exploit this tension. A small, heterogeneous group, it had been dominated until 1820 by Benjamin Constant and the parliamentary liberals. Horrified by the authoritarian excesses of the Republic and the Empire, liberals welcomed the monarchy in 1815 and worked to place it on a sound constitutional basis. Ministers, they said, should be responsible to a parliamentary majority rather than to the king. The judicial system should be separated from the administration to minimize political influence. Exceptional courts, secret trials and torture should be outlawed. The Council of State, the Napoleonic advisory body and court of appeals retained by the Restoration, was attacked for uniting administrative and judicial functions. Liberals also demanded an end to press censorship and an increase in the number of electors to give the middle class a larger voice in government. Economically, they were measured free-traders, although many admitted that tariffs were made necessary by foreign protectionism. Constant especially criticized restrictions on cereal imports and the consequent inflation of bread prices. The economist, Bastiat, attempted to popularize the free trade theories of Cobden through the 'Association pour la liberté des échanges'.[16]

Between 1816 and 1819 the moderate tactics of the parliamentary

Left appeared to show dividends. Press censorship was abolished and a liberal press law voted in. The army was reorganized on a liberal basis and a trained reserve established. In the elections of September 1819, the Left won twenty-five new seats while the Right lost ten. But the election of Grégoire, a regicide deputy of the Convention and a constitutionalist bishop in the Revolution, frightened the moderate chief minister, Decazes, who abandoned his left-centre supporters and sought a majority on the Right. When Saint-Cyr protested, he was replaced by Latour-Maubourg.[17]

But this mild reaction escalated after Louvel assassinated the Duc de Berry, the last Bourbon heir, on 13 February 1820. The Right claimed that liberals had created an atmosphere conducive to anarchy. Nodier wrote in the *Journal des Débats*: 'I saw Louvel's dagger, it was a liberal idea', while Chateaubriand cried: 'The hand which held the dagger is not the most culpable.'[18]

Decazes quickly pushed through two measures re-establishing press censorship and legalizing internment without trial. But the Right refused to forgive his past alliances with the liberals, and he was soon replaced by Richelieu. The new government, despite opposition from Constant, Lafayette, Manuel and General Foy in the Chamber, tightened press censorship still further and authorized fines and imprisonment for offending journalists. A new electoral law was passed on 12 June, as demonstrations rocked the streets of Paris, creating 172 new seats to be voted for by the wealthier electors.[19]

With the parliamentary liberals reduced to silence, the militant Left organized to exploit popular discontent. It had few positive ideas on the form of a future French government, but was motivated by a fierce patriotism and a hatred of the Bourbons. Led by young men like Cavaignac, Marrast, Teste, Blanqui, Trélat, Raspail and Rey, it drew its support mainly from Paris students and a handful of ex-Napoleonic soldiers both inside and outside the army. In the provinces, and especially in the east, ex-students and young lawyers and doctors were often attracted to the Left, though not in great numbers.[20] They believed that the army, because of its Imperial heritage, would spearhead the revolution.

Indeed, the army appeared ripe for revolution. Waterloo and the return of the French royal family in the baggage trains of the allies had marked a humiliating end to a period of military success unparalleled since the Romans. The application of the Revolutionary *levée en masse* in the face of foreign invasion in 1792 had transformed the French army from the small professional force then common in Europe into a large national army. This army, bearing the torch of the Revolution, streamed across the frontiers to liberate

Europe from its repressive aristocracy. At the height of its Imperial power in 1812, France stretched from the Pyrenees to Hamburg, from Parma to the Atlantic. The Dalmatian coast was under its control; Spain, the Confederation of the Rhine, Switzerland, Italy and the Duchy of Warsaw were client states; Prussia, Austria and the Kingdom of Denmark and Norway were reduced, through military force, to reluctant allies. European hegemony had been won on the battlefield and French regimental standards bore the names of stunning victories such as those of Valmy, Rivoli, Jena, Wagram, Austerlitz and Borodino. 'Among the people', wrote the historian George Bourgin of the generation of 1848, 'the idea of France as the source and propagator of liberty, lived on as an instinctive ideal. The glories of the Revolutionary and Imperial wars were not forgotten – Waterloo had been a catastrophe for France and for humanity. The treaties of 1815 were detested, not just because France had suffered, but because they had enslaved the peoples of Europe.'[21]

The success of nationalist revolutions in Piedmont and Spain encouraged the Left to plot the government's overthrow. The first attempt by ex-Napoleonic Colonel Fabvier and other *demi-soldes* backed by students to lead the legions of the Meurthe and the Côtes-du-Nord and the 2nd and 5th Royal Guard Regiments in Paris to revolt in August 1820 fizzled out when officers warned police, who jumped on the conspirators. The plotters had counted on ex-colleagues in these regiments who, though at first friendly, refused to support an insurrection. The following year, republicans turned to the east hoping to provoke a rebellion in one of the large frontier garrisons which would gain the support of the notoriously patriotic Alsatians. Colonel Caron, a *demi-solde*, was arrested in July 1821 by soldiers in the Colmar garrison who, warned by officials, at first pretended to follow him. Plans to raise the garrisons at Belfort and Neufbrisach in December collapsed when local republicans refused to join until the insurrection promised success. The same year, the retired General Berton was arrested when students at the cavalry school at Saumur refused to join his conspiracy. In June 1822 four sergeants in the 45th Infantry Regiment at La Rochelle, led by Napoleonic veteran, Sergeant Boirès, were arrested and executed for plotting to overthrow the government.[22]

Though Leftist attempts to provoke a military rebellion failed, army opposition to the Bourbons seemed to be so widespread that many doubted the government would move to crush the Spanish revolutionaries in 1823. But the army, with the exception of Saint-Cyr's reserve, remained loyal throughout the nine-month campaign. The Bourbons seized the opportunity to abolish the reserve in

1824 to insulate the army against outside political influence: maximum army strength was increased from 240,000 to 400,000 men organized into sixty-five infantry regiments, twenty light infantry regiments, fifty cavalry regiments, ten artillery regiments and three regiments of engineers. The length of service was raised from six to eight years.

This law reintroduced the traditional concept of a small professional army. It encouraged re-enlistment and the professionalization of cadres, nullifying in part the liberal principles of 1818.

As no military plots or insurrections were recorded in the last seven years of the régime, Guillon concluded that the Spanish campaign had reconciled the diverse political elements in the army into a single force dedicated to serving France.[23]

Although the political effects of the Spanish campaign were undeniably salutary, the root causes of unrest and revolution in the army were not political, but rather economic and personal. Here lies the key to the continued discontent in the army and its desertion of the Bourbons in 1830.

The world of great issues had disappeared in 1814, and with it that of great opportunities. The real attraction of the Revolution and the Empire lay not so much in their political idealism as in the possibility of rapid personal advancement.

The government, the civil service and the army aged greatly after 1815. A young soldier could no longer hope to imitate the career of Marshal Ney – son of an artisan, volunteer in 1787 and Marshal of France in 1804 at the age of thirty-six. The Restoration only offered the sixty-two-year-old Prince de Hohenlohe, promoted to Marshal in 1827. This tension between the generations was a major literary theme of the period: Stendhal, Balzac and others portrayed young heroes attempting to carve out careers in an overcrowded capital. Julien Sorel lamented the passing of Napoleon for those who, like himself, were well educated but financially unable to stake out a career. Vigny echoed the frustrations of an unrewarding military career:

> J'ai servi seize ans la Restauration
> Moi, dont elle a laissé vieillir l'ambition
> Dans les honneurs obscurs de quelque légion.

In short, opposition to the Bourbons in the army cannot be reduced to political discontent. It was also rooted in the reaction against the gerontocracy which dominated the Restoration and the July Monarchy. Castellane realized this when he complained that 1830 was a repeat performance of 1815, with the *voltigeurs de Napoléon* succeeding the *voltigeurs de Louis XIV*. The reinstatement of ex-Napoleonic soldiers did not appease military discontent, but rather aggravated it.

The history of the Restoration army after 1823 demonstrates that political opposition in the army went hand in hand with frustrated ambition.

The 1823 reserve mobilization and the 1824 law

The Spanish War of 1823 marked a turning point for the French army. The military conspiracies of the previous years had increased conservative anxieties over the political reliability of the army and liberals seized the unpopular war as an opportunity to provoke a military rebellion and overthrow the government.

The Spanish revolution had been touched off in January 1820 in Cadiz as troops bound for South America mutinied in protest against irregular pay, poor equipment and bad food. By March other regiments had mutinied in Galicia, Navarre and Madrid, as a severe economic depression induced many civilians to follow the army's example and to agitate for constitutional reforms.

This situation was aggravated in June 1822 when conservative royalists, backed by King Ferdinand VII, attempted unsuccessfully to occupy Madrid with loyal guard regiments. In the wake of the attempted coup, leftists forced the moderate constitutionalist government to resign. Rather than serve the new extremist government which had made the king a virtual prisoner, royalists in Catalonia, Navarre and Aragon revolted and proclaimed a regency.

The French government, led by Chateaubriand, decided that military intervention was imperative to end the anarchy across the Pyrenees and to remove the home threat from left-wing supporters of the Spanish rebels. And in April 1823, ignoring the advice of chief minister Joseph de Villèle who feared a protracted guerilla struggle and who expressed reservations over the reliability of the army, the government gave the order to invade.

Liberals saw the chance of striking a blow against the monarchy. Béranger urged the army to turn the tables on the government in a popular song: 'Brav' soldats, v'la l'ord' du jour; Gard' à vous! Demi-tour!' Simultaneously, French exiles in Spain bombarded the army mustering on the Pyrenees with propaganda reminding them of their proud imperial heritage and demanding a regency for the young Napoleon II, in Austrian exile.

Armand Carrel, a Saint-Cyr graduate and future editor of the liberal daily, *National*, reported that the Spanish liberals were

9

themselves confident the French army would turn against the government rather than break with its revolutionary tradition: 'The insurgents' faith in the feelings of a country which they looked on as the guardian of liberty, extended to the very army which was preparing to move against them.'[1]

The Prussian ambassador to France corroborated this opinion: 'The King', he said, 'cannot depend on any regiment in such a controversial war. A tricolour, even one waved by Spaniards in the South of France, would be enough to touch off a civil war and topple the government.'[2]

However, Colonel Saint-Chamans claimed that the threat of a military revolution was exaggerated by the Director of Police, Franchet-Despérey, who dispatched to French officials unfounded accusations of treason against many ex-Napoleonic officers. The Duc d'Angoulême, commander of the Spanish expedition, burned these reports and told accused officers to prove their loyalty in the coming campaign.[3]

General Pelleport also believed that the army's loyalty was never in question:[4]

> The so-called liberal spirit of the army in the Pyrenees was discussed at length at the time. Some people even said that the general staffs were involved in the conspiracy which, through lack of energy, never got off the ground. I did not know just how much truth there was in this assertion. Nevertheless, I do believe that agitators tried to use the war to induce the army to make, in their own words, an about-face. But I also think that the importance of this attempt, scotched by the aloofness of the army, always loyal to its standard, was exaggerated by both sides.

Pelleport's opinion was confirmed when on 7 April a French column under Waterloo veteran General Vallin fired on a band of 150 French and Italian liberals who had urged them to revolt.

Carrel, bitterly disappointed, reasoned that ex-Napoleonic officers had been brought to heel by periodic Bourbon purges, while younger officers welcomed any chance for war and promotion: 'They were just as ready to march against the Holy Alliance as against the Cortez [the Spanish Parliament] . . . the cause did not matter to them. This is not a very laudable attitude, but it is drilled in the military schools – unfortunately, with some success.'[5]

Furthermore, he said, the La Rochelle affair had intimidated dissidents: 'These young men were chosen for their example, for their belief in liberty in all its nobility, impartiality, unattainability.

After their deaths, observed only by indifferent eyes, the dream was seen for what it was worth.'[6]

Although the liberals failed to provoke a military rebellion, they were successful in their efforts to undermine Saint-Cyr's reserve. The Saint-Cyr law of 1818 required six years' active service followed by six years' reserve duty. In 1818 conservatives had opposed the reserve measure fearing the political unreliability of a citizen reserve. Nevertheless, on the eve of the invasion, the government brought the army up to strength by mobilizing a portion of this reserve. Article 2 of the law stipulated that, in the event of a reserve call-up, the last conscript contingent to be released from active service should be the first recalled. Accordingly, the government directed the class of 1816, released from active service only three months previously, to report to designated assembly points for assignment to line regiments.

As reservists gathered in late May and early June, reports of rioting and insubordination began to reach Paris. The Prefect of the Bas-Rhin reported that angry reservists at Strasbourg had cut off their buttons and torn their insignia from their shakos. Strasbourg liberals, organized into a 'Council of Regence for Napoleon II', urged veterans to revolt and proclaim the empire:[7]

THE REGENCY COUNCIL OF NAPOLEON II TO THE
WORTHY ALSATIANS

The lily is about to blossom. Your sweet youth, filled with memories of the glorious and immortal Napoleon, will be acclaimed by the good people of France in re-establishing the dynasty which has never ceased to reign in your hearts. You will joyfully welcome the august heir in the venerated name of Napoleon II. This empire, the only one worthy of France, will make you forget the odious reign of the Bourbons.

Henceforth, you will no longer bow to the demands of the Holy Alliance. Rally to the tricolour.

Alsatians! The hour is at hand! The Fatherland expects you to vindicate the reputation won in 1814 and 1815!

Long Live Napoleon II!

Long Live Liberty!

Elsewhere in the east, veterans at Colmar threatened mass desertions and the Prefect at Metz expressed the fear that the incorporation into line regiments of the city's 900 mutinous reservists would seriously undermine discipline. Vosges reservists openly declared their desire to join the Spanish revolutionaries: 'We have served six years for the King! We shall serve six for Mina! [an insurgent Spanish general].'[8] And police in the Jura underlined the rebellious mood of reservists there: 'They said that nothing could force them to cross the Spanish frontier. That they would rather take on the whole army, and that if they were led there, they would turn on the French.'[9] Trouble was also reported among veterans at Besançon, Givet and Chalôns. Reservists from the Yonne insulted priests at Auxerre and shouted, 'Vive Napoléon! Vive la liberté! Vive Mina!'

In the north and west, shouts of 'à moi la bande de Mina' were heard among veterans from Pas-de-Calais, Aisne and the Nord, while the Prefect of Calvados had to call in police to put down a mutiny of reservists from his department and neighbouring Manche. Officers crushed mutinies at Alençon and Rouen with drawn swords. A report to the Minister of the Interior pointed out that republicans had been especially successful in undermining reserve discipline in departments bordering the Loire and even in the conservative Ille-et-Vilaine.[10]

Liberals upbraided Nantes reservists for marching against the Spanish liberals in the name of the absolutist Bourbons: 'They said they were fools to prop up an absolutist foreign government while their own was much the same.'[11]

Trouble was also reported among veterans at La Rochelle, Clermont-Ferrand, Lyon and Grenoble, and in the Midi at Toulon, Marseille, Nîmes, Mende and Toulouse. Trouble was so widespread that Franchet-Despérey instructed the War Minister to hold troops in reserve to put down the revolution he believed was imminent.[12]

In all, thirty-five departmental legions were cited for insubordination and seditious behaviour. Discontent, however, was probably more widespread than this; many departmental reports are missing, while Prefects tended to stress the disloyalty of visiting detachments over local misbehaviour.

Frequent cries of 'Vive Mina' testify that liberals had successfully canvassed reserve detachments. Yet closer examination reveals that political opposition to the Spanish war among reservists masked a more fundamental discontent over the conditions of their mobilization.

Prefect reports confirm that veterans were enraged over being called up barely three months after their release from six years' active service. The Prefect of the Basses-Alpes claimed that this was the root cause of reserve discontent:[13]

These soldiers are generally very discontented and very loath to be mobilized. They complain that they were discharged on 31 December only to be recalled a few months later. There has even been some indiscreet – not to put too fine a point on it – criticism of the government. Their contact with local men in the inns was bound to lead to trouble.

At La Rochelle, veterans refused to accept uniforms of the 52nd Infantry Regiment claiming that the government planned to keep them for several years more. In many towns, wives of newly released soldiers attempted to prevent their departure. And in Metz, civilians came to blows with soldiers and police ordered to arrest absentee veterans.

Elsewhere, government unpreparedness brought reserve discontent to the boil. In Troyes, for example, 181 veterans from the Seine-et-Marne rioted after having gone without food all day: 'We are no longer soldiers, we are slaves; if we are given arms, we will not use them.' The rioters were appeased only when the mayor ordered food to be distributed.[14] This same scene was repeated in Alençon and several other towns.

General Villette, commander of the 3rd Military Division at Metz, complained that as the War Minister had laid down no instructions for the incorporation of reservists into line regiments, reserve contingents had joined their regiments amid complete confusion. In most cases colonels could not provide uniforms for the new men, much less adequate quarters and rations.[15]

Several Prefects pointed out that reservists, many of whom had retired with the rank of corporal or sergeant, were enraged at being placed in line regiments as private soldiers: 'They were therefore very eager to return home and forget about the army.'

Only 16,000 of 22,000 reservists answered the call-up. And Prefects agreed that those who did report would cause trouble.

The Spanish expedition was hailed as a great conservative victory. Not only had the army remained loyal, but in the March 1824 general elections the 110 seats held by the liberals were reduced to nineteen. Having defeated the Left both at home and abroad, the government now turned its new power against the reserve, viewed as a liberal spanner in basically sound works.

In May 1824 the government presented the new chamber with a proposal to raise maximum army strength from 240,000 to 400,000 men, the annual call-up from 40,000 to 60,000, the term of service from six to eight years, and to modify reserve organization by abolishing the reserve requirement for veterans: 'After careful consideration of past experience, His Majesty's government decided to reorganize the reserve . . . our bill replaces the veterans' reserve with a reserve of young soldiers.'[16] The reserve was henceforth to be composed of conscripts who, for financial or other reasons, were not incorporated into the active army but sent home untrained to await call-up in case of a national emergency. This usually amounted to half of the annual contingent.

But parliamentary liberals refused to let the conservative proposal go unchallenged, and on 11 May Marshal Gouvion-Saint-Cyr rose to defend his reserve in the Chamber of Peers. The fault, he claimed, lay not in the citizen reserve but in poor organization. He pointed out that article 23 of his 1818 law required parliament to organize a company of *légionnaires-vétérans* in each canton; but as these never materialized, smooth reserve mobilization had been rendered impossible.

Poor organization and planning created other problems. Saint-Cyr said that to avoid recalling reservists immediately after their release and realizing war was imminent, the government should have postponed the release of the 1816 contingent. He also criticized the government for returning the reservists as private soldiers. This, he said, would never have happened had a proper reserve cadre existed: 'The NCOs who formed it [the reserve] and who would have kept their rank had they joined a veterans corps, had to enter their new regiments as privates, and were therefore undeservedly demoted.'[17]

Saint-Cyr contended that the reserve mobilization was in any case unnecessary, as only 40,000 troops had participated in the Spanish war. Criticizing the nationwide call-up, he suggested it would have been preferable to mobilize several reserve classes in the departments bordering Spain. Southerners, he noted, were always eager to participate in a Spanish war. The behaviour of reservists in the Midi, however, casts doubts on this assumption.

Saint-Cyr concluded that the government had betrayed the spirit of 1818 which laid down that locally organized reserve units would be called out only in case of a national emergency; the Spanish war was not a national emergency:[18]

> In the conviction [he said] that the King will find in the
> veterans, in the event of a real crisis, an effective reserve,
> enthusiastic and capable of repulsing enemies foolish enough
> to invade our land, I consider this proposal unnecessary,
> unjust . . . and, moreover, impossible to execute.

But Saint-Cyr found little support among the peers and the new proposal was passed by 110 to 28 votes.

Poor reserve organization was also criticized in the Chamber of Deputies by ex-Napoleonic General Foy, who argued that the mustering of 16,000 reservists in such inauspicious circumstances had proved the viability of a citizen reserve:[19]

> The situation demanded not a reserve mobilization, but an
> additional conscript levy . . . The men called up were
> stunned . . . These were young men humiliated by being
> stripped of their rank . . . dissatisfied by having been cheated
> of the opportunity to sell themselves as replacements in the
> 1822 call-up . . . After what happened in 1823, if I find
> anything surprising, it is not that 6,000 veterans were missing,
> but that 16,000 reported to their assigned destinations.

He objected that the two years' additional service prescribed by
the new proposal did not compensate for a trained reserve. He also
pointed out that military expenditure would climb drastically.

But many conservatives refused to believe that reserve discontent-
ment had been provoked by dissatisfaction over material conditions
and saw it rather as a preplanned political conspiracy. General
Paultre de la Motte, commander of the 19th Military Division at
Lyon, had claimed in June 1823 that republicans had converted the
reservists in the five months between their release from active service
and their mobilization: 'Your Excellency is aware that the enemies
of the government began to subvert that part of the army they knew
to be the most experienced and whose recall appeared imminent from
the moment the conscript class of 1816 was discharged. These
trouble-makers seem to me to have been remarkably successful.'[20]
'Since their discharge from the service', wrote General Villette,
echoing General Paultre de la Motte, 'they have been badly
indoctrinated.'[21]
In the Chamber, conservatives argued that civilian life was
incompatible with military discipline. General Partouneaux pointed
out that veteran reluctance to return to active duty was often
exploited by opponents of the government:[22]

> He returns home: he soon grows used to the pleasures and
> independence of civilian life; he can marry, own property,
> go back to his work; but he can still be called up and taken
> away from his wife and children. He is worried, dissatisfied
> with his position . . . very often he refuses to rejoin his regiment.
> Now you have a deserter, a malcontent, a fugitive, ready to
> break any law and take up arms against the government.

Viscount Dutertre, representing the Pas-de-Calais, argued that
the political unreliability of a citizen reserve had been conclusively
demonstrated in 1823: 'The departments which they crossed', he
contended, 'heard treacherous shouts and witnessed serious insubordination . . . These are the facts of the matter.' He suggested
that a trained reserve was good in theory but unmanageable in

practice: 'A veteran reserve is better trained, but far harder to mobilize.'[23]

In a last-ditch attempt to salvage the reserve, Baron Cuivier, a member of the Conseil d'Etat, attacked conservative fears of a military revolution. The military, he pointed out, had never spearheaded revolution: 'They have tried to raise other bogeys and to present a large call-up as a way of getting rid of parliament and subjugating the country . . . but a large army has never given rise to revolution.'[24]

However, partisans of the reserve were overwhelmed by a massive 248–70 majority.

The abolition of the reserve eliminated one element of political instability in the army. But by removing the last vestiges of the revolutionary 'nation in arms' from French military organization, conservatives left the army open to defeat by a numerically superior enemy.

The year 1824 also signalled a new era in military opposition. The plots and rebellions which had racked the army before 1822 were inspired by ex-imperial officers and NCOs who hoped a military insurrection would bring back the Empire.

At the time, liberals and conservatives viewed veteran agitation as yet another of these post-1815, politically inspired insurrections. Carrel blamed the failure of the liberal attempts to provoke a military rebellion in 1823 on, among other things, the scarcity of hostile ex-Napoleonic officers and NCOs in the army: 'No more old soldiers in the army of the Pyrenees, and so no more bitter memories associated with the new regime.' He also claimed that most infantry and cavalry soldiers were from rural areas and consequently ignorant of politics.[25]

But the 1823 reserve revolt was none of these things. Young soldiers with no Imperial service were simply angered by the harsh conditions forced on them by the government. The era of political conspiracies in the army was at an end, but the government had not yet realized that discontent with the conditions of service posed a greater threat to military stability than political militancy.

Chapter 2

The Restoration army, 1824–30

A study of the army's role in the 1830 revolution must begin with a discussion of France and the Restoration army after the 1823 Spanish campaign. This chapter examines the reasons behind the military inertia of 1830 when, for the most part, the army either refused or only half-heartedly defended the Bourbon regime. Although Restoration France did not subsequently witness the spectacular series of plots and military insurrections which characterized military instability before 1823, an undercurrent of political opposition nevertheless permeated the army. This latent political resentment was aggravated by discontent over certain Restoration military policies. Together, they help to explain the pessimistic mood of many officers in the last years of the Restoration.

Political opposition under the Restoration presented an informal array of political opinions ranging from Bonapartism to liberalism. Though powerful, this opposition was without a formal party structure and was committed only to a relatively vague programme of press freedom, requiring the Cabinet to be responsible to the Chamber rather than to the king, and electoral reform.

The Church especially was attacked by the Left for its strong support of the regime. In 1815 returning émigrés realized that the fashionable agnosticism of the *ancien régime* had helped to undermine the religious faith they believed so essential to social stability. 'The throne of Saint-Louis', Chateaubriand wrote, 'without the religion of Saint-Louis is an absurd supposition.'[1]

The Church, they thought, must be the regime's cornerstone: Catholicism was established in France by the Charter, and religious orders, including the Jesuits, were encouraged. Bishops were permitted one school in their diocese free from central University control. Seminaries increased in number and religious orders flourished.[2]

Conservative lay groups like the Chevaliers de la Foi, formed in 1801 to counter masonic influence, embroiled the Church in political battles. In 1821 the conservative Richelieu government named Monsignor Frayssinous to head the University, thereby placing a cleric in control of the nation's educational system. He promptly dismissed unpopular and controversial professors, and replaced many with priests. By 1830 fully one-third of University teaching posts were in the hands of the Church. A February 1821 ordinance also gave bishops the right to inspect royal colleges in their dioceses.[3]

Liberals, however, resented Church attempts to gain political influence and, especially after their 1824 election defeat, hoped to undermine the regime with an anti-clerical counter-offensive. They claimed that traditional Gallican rights were threatened by Rome's influence on the government through the Congregation, a secret, aristocrat-dominated society. The liberal press, led by the *Constitutionnel*, launched a vituperative offensive against clerical abuses, including the refusal of sacraments to liberals, to owners of church lands appropriated in the Revolution, and to parents with children in state schools. Priests were accused of forcing young girls to take the veil, of burning books and of immorality. Béranger attacked the Church in verse; Voltaire's anti-clerical tracts reappeared, satirical plays like *Tartuffe* played to full houses, and religious services were often interrupted by exploding firecrackers.[4]

The Right reacted vigorously. Many priests rallied to the Church's defence, while lay groups were formed to combat the liberal press. The Société Catholique des Bons Livres was soon joined by the Association pour la Défense de la Réligion Catholique and the Société pour la Propagation de la Foi, among others. The death penalty for sacrilege passed into law in 1825, but was never applied. None the less, it was denounced by the Left as an example of right-wing fanaticism.[5]

Equated with the Terror, republicanism was largely discredited in the Restoration. 'The idea of a republican executive', Lafayette wrote to Jefferson in 1814, 'is synonymous with the excesses committed in its name.'[6] In the early years of the Restoration, Destutt de Tracy, Lanjuinais, Garat and Grégoire kept the republican tradition alive, aided by masonic lodges and a few other, mostly Paris-based, secret societies.[7] After 1824 liberals began to popularize moderate American republicanism: Armand Carrel founded *La Revue Américaine* in the wake of Lafayette's triumphal 1825 American tour. In the last years of the Restoration, left-wing journals like *La Jeune France, La Révolution, La Patriote, La Tribune des Départements*, the *Tribune* and the *National* mushroomed. Dissidents of all persuasions closed ranks against the conservative Polignac ministry. The society Aide-Toi grouped Guizot, Casimir Périer and other moderate liberals agitating for administrative decentralization, reorganization of the National Guard – disbanded in 1827 – and a programme of education, tax and tariff reform.[8]

In June 1829 Plagniol, editor of *La Jeune France*, claimed that many believed republicanism had abandoned its Terrorist origins: 'By a republic,' he wrote, 'I mean a thirst for equality and justice, a disdain for unmerited honours, a need to control government, and a consciousness of the dignity of man and of the citizen which leads him to oppose arbitrary power and to become indignant at the suggestion of despotism.'[9]

By 1829 the republican Littré could write that the idea of a republic was 'a little less objectionable'.[10]

By 1830 Lafayette and the 'Americans' had erased some of the social stigma of republicanism. Secret societies flourished, but not as a powerful political force. Much of the political opposition in the army centred around an attachment to the military glories of the Empire and the egalitarian principles of the Revolution. To simplify matters, political opponents of the Bourbons between 1824 and 1830 will be referred to as liberals.

Although less critical than in the years preceding the Spanish campaign, political activity in the army after 1823 continued to worry Restoration officials. In January 1824 Belgian liberals began canvassing among troops in the Cuirassiers du Dauphin stationed near the frontier.[11] In June of that year, a tricolour was found on two officers of the 51st Infantry Regiment at La Rochelle. Though they were dismissed from the service, political activity in the regiment continued to cause concern. A regimental address to Charles X on the death of his brother, Louis XVIII, was considered in such poor taste that it earned the Colonel a reprimand from the War Minister.[12] After a plot to assassinate the Colonel and several officers was uncovered in the ranks, the regiment was sent to Guadeloupe where it remained until 1830.[13]

Though the 51st was the most rebellious regiment in the years after the Spanish campaign, political opposition occasionally surfaced in other regiments. Encouraged by political activists, soldiers of the 36th Infantry Regiment and the Dragons de la Manche attacked tax collectors at Poitiers who were a particularly unpopular symbol of the Restoration,[14] while soldiers in the 5th Infantry Regiment joined an anti-governmental riot at Gap in October 1824.[15] In 1825 political opposition spread throughout France as anti-Bourbon placards appeared in Evreux, Rouen, Orléans, Bordeaux and Toulouse and a secret society was unearthed among officers in the 17th Light Infantry Regiment.[16]

In 1826 Strasbourg liberals launched a campaign to strengthen their following in the local garrison. The Prefect of the Bas-Rhin reported in March that the opposition 'is working hard to undermine the morale of Strasbourg NCOs'[17] and ordered local police to inspect the barracks regularly after soldiers were found with opposition propaganda. The Prefect's unprecedented step provoked a strong complaint from the garrison commander, who viewed the intrusion as an encroachment on his authority and another example of government interference in military matters.[18] Opposition influence on the Strasbourg garrison continued throughout the Restoration into the July Monarchy, especially in the two artillery regiments and the battalion of bridge builders permanently stationed there. News of the 1830 Paris revolution was greeted with unrestrained joy by the garrison and artillery officers immediately circulated a denunciation of Charles X's government for all military and civilian officials to sign.

Public opposition to the government had made up the ground lost during the successful Spanish war by 1827.

The Villèle government alienated much of the country with a December 1826 proposal requiring newspapers and pamphlets to affix a stamp to each page or suffer heavy fines, in the hope of bankrupting financially troubled left-wing journals. Both the Left and the printing trade were outraged, and the bill was shelved by a peers committee in a sharp blow to both the Villèle administration and the monarchy.[19] Discontent was such that the French Ambassador to Russia, Count de la Férronays, confided to General Marmont that the Czar feared for the stability of Charles X's government.[20] And when the king reviewed the Paris National Guard on 29 April 1827, he was met with cries of 'Vive la liberté de la presse! A bas les ministres! A bas les Jésuites!' Villèle disbanded the National Guard that very same night, infuriating many middle-class Parisians, the National Guard's traditional recruiting base, and bringing further discredit on the throne.[21] Press censorship was reintroduced in June.

As the November elections approached, Benjamin Constant, Lafayette and other liberals stumped the country criticizing the government's domestic record and foreign policy which, they claimed, placed France in England's shadow. On the eve of the elections, anti-Bourbon placards reappeared in many towns. The vote in the *arrondissement* colleges spelled a resounding victory for the Left, although the government was able to redress the balance in the departmental vote, restricted to the wealthier electors. But Villèle's unpopularity forced his resignation in January 1828 as grain riots signalled the beginning of the economic depression which lasted until 1832.

The army was hardly an island of tranquillity in this sea of political turmoil. General Dumoulin, commander of the 5th Military Division at Strasbourg, attacked the press campaign to spread dissension in the army and criticized 'the disadvantages of press freedom for military discipline'.[22] A plot to kill the king was discovered in the 4th Infantry Regiment at Dieppe.[23] A soldier in the 21st Infantry Regiment in Paris was arrested for shouting seditiously, soldiers in the 13th Infantry Regiment were reprimanded for insulting priests at Lille and a secret society was uncovered in the 17th Infantry Regiment at Lyon.[24] The 2nd Artillery band serenaded Benjamin Constant after his electoral victory in Strasbourg[25] and police director Franchet-Despérey warned in December that republicans were attempting to win over the army. This caution was followed by a circular from the War Minister, Clermont-Tonnerre, ordering all prefects and division commanders to watch out for republican activity in the army and especially in the Toulouse garrison.[26]

By 1828 the economic squeeze was felt all over France. Industrial wages fell by a quarter to a third and the price of bread rose by 125 per cent between 1825 and 1829. Three thousand looms stood idle in Lyon, centre of the silk industry, and an estimated 3,000 unemployed were forced to leave Paris for the provinces. In July 1830 227,000 of 755,000 Parisians applied for relief. Ninety attacks on tax collectors were registered in 1829 alone, while grain riots continued across France and workers rioted in Paris, Lyon and Nantes.

Parliamentary liberals scored successes in their anti-clerical campaign. The Jesuits were banished and the Church was forced to stop using seminaries as a front for secondary schools. Henceforth, all seminaries would be limited to 20,000 students who received their *baccalauréat* only after taking orders.[27] But the liberal press continued to lambast Villèlists like Frayssinous in the Martignac ministry and to agitate for administrative reform to lessen the influence of government-appointed prefects, sub-prefects and local mayors.

The political agitation in France was marked by a corresponding increase in political activity in the army. In January 1828 a book of 'seditious' songs was discovered in the Paris barracks of the Royal Guard[28] and after 'désordres graves' in September four dragoons of the Royal Guard were brought to trial for organizing a regimental secret society.[29] Several artillery regiments and student officers at the artillery Ecole d'Application at Metz were cited for opposition activity in 1829. Soldiers were arrested for seditious shouts at Tours and several soldiers in the Besançon garrison joined a protest demonstration against high taxes.[30] Aware that the army had been influenced by the political turmoil sweeping the country, the War Minister rejected the Minister of the Interior's request for troops to break up an illegal political society at Romans: 'The army would be exposed to malicious attempts to sow the seeds of insubordination and indiscipline in the ranks.'[31] Secret societies were also discovered in the 2nd Light Infantry Regiment at Strasbourg and the 2nd Discipline Company, which contained men convicted of a felony, insubordination and, especially after 1830, political crimes, at Besançon.[32]

Although political opposition in the army never again reached the 1815–23 peak, part of the army was caught up in the wave of political agitation sweeping France. Though opposition to the regime never crystallized into military insurrection, it smouldered continuously both in the officer corps and in the ranks. Much of this overt political activity was motivated by increasing discontent in the army over certain Restoration military policies. This discontent affected the army's morale and consequently its willingness and even its ability to defend the regime in 1830.

A major military complaint under the Restoration and especially after 1827 was the low rate of pay. Set out in 1799, the pay scales were out of date by 1827. Low pay had not been an issue before the Revolution when most officers, as aristocrats, had private sources of income. During the Revolution, however, the officer corps had been taken over by middle-class and lower middle-class officers who depended exclusively on their army pay. Consequently, the 1827 depression lowered the French officer's standard of living quite considerably.

In 1828 one writer discussed the financial difficulties confronting an army officer. The basic rate of pay in francs in this period was as shown in Table 1:

TABLE 1   *French army officers' pay (in francs)*

	Infantry	Artillery
Colonel	5,000	6,250
Lieut. colonel	4,300	5,300
Chef de bataillon	3,600	4,500
Capitaine 1e	2,400	2,500
Capitaine 2e	2,000	2,000
Lieutenant	1,250	1,500
Sous-lieutenant	1,100	1,300

The equivalent British army pay scales in francs for the same period were substantially higher (Table 2):[33]

TABLE 2   *British army officers' pay (in francs)*

	Horse Guards	*Cavalry*	*Infantry*
Colonel	17,725	15,000	10,275
Lieut. colonel	12,750	10,500	7,750
Major	11,675	8,775	7,300
Captain	9,300	6,675	5,300
Lieutenant	6,500	4,125	2,975
Cornet	6,175	3,775	—
Ensign	—	—	2,400

The writer gives a typical budget for a cavalry colonel whose basic pay was 5,500 francs a year, plus a 600-franc housing allowance and 1,500 francs for extra expenses (frais de représentation) – an annual total of 7,600 francs:

	francs
lodging	1,000
food	3,650 (10 francs a day)
servant	600
maintenance of two horses	100
annual loss on horses	150
entertainment	180
regimental dinner	50
	5,730

A colonel wholly dependent on his army salary was therefore not a wealthy man. And this budget is probably a conservative estimate. The additional expenses of a married officer, for whom the costs of yearly garrison changes were prodigious, and marginal expenses such as heating and light are not considered. Superior officers were expected to give three to four large dinners a year and several smaller ones which added considerably to their expenses. Officers living in large cities and in the east, which depended on Germany for many of its goods, also faced a higher cost of living. The government was careful to change regiments stationed in Paris, Lyon, Strasbourg and other large cities where political opposition was strong, almost annually. But the high cost of living also made these towns unsuitable from an officer's point of view and contributed to the strength of the opposition in the local garrisons.

If a colonel was forced to economize, a young second lieutenant was bound to fall into debt on a basic salary of 95 francs 83 centimes

a month plus a small housing allowance. The writer sketched out
his monthly budget as follows:

	francs
lodging	18
horseshoes	2.50
clean room and board horse	6
pension	45
equipment maintenance	40
laundry	5
heating	3
light	1
entertainment	3.19
	123.69

Polytechnicians who joined the *ponts et chaussées* or the civil service,
however, received a starting salary of 4,000 francs a year. Three to
four years after graduation, Polytechnicians who became civil
engineers were promoted to second-class engineer with a basic
salary of 4,500 francs, plus 800 francs for expenses and a percentage
of the cost of their projects which boosted their annual salary to
between 5,000 and 6,000 francs. They could expect to earn at least
7,000 francs a year as first-class engineers, while their former classmates were earning only 1,700 to 2,000 francs as lieutenants or
second-class captains and faced the grim prospect of early retirement
on a low pension. Mining engineers could look forward to an even
more lucrative future.

Polytechnicians entering the army were aware of this pay dis-
crepancy. 'Those who are forced to stay serve only reluctantly',
noted one contemporary observer.[34] In 1837 Baron Pelletier,
commanding general of the Ecole d'Application, suggested that the
financial difficulties of student officers were a major reason for the
school's notorious republicanism.[35]

Complaints of low pay were especially numerous among Polytechnicians who entered the artillery and army engineers. Engineering officers, who were often stationed in non-garrison towns to
maintain the fortifications, complained that their housing allowance
of 18 francs a month was inadequate. In garrison towns, officers
negotiated a uniform price for room and pension with a local inn-
keeper. Detached engineering officers, however, who did not enjoy
this advantage were forced to pay 36 to 40 francs a month for their
room and, because they worked in this room, burned more wood.
They were also saddled with additional expenses such as books
and medical care when an army doctor was not available. And as

they seldom went on campaign, they were denied the 600 francs combat pay accorded to officers as well as an additional chance of promotion.

As most officers ended their career as captain, few could look forward to a substantial improvement in their standard of living. While a Prussian captain earned the equivalent of 4,800 francs a year in a country with a lower cost of living, a French captain could only expect to earn 2,000 to 2,500 francs at the height of his career. In 1828, one writer declared, 'Captains . . . are disinherited in France, where their pay has stayed the same since 1764.'[36] The writer points out the adverse effect this had on the discipline of the entire company: 'The enthusiasm or apathy of the captain soon influences even the lowest private.'

Lower down, NCOs and soldiers barely had enough to live on. Their daily pay was:[37]

	francs
Adjutant	1.65
Sergent-major	0.85
Sergent	0.67
Caporal	0.55
Simple soldat	0.45

British NCOs and soldiers earned considerably more than their French counterparts.

TABLE 3   *British NCOs and soldiers – annual pay in francs*

	Horse Guards	*Cavalry*	*Infantry*
Sergeant-major	1,650	1,600	1,370
Corporal	1,200	750	625
Private	950	575	475

A sergeant-major was barely able to make ends meet on a monthly salary of 25 francs 50 centimes, as a typical budget demonstrates:

	francs
food	13.50
clerk	2.00
barber	0.50
laundry	3.00
equipment maintenance, etc.	2.50
	21.50

The small 4-franc margin usually disappeared in the summer when the army wore white trousers which had to be laundered daily at 10 centimes a time.[38]

Sergeant-majors were also required to provide the regiment's daily requirement of paper and pens and even the paper for the inspector general's reports. For this they were given a yearly stipend of 18 francs, of which 7.50 francs were retained by the regimental treasury leaving them 10.50 francs or approximately 88 centimes a month for this expense. A monthly budget demonstrates that this put sergeant-majors considerably out of pocket.[39]

	francs
2½ hands of paper at 40 centimes each	1.00
pens	0.25
ink	0.35
pencils	0.25
sharpen penknife and quills	0.15
upkeep of regulations, etc.	0.10
	2.10

Soldiers were paid 45 centimes a day, of which 30 were kept for food and 10 for laundry and shoes. This left 5 centimes a day for soap and other necessities – and none for wine or entertainment. The constant lack of entertainment made soldiers vulnerable to republicans who spent money liberally on them, invited them to join social clubs which soon became political cells and sometimes offered them bribes to desert.

But if salaries were low, pensions were too meagre to live on. 'Officers are crying out to see pensions raised,' Maréchal de Camp Dejean pointed out in 1828.[40] French military pensions, reckoned on the number of years' service and the number of campaigns, were the lowest in Europe:[41]

Lieutenant général	3,000	Chef de bataillon	900
Maréchal de camp	2,000	Capitaine	600
Colonel	1,200	Lieutenant	450
Lieut. colonel	1,000	Sous-lieutenant	350
		Sergent-major	182.50
		Sergent	136.87
		Simple soldat	91.25

In Austria a retired captain received the equivalent of 1,728 francs, in Bavaria 2,600, in Prussia 2,000 and in Britain officers were retired on half pay.[42] Maréchal de Camp Dejean, who was no enemy of the Restoration, points out that the pension question had not been serious when most officers had an outside income, but that by the Restoration many officers were forced to retire to small rural villages, 'to hide their wretched condition'. In 1827 the Prefect of Corsica reported that ninety-six retired officers in his department were living in poverty: 'They are almost all penniless and will find themselves in dire straits if the government does not do something to help them ... Your Excellency will certainly realize that for humanitarian as well as political reasons it is vital not to leave them without adequate means of support.'[43] A report to the War Minister in 1825 noted that retired NCOs were paid barely enough to buy bread.[44]

The prospect of retirement on such low pensions seriously damaged army morale. 'Officers both dread and desire retirement ... They dread it because they know that having no personal fortune and depending entirely on their army pay, retirement breeds only indifference.'[45] Most officers and NCOs had nothing to look forward to but a life of 'humiliating near-poverty ... The pension situation worries even young officers.'[46] General Villette, commander of the 3rd Military Division at Metz, seconded Dejean in 1829 when he reported to the War Minister that the defeat in parliament of General Sebastiani's proposal to raise pensions had seriously affected army morale and performance:[47]

> It is my duty to point out to your Excellency, given my love and devotion to the King, that the vote taken in closed committee on General Sebastiani's pension proposal has had a disastrous effect among the officers and has given rise to observations, discussions and ill-natured talk which has undermined morale.
>
> Especially of late, I have observed much apathy and dis-affection among officers of all ranks. It is a kind of disease. What are its causes? What is the cure? Your Excellency can decide that, being more experienced than I in these matters. But it is a fact that officers serve only half-heartedly, and that this indifference rubs off on NCOs and soldiers. The present calm certainly contributes to this state of affairs. But newspapers and periodicals – which cannot be banned – have a great influence on officers, who, comparing their status to that of civil servants, say their privileges have been forfeited.

Together with low pay and inadequate pensions, the slow pro-motion rate of a peacetime army also damaged morale. This was exacerbated by the fact that many officers had gained their rank during the Empire while still young. Consequently, few officers retired during the Restoration and early years of the July Monarchy to make way for younger men. Marshal Jourdan was 68 years old in 1830, but Marshal Soult was only 61, Marshal Clauzel 58 and General Gérard, appointed War Minister in 1830, only 57.

In 1828 most lieutenants averaged fifteen years' service and captains eighteen years'. 'As an inevitable result of peace, promotion has become so slow that most officers will end their careers with no more than a captaincy.'[48] 'Promotion was so difficult and slow before the 1830 revolution [General Trochu claimed in 1867] that it was at a virtual standstill. Everyone gradually realized this and, shelving his ambitious dreams, accepted the immobility which all were forced to endure.'[49] In 1829 General Madelaine, who faithfully served the Bourbons, complained that slow promotion, peacetime inactivity and inadequate pensions had created a malaise in the army: 'A restlessness has taken hold of many young officers condemned by a lengthy peace to vegetate in junior grades without prospect of a more comfortable old age thanks to excessively low pensions.'[50] Even La Motte Rouge, an ardent apologist for the Restoration, admitted that the officers were discouraged after waiting six years without one promotion in the regiment: 'It was rather long and discouraging.'[51] Chalmin points out that 646 of 2,934 captains in 1831 received their rank before 1816[52] and this was after the plethora of promotions which followed the 1830 revolution.

In October 1829 Cadudal, commander of the 22nd Légion de Gendarmerie at Nancy, reported that because of slow promotion and inadequate pensions army morale had fallen to a dangerously low level. His assurance to the War Minister that the army would remain faithful to the government is an admission that the issues were important enough to alter the army's political disposition:[53]

> The army deserves special attention. Naturally obedient, law-abiding and devoted to the King, it would be a grave mistake to assume that it is happy with the present state of affairs and that reform is unnecessary. The entire army is disaffected and seriously concerned about the future because of the dearth of promotion and meagre pensions which do not reflect the cost of living. It is therefore vital to increase pensions.

Living conditions for NCOs and soldiers under the Restoration were harsh. Most of the barracks were constructed in the eighteenth century and had provided adequate housing until the Revolution. However, Revolutionary and Imperial governments had neglected to build new barracks as most of their armies were stationed abroad and because soldiers were billeted with civilians to educate the population to the goals of the Revolution. The Bourbons, fearing liberal influence in the army, were reluctant to quarter troops with civilians. In 1825 a report to the War Minister complained that most barracks were dangerously dilapidated and badly overcrowded. Regiments assigned barracks seldom had half enough beds for their men. Consequently, soldiers were forced to sleep in shifts or share the same bed and linen. Others slept on boards in the attics, often without blankets. Without a mess, soldiers were forced to eat in barracks, with four to eight men sharing a dirty pot. The Inspector General complained that soldiers were continually plagued by insects and rats. Latrines were far from the barracks and were considered notoriously insanitary even by the lax standards of the age.

Soldiers had little respite from the drudgery of garrison duty. Regulations stipulated that a soldier was to have guard duty no more than one night in five. However, because Restoration regiments were under strength, they were often required to go on guard duty every other night. Consequently, soldiers complained of constant fatigue. Inspectors pointed out that morale suffered because the men were not given enough free time, but were kept continually under surveillance. Even NCOs were required to sleep in one room and enjoyed little privacy.[54]

Young peasant conscripts were already used to a hard existence and were probably least affected by the privations of military life. Yet young soldiers from a lower middle-class background who volunteered for military service hoping to be commissioned and win social advancement considered these living conditions degrading. These men who had a basic education and were raised in reasonably comfortable surroundings formed the NCO class in the army and they resented the low pay, lack of privacy and inhuman barrack conditions forced on them by the Restoration. Consequently, they were eager for a commission even at the price of revolution, and not unwilling to aid in the overthrow of a regime which neglected their interests. The Restoration's alienation of the NCO class explains why this group was quick to join the revolutionaries in 1830.

Garrison duty demanded little from officers and inspection reports constantly decried its demoralizing effects. To occupy officers and increase army efficiency, officials proposed to establish regimental schools to teach writing and basic tactics to soldiers and NCOs. Yet two years after the government circular of March 1827 encouraging the establishment of regimental schools, General Villette complained that few regiments had them. Consequently, officers continued to spend a large part of their day in cafés where they were exposed to opposition newspapers:[55]

On the subject of training [wrote General Villette] it would be useful to busy the idle infantry and cavalry officers who pass the time of day in cafés, reading newspapers and talking politics. If each regiment established a school to run courses on strategy and field fortifications, they would gain knowledge which few now possess and would forget those ideas which idleness and boredom inspire.

The July Monarchy promoted regimental schools so that by 1836 virtually every metropolitan regiment had one.

The oppressive political climate of the Restoration army also heightened army pessimism. In December 1824 War Minister Clermont-Tonnerre signed an ordinance dismissing fifty-six lieutenant generals and 117 brigadiers 'whose political opinions clashed with those of the regime'.[56] The liberal General Foy called this act 'the last shot fired at Waterloo'.[57] Many officers were upset by the presence of chaplains who served as informers for the regime. Marmont complained that they sent notes on the conduct of officers which often influenced promotions.[58] General Madelaine objected that anyone who proposed using the army for public works was viewed with suspicion: 'He is considered untrustworthy and treated as such.'[59] 'The army was subjected to a most deplorable inquisition', claimed the *National* when speaking of the perpetual fear of political reprisals in regiments commanded by royalist officers.[60] Many officers opposed the 1829 appointment to the war ministry of General Bourmont, who had abandoned Napoleon on the eve of Waterloo and whose treason was blamed for the emperor's defeat. The Prefect of the Moselle at Metz reported that Bourmont's nomination 'has rocked the garrison'.[61] Some liberals claimed that Wellington was responsible for his appointment and the *Figaro* invited deserters to call at the War Ministry where they would be given employment.[62] The Naval Minister resigned rather than serve in the Cabinet with him. Both Major Barrès and General Castellane noted that few officers approved of either the Polignac ministry or the July ordinances which sparked off the revolution: 'A very small number approved the ordinances, the great majority condemned them.'[63] Castellane condemned 'the deplorable ordinances of 25 July' and concluded, 'there is every chance that they [the Bourbons] will eventually pay for this with their lives.' He summed up the indignation of a number of generals with whom he was on holiday in 1830: 'Everyone here is amazed and outraged.'[64]

Hand in hand with these issues goes the favoured position of the Royal Guard in the Restoration. Low pay and slow promotion would have lost some of their political overtones had line officers and NCOs enjoyed the same status as the Royal Guard. Royal Guard and Swiss officers, however, enjoyed one rank above the equivalent command position in a line regiment and their pay was substantially higher (see Table 4). They were often promoted through court intrigue, regardless of the legal time requirements for promotion.

TABLE 4   *Military pay scales under the restoration*

		Guard			Line	
	Swiss	*French*	*Differ-ence*	*Swiss*	*French*	*Differ-ence*
Colonel	15,000	6,250	8,750	6,000	5,000	1,000
Lieut. colonel	12,000	5,375	6,625	5,000	4,300	700
Chef de bataillon	8,000	4,500	3,500	4,000	3,600	400
Capitaine 1ᵉ	5,400	3,600	1,800	2,800	2,400	400
Capitaine 2ᵉ	5,000	3,000	2,000	2,400	2,000	400
Lieutenant 1ᵉ	3,000	1,875	1,125	1,800	1,450	350
Lieutenant 2ᵉ	2,500	1,650	850	1,500	1,300	200
NCOs – daily pay						
Sergent-major	1.625	1.425	0.20	1.20	0.85	0.35
Sergent	1.36	1.23	0.13	1.00	0.67	0.33
Caporal	0.95	0.95	—	0.75	0.55	0.20

During the debates on the 1832 promotion law, deputies frequently cited promotional abuses under the Restoration. 'It was not so long ago', stated Roget, deputy for the Loiret in November 1831, 'that we were shocked by countless promotional abuses in the highest echelons of the army.'[65] General Demarçay castigated the Bourbons for promoting court favourites who had no command experience,[66] while General Laidet claimed that the abolition of the Royal Guard was one of the greatest accomplishments of the July revolution.[67] 'The government learned', said Martin du Nord, chairman of the parliamentary committee set up to study the promotion bill, '. . . by brief but fateful experience the consequences of despotism. It had seen men who had nothing to recommend them but influence at court rise to the highest military positions; the army was demoralized, discipline was undermined, authority vilified.'[68]

On 6 March 1828 the *conseil supérieur de la guerre*, for which ex-

Napoleonic officers actively lobbied throughout the Restoration, was established. This interarm council was designed to review ordinances and propose reforms. The council met with dubious success under the Bourbons. Under the direction of ex-Napoleonic officers, it first proposed shortening the term of service from eight to five years and forming a trained reserve of those released from active duty. It also attacked the composition of the general staff. Pelleport reports, however, that War Minister Bourmont definitively dismissed the council after it recommended the abolition of many privileges enjoyed by the Royal Guard.[69]

Anti-Royal Guard feeling ran high both among soldiers and civilians. Paris workers attacked Royal Guards in January 1827[70] and August 1829.[71] Petit Chesnay near Versailles was declared off-limits to Royal Guards after soldiers from line regiments stationed there provoked fights and refused to let them enter the town.[72] A regimental scrap broke out between the 15th Light Infantry Regiment and a detachment of Royal Guards at the barrière du Maine in August 1829.[73]

The resentment of officers towards the Royal Guard became most apparent in the first few months of the July Monarchy. In November 1830 the commander of the 5th Military Division at Strasbourg reported with some surprise that ex-Royal Guard officers sent to regiments in the Bas-Rhin had neither deserted nor met much hostility from the other officers. This was unusual, however. Marshal Soult wrote to Maréchal de Camp Dermoncourt in 1830 that a reserve could incorporate ex-Royal Guards who were discriminated against in the line regiments:[74]

> The existence of a reserve – which would return to the ranks many loyal and upstanding veterans and many ex-Royal Guard soldiers and NCOs ill-received in line regiments because of, for the most part, undeserved prejudice – would boost the morale of our young army.

Yet, if the Royal Guards were disliked as a symbol of royal privilege, the mercenary Swiss Guards were hated. Civilians at Abbeville fought Swiss Guards in January 1825,[75] while Paris workers sought trouble with the Swiss in July 1827 and June 1828[76] and the 2nd Grenadiers attacked the 8th Swiss Regiment at Versailles in November 1828.[77] In October 1829 police reported that groups of Swiss Guards from the Babylone barracks frequently mistreated civilians there. Barrès reported that in the 1830 revolution the fury of the crowds was directed especially at the Swiss and that when the insurgents attacked the Babylone barracks, many of the defenders were killed. After the revolution, the government provided the

Swiss regiments with safe conduct passes back to their homes to protect them from reprisals.

Favouritism shown to the Royal Guard, low pay and inadequate pensions geared for an aristocratic army prove that the Bourbons were in many ways out of touch with the post-Revolutionary French army. They failed to realize that the social composition of the Restoration army was different from that of the *ancien régime* and neglected to push through the minor reforms which could have dispelled the pessimism permeating the army.

By the end of the Restoration, army morale was dangerously low. Madelaine saw 'no future' in the army and concluded: 'the army's morale has already slumped.'[78] This pessimism encouraged at best a tepid affection for the Restoration. Barrès's observations after his court presentation in 1828 are probably typical of many officers who like himself supported no political faction: 'Glory had given way to devout hypocrisy, the famous men of the Empire to the little men of the emigration, and the great doings of Napoleon to the intrigues of an insecure government.'[79] This feeling was shared by many in the army. Barrès noted that during a royal troop review in 1829, the ranks were conspicuously silent as they passed the King and only a few isolated shouts of 'Vive le Roi' were heard.

Though the army was not on the verge of revolt, a general feeling of despondency permeated the ranks on the eve of the revolution. One contemporary observer sums up this feeling perhaps too pessimistically. But his assessment of the army's morale is important, for a large part of the army felt only slightly less gloomy:[80]

> The French army is no more. How could these thin corps of bored, demoralized men be called an army? Enthusiasm for the service, pride in the uniform, camaraderie have disappeared. Officers and men alike are afflicted by a general malaise, a need for change, a constant anxiety. Duty without pleasure is onerous.

With this in mind, it becomes easier to explain why the army abandoned the regime in 1830, as the scales tipped in favour of the opposition.

Chapter 3

1830

In July 1830 the nation and the army abandoned the Bourbons with amazing ease. With the exception of a few royalist officers, the army was not unfavourable to the change of government. But the revolution placed the army in a politically delicate situation and military leaders soon faced a serious breakdown of discipline both in Paris and in the provinces.

The appointment of Polignac in 1829 as chief minister provoked dismay throughout France. The Left especially objected to the presence of the reactionary, La Bourdonnaye, in the Interior Ministry and General Bourmont in the War Ministry. 'The new ministry . . .', the *Globe* declared, 'divides France in two: the court on one side, the nation on the other.'[1] La Bourdonnaye was dismissed in a vain effort to gain confidence for the administration. But left-wing newspapers, encouraged by judicial reluctance to convict them, continued their anti-government diatribes. The *Journal du Commerce* suggested refusing to pay taxes if the budget were passed, while Carrel, Thiers and Mignet at the *National* exhorted the monarchy to remain true to its constitutional foundations. The debate over royal prerogative climaxed with a vote by 221 deputies supporting the sovereignty of the charter. Parliament was dissolved on 16 May and Aide-Toi immediately set up electoral committees in Paris and the provinces. The July elections resulted in a resounding victory for the Left, which gained 274 seats against 143 for the ministry.[2]

After their election defeat, Polignac and Charles X decided to impose the emergency powers granted the king under article 14 of the charter to silence the liberal opposition once and for all. On 6 July they adopted Peyronnet's proposal that the king should dissolve parliament, call for a new election according to a modified electoral list and impose press censorship. 'The revolutionary spirit is still very much alive on the Left', Charles reasoned. 'By attacking the ministry, it is the king, the monarchy they wish to destroy . . . if I give in to their demands now, they will end by treating me like they treated my brother.'[3] The final text of the ordinances was adopted on 24 June, and signed on Sunday the 25th after the prefect of police, Mangin, assured the council, 'Paris will not stir.' The government was counting on the news of the capture of Algiers by French troops to carry it over the crisis and was not prepared for a large civilian protest. Consequently, it failed to reinforce the under-strength Paris garrison. As the War Minister, Bourmont, had assumed command of the Algerian expedition, the army had operated without his direction for several months; every general and most senior officers had returned home to vote and the 4th Regiment of the Royal Guard was in Normandy. General Marmont, who was placed in command of the garrison only on Tuesday 27 July, inventoried his troops at 5,500 Royal Guard and Swiss infantry, 4,000 regular infantry, 750 cavalry, 1,526 police and 12 cannon. He noted that the Royal Guard was 'the only infantry we could trust.'[4]

The crowds which had gathered on the 26th after the publication of the ordinances grew increasingly hostile on the 27th, undoubtedly incensed by the presence of Marmont, who had deserted Napoleon in March 1814 as the allies approached Paris. Troops were stationed at several points in the city but met only sporadic opposition.[5] 'The resistance of the Parisians', Marmont concluded of the crowd activity on the 27th, 'was not meant in earnest. They seemed to want only to provoke and to test the mood of the soldiers by building the barricades so close to the troop concentrations.' The troops returned to their barracks for the night, but large crowds appeared once again on the morning of the 28th crying: 'à bas les Bourbons', and once again Marmont deployed his forces. The events of the 28th are well known. In the face of a hostile population, under a blazing sun and without food and water, the soldiers began to falter. The 50th Infantry Regiment refused to fight and gave away its ammunition. By mid-afternoon, other regular troops had begun to desert; Marmont was forced to draw his troops into a defensive position around the Louvre and Tuileries. The 5th and 53rd Infantry Regiments stationed on the Place Vendôme, harangued by Casimir Périer, defected *en masse* and joined the insurgents. Marmont pulled a battalion of Swiss out of their position on the east front of the Louvre to fill the gap left by the deserting regiments. Through a misunderstanding no replacements arrived, however, and the insurgents, spotting the gap in the defences, attacked, sending the demoralized troops reeling up the Champs Elysées in panic.

The dispirited army fell back on Saint-Cloud and Royal Guards began to desert. On the night of the 28th, Lieutenant-Colonel Vielbans, commander of the 1st Guard Regiment, informed

35

Colonel Saint-Chamans that his troops refused to fight any longer. Saint-Chamans, afraid that if this regiment deserted other troops would follow its example, promised them that the army was withdrawing from Paris. In an attempt to prevent more desertions, Marmont announced on the 29th that the king had appointed the Duc de Mortmart Prime Minister, and opened negotiations with the provisional government. The Dauphin, furious with Marmont for discussing politics with the troops, called him a traitor and placed him under house arrest. The arrest of the commanding general aggravated the deteriorating military situation. Because the Dauphin, the new commanding general, refused to retreat from Saint-Cloud, the troops believed that he was preparing to retake Paris and began deserting in even larger numbers. The Dauphin directed the 3rd Royal Guard and the 1st Swiss Regiments to Sèvres and Meudon to suppress uprisings there, but they refused to fire. By Friday, even officers were abandoning the throne; Lieutenant-General Bordesoulle pledged his support to the provisional government. The king retreated to Rambouillet and the Dauphin took the remaining troops to Trappes. On Saturday, six companies of Swiss Guards threw down their weapons and headed for Paris to join the insurrection. On Sunday morning the colonels of the Royal Guard and Swiss Regiments met at Trappes. After consultation, Farincourt, Revel, Salis, Bésenval, Fontenille and Dandrie, commander of the *gendarmerie d'élite*, decided to submit to the Paris government. Three Royal Guard cavalry regiments deserted to Paris the next day. The Swiss received a safe conduct pass from the provisional government which, Marmont pointed out, must have been solicited on Friday while still at Saint-Cloud.

When he abdicated on 2 August, the king had barely 1,350 men, many of them officers without regiments, and his Garde du Corps. Plans to prolong the struggle on the Loire were unrealistic, for virtually every garrison within fifty miles of Paris had declared for the provisional government. Few regiments waited to be notified of the abdication before switching allegiance. Only the Royal Guards had opposed the insurgents with vigour and they quickly abandoned the throne after the 28th. Provincial garrisons, removed from the pressures of insurrection, looked on apathetically as the Bourbons were forced out of France. Yet, repercussions from the revolution demonstrated the relationship between governmental instability, indiscipline and republican activity in the army.

In the provinces, news of the revolution was greeted with unrestrained joy. Large crowds gathered in Metz, Strasbourg, Bordeaux, Caen, Lyon, Clermont-Ferrand and many other towns to await news from Paris. Opposition leaders demanding the resurrection of the National Guard and that the tricolour replace the white flag immediately challenged the authority of local government officials; local hierarchies either resigned or teetered dangerously on the brink of collapse. The breakdown of civil discipline also tainted the army. Faced with a revolutionary *fait accompli* and an armed citizenry, most commanders hesitated between duty and their sympathy for the revolution or their impotence before the aroused town. This refusal to assert authority proved fatal to military discipline.

The revolution in the army at Strasbourg and Metz was carried out by young artillery officers. In Strasbourg they drew up an indictment of Charles's government and demanded that every senior officer and government official sign it. The Prefect, Esmangart, complained that this document, 'full of vulgar abuse', was signed by every officer except one general and one colonel, 'the alternative being a breakdown of discipline'.[6] 'Young officers, carried away by youthful ardour,' reports said of Metz artillery regiments, 'forgot their duty to their leaders and ignored the demands of discipline.'[7] Elsewhere, however, NCOs took the initiative.

As news of the revolution threw garrison towns into turmoil, and as officers nervously awaited orders from Paris, NCOs wasted little time in disrupting their regiments. In most cases they seized as a pretext for revolt their superiors' refusal to let them wear the tricoloured cockade which the National Guard had taken up immediately until orders arrived from Paris. For this reason many NCOs, egged on by local republicans who were buying drinks and passing out money, reasoned that their officers were holding the regiments in check until the Bourbons could consolidate their forces and retake Paris. Consequently, many NCOs and soldiers stationed near Paris deserted to ride to Paris and protect the revolution.

On 3 August a Maréchal des Logis Chef of the 6th Chasseurs at Givet, ordered two hundred men to saddle up and prepare to ride on the capital. Colonel Etang quickly ordered the city gates closed, halted the group and demanded to know where they were going. They answered that they were riding to Paris themselves because he refused to take them there. The colonel objected that he could not lead them to Paris without orders, but they insisted that he had received orders and was holding them back. They also accused him of plotting to abandon them. Despite the colonel's protests, eighty-four NCOs and soldiers broke past him and galloped for Paris.[8]

This scene was repeated elsewhere, especially in cavalry regiments as mounted soldiers could easily reach the capital and not, as Rémusat suggests, because NCOs especially resented the aristocratic officers who dominated that arm. A Maréchal des Logis led a revolt in the 5th Cuirassiers at Nevers and attempted to take the regiment to Paris. Forty-four NCOs and soldiers of the 4th Artillery at La Fère deserted for Paris and only thirty officers and men were left in the 4th Cuirassiers at Chateaudun after desertions. 'Unrest is evident among officers, NCOs and soldiers of the 2nd Carabineers', reported the Lille Prefect and Colonel Gustler of the 2nd Carabineers reported on 7 August that 'all the NCOs and a large number of soldiers are ready to desert and ride to Paris.'[9]

Forty-one NCOs later deserted the regiment. Mass desertions were reported in the 43rd Infantry Regiment at Dieppe, the 64th at Cherbourg, the 33rd Infantry and 5th Hussards at Thionville, the 13th Infantry Regiment at Nancy, the 6th Artillery at Strasbourg and the 12th Dragoons. NCOs in the 10th Chasseurs revolted and marched to Paris after their officers tried to lead the regiment to the Vendée.

Reports of trouble in thirty-two out of 148 French regiments reached the War Ministry. It is certain that these reports understate the real extent of unrest. Later estimates of desertion were much greater than contemporary records suggest. According to a report drawn up in 1841, army strength, which stood at 223,073 officers and men in January 1830, plummeted to 183,311 in August, a loss of 40,000 men.[10]

Yet the deserters rode to Paris for reasons other than to save the revolution. The prospect of higher pay and a promotion promised to those who joined the Paris National Guard played a decisive part in the decision of NCOs and soldiers to desert. A soldier who received 45 centimes a day was clearly attracted by the daily wage of 1 franc 50 centimes supposedly offered by the Paris National Guard. 'Their friends have written to tell them', said the colonel of the 4th Artillery Regiment about deserters in his regiment, 'that they are welcomed in Paris and placed in a regiment (the National Guard, I assume) where they receive 1 franc 50 centimes a day.'[11]

> I am convinced [reported Colonel Chepy of the Givet revolt] that their desire to join the newly organized National Guard was the only reason for their desertion. They were attracted by the pay, and the leaders by the chance of a commission. They claim they were told only lies and given orders designed to prevent them from joining it. The leaders were responsible, and they alone should be punished. The men were misled [by them], and wanted only to join the good people of Paris and to enjoy the benefits proclaimed in the newspapers and misrepresented to them.[12]

Yet the War Ministry believed that the mutiny in the ranks could have been prevented had the officers acted firmly to prevent civil indiscipline from spreading to the garrison. Faced with an unstable political situation and without orders from Paris, officers hesitated to take strong measures for which they could later be held accountable. La Motte Rouge reports the reticence of officers in the Lille garrison to express an opinion about the July ordinances and the atmosphere of mistrust in the garrison on the eve of the revolution.[13]

> We met, we eyed each other, we conversed without daring to utter a candid opinion on the situation or on its likely outcome. I was struck by the expressions of uncertainty and anticipation which marked every face and many of my friends. Normally open discussion gave way to caution, to a defiance born of the fear of compromising oneself by an ambiguous word or sentence.

As long as the government remained unstable, the army was continually threatened by republican activists who took advantage of the officers' weakened authority. In November 1831 Castellane noted the adverse effects of governmental instability on military discipline. He pointed out that officers were wary of taking decisive action, for junior officers and NCOs often denounced the strict disciplinarian as a Carlist, a follower of the deposed Charles X. Consequently most officers turned a blind eye on insubordination.[14] He also pointed out that governmental instability encouraged military indecision even on the ministerial level and accused the War Minister, ex-Napoleonic Marshal Soult, of not punishing indiscipline for fear of revolution: 'Marshal Soult is afraid of the so-called patriots; he also cultivates Napoleon II's partisans for, like many people, he is not sure this situation will last.'[15] Rémusat also noted that Soult maintained his connections with the Left in case the government fell:[16]

> Soult cast his lot with what he considered the most revolutionary faction . . . Today's government might not be tomorrow's, and Soult always contrived to look after the future . . . He continued to court the Leftist opposition, making secret deals with them, always consulting Carrel, who was promised eventual appointment as Under-Secretary of State for war, and, on the pretext of keeping himself informed through inside sources on movements and military preparations throughout Europe, maintaining itinerant revolutionaries from secret funds.

Officers blamed indecision in the War Ministry for their hesitation before mutinous troops. Colonel Etang claimed that responsibility for the desertions in the 2nd Carabineers lay with the War Ministry which had failed to send the necessary directives clarifying the army's position *vis-à-vis* the revolution. General Gérard, who was appointed War Minister on 1 August, only ordered army regiments to take the tricoloured cockade on the 3rd. Officers who only received these orders a few days later claimed that Paris's indecision undermined their authority. 'Because you had not given the order to take up the tricoloured cockade, I could not act as decisively as I would otherwise have done. In short, General, while I have always been a staunch constitutionalist, it was clear I would abide by my oath.'[17] Yet, had Colonel Etang been loyal to the Restoration, he would have taken positive action against the revolution. He was simply waiting for the political situation to clarify. Charpentier, the public prosecutor at Metz, also blamed the Ministry for the indiscipline: 'The timidity and indecision of the supreme military command were to blame . . . They [the officers] must be given support, they must be given orders. These orders are not forthcoming.'[18] La Motte Rouge reported that civil and military officials without orders from Paris simply stayed at home to await the outcome of the revolution. 'Both groups [prefects and generals] remained at home without orders, and like most officials of any rank or position, waited for the situation to develop. They limited themselves to calling the troops out of the barracks and on to the squares and main streets, without issuing instructions as to what to do in case of trouble.'[19]

At Lyon Lieutenant Canrobert witnessed official hesitation before left-wing demands that the government evacuate the town hall and place the responsibility for public order in the hands of the National Guard. 'Neither the Prefect nor the generals dared take a decision. They negotiated to gain time but never issued a categorical refusal.'[20]

The interruption of pay after the 27th, on which soldiers depended for their daily rations, contributed to unrest in several garrisons. Royal Guard officers pointed out that this lay behind their massive desertions in Paris.[21] At Strasbourg the Prefect was forced to pay the soldiers from public funds or face a military revolt. Esmangart complained that the authority of the officers was undermined and concluded that they could never be trusted to act firmly in a political crisis: 'The generals had no authority and the officers had no influence. This deficiency, together with the suspension of pay, could have been disastrous . . . These old soldiers, so brave on the battlefield, rarely show courage in a civil crisis.'[22] Colonel Gustler of the 2nd Carabineers pointed out that had he attempted to arrest even one mutinous NCO, he would have had a full-scale revolution on his hands. Barrès also noted officers' reluctance to give orders to their mutinous troops after the revolution.[23]

Officers could easily justify their hesitation before the revolution and the rapid desertion of the Restoration. Most regiments, especially those stationed in the cities, realized that opposition was futile. Castellane pointed out that had the 8th Infantry Regiment at Clermont fired on the town as General Saint-Suzanne ordered, it would have been massacred. This is not an isolated example. The future Marshal Canrobert observed that at Lyon the garrison was at the town's mercy:[24]

> Our situation was hardly encouraging. The crowd was pressing
> so close that we were virtual prisoners. We could not have
> manoeuvred or even changed position. The slightest incident
> would have brought the people, who were not yet hostile,
> down on our heads. We could not use our weapons, in the
> first place because there was not room enough, and second,
> because we did not dare fire on a crowd composed mainly of
> women and children. Had we done so, improvised projectiles
> would have been hurled in their thousands from every window.
> We would have been knocked senseless by stones, tiles and
> furniture pelting down thick as hail on our heads. Had one
> jumpy, blundering soldier fired a shot, had the crowd misread
> one order, we would have been finished for sure. Both officers
> and soldiers understood the seriousness of the situation, and,
> probably thanks to this awareness of imminent danger, they
> stayed calm and averted possible catastrophe. Besides, what
> could we have expected of the men in such a hopeless position?

Canrobert concluded that the bravest soldiers often broke in the face of civil disorder: 'The soldier dreads civil war. He does not know if the cause he is defending will be victorious, or if perhaps tomorrow he will be serving the insurgents . . . He becomes restless, manifesting a lethargy and mistrust which sometimes leads him to desert, to disobey and panic.'[25]

Barrès admitted the futility of resistance when he allowed his men to desert after only half-heartedly opposing their exit. His reasons must have occurred to many other officers:[26]

> To accept battle would have been to doom to certain death
> the fifteen officers and two hundred men whom I had with me
> and to doom to destruction the barracks, the valuable stores
> and the neighbouring houses. Torrents of blood would flow
> and my memory would be held responsible for all these
> calamities; and for whom? For a perjured King, for an inept

government imposed on France by foreign bayonets. Until then I had served faithfully and conscientiously. I had nothing with which to reproach myself as regards the Bourbons, but this wretched, ill-advised sovereign had broken his oaths, had he not freed me from mine?

Although the army was ready to do its duty, it was not morally committed to the Restoration and yielded with few pangs of conscience to the revolutionary will. Conscious of their past association with the Bourbons, officers carefully avoided compromising themselves before the wave of patriotism and indiscipline which swept through the ranks. They went underground until the political situation was stable enough to allow them to re-establish discipline without fear of political reprisals. Consequently, republican activity in the army increased in direct proportion to governmental instability.

The revolution in the army quickly entered a second and more prolonged phase as NCOs, conscious that the authority of the officers was undermined, began to denounce their superiors as Carlists and counter-revolutionaries in an attempt to have them suspended and to take their places. Here begins a study of the special position of the French NCO which caused him to play such an active role in the July revolution and subsequent republican activity in the army after 1830.

La Motte Rouge noted that NCOs and soldiers were quick to take advantage of the insecure position of the officers following the revolution: 'If discipline was at first maintained and riots and disorder opposed, it later broke down. NCOs and soldiers were driven to insubordination, disobedience and disrespect by provocative, bad advice. In several infantry and cavalry regiments, indiscipline knew no bounds.'[27] He reports that after an NCO he arrested for insubordination claimed that he was being persecuted for his liberal opinions, the colonel begged him to set the offender free.[28] Soon, everyone who was punished for discontent claimed political discrimination.

On 7 August Colonel Gustler reported that the NCOs in his regiment presented him with a list of six captains, two lieutenants and six second-lieutenants who they claimed were 'traitors' and should be dismissed.[29] Soon NCOs in other regiments began to denounce their superiors. NCOs in the 5th Chasseurs at Poitiers forced their colonel, two majors and several other officers to leave the regiment after denouncing them as Carlists. Several officers in the 16th Infantry Regiment at Tours were denounced, as were officers in the 10th, 11th and 13th Chasseurs and the 5th Cuirassiers. On 29 August NCOs of the 6th Artillery at Metz told General Barrois that they no longer wanted to serve under their colonel, who was too strict and anti-patriotic: 'He always treated them harshly, and during the events of July he called the tricolour a horseblanket.'[30] They revolted, pulled the regimental standard from the colonel's door and broke into his house; the colonel was forced to hide in a closet until a servant persuaded the soldiers to leave. Metz police reported that the trouble was provoked by 'some of the common people'.[31]

The trouble quickly spread to near-by Thionville, where the 5th Hussards and 33rd Infantry Regiment revolted against their officers. Confusion broke out in the 5th Hussards after the colonel, a major, six captains, two lieutenants and two second-lieutenants who had resigned after learning of the revolution attempted to rejoin their regiment. Both officers and NCOs refused to let them rejoin and the NCOs, encouraged by republicans, claimed that they were returning to order both the 5th and the 33rd to march against the people. NCOs in the 13th Infantry Regiment presented a list of nineteen officers whose dismissal they demanded. Similar incidents were reported in the 1st and 4th Dragoons, the 2nd Engineers, the 10th, 19th, 31st, 36th, 47th and 49th Infantry Regiments and the 7th Cuirassiers. 'A Carlist', the saying went, 'is a man who has a job that someone else wants.'[32]

The revolutionary NCO is a phenomenon peculiar to the post-Revolutionary French army. Hoping to democratize the class-structured army of the *ancien régime*, revolutionary governments worked to open the officer corps to the lower classes. To facilitate direct promotion from sergeant to second-lieutenant, they struck down the 1780 ordinance which restricted the officer corps to the nobility. As Saint-Cyr was too small to fill the yearly officer quota, most French officers came up through the ranks in the infantry and cavalry, though the artillery continued to be dominated by school-trained men. In 1832 Soult pointed out that of 4,489 men commissioned as second-lieutenants between 1821 and 1831, 2,537 were promoted through the ranks and 1,952 through military schools.[33] Well over half of the officers were ex-NCOs.

This promotion system had a peculiar effect on the French army. Most armies were stratified according to class, with the soldier's career terminating at the relative position of his class in the military hierarchy; lower middle-class soldiers could hope to be sergeants or sergeant-majors, middle-class officers ended their careers as captains or majors, while aristocrats hoped for a higher command. Each soldier realized that his ambitions were limited by his social class. The revolutionary application of the promotional system in the

French army broke down class barriers and weakened the traditional social authority of the military hierarchy: a lower middle-class soldier now aspired to a commission and was no longer content with a lower rank. Consequently, the NCO 'class' was fluid and socially unstable. It welcomed the prospect of political turmoil which undermined the officers' authority and created opportunity for promotion. Carrel noted that 'this insubordination has revealed the dormant ambition and disaffection of the army.'[34]

Contemporary writers were aware of the revolutionary tendencies of the French NCO. Morand noted in 1829 that the French NCO was in fact an apprentice officer and that this had an unsettling effect on military organization. He called for the establishment of several levels in the military hierarchy where a soldier could end his career with a sense of accomplishment. He suggested that these ranks should be sergeant-major, captain and colonel.[35] Tocqueville noted that military revolutions were rare in 'aristocratic' armies – or armies where rank corresponded to the soldier's equivalent social position; 'democratic' armies, however, were revolution-prone because ambitious NCOs looked for ways to gain quick promotion. Rémusat interpreted the 1830 military revolution as the rebellion of middle-class NCOs against their aristocratic officers: 'The tricolour did not replace the white flag, especially in the cavalry, without something of a military bourgeois uprising against noble officers.'[36]

As Napoleon recognized when he observed that every French soldier carried a marshal's baton in his knapsack, the post-Revolutionary French army offered lower middle-class soldiers an excellent opportunity to improve their social position. The ambition of these NCOs explains their indiscipline and the large-scale denunciations following the revolution.

Officials repeatedly advised the War Ministry to make every effort to ensure NCO loyalty to the Orléans government. 'They [NCOs] must be persuaded', warned Charpentier in September 1830, 'to support the present government, and the best way is to promote them. Above all, officers and NCOs from disbanded guard regiments must not be sent to line regiments. This would only cause new trouble and new disorder.'[37]

General Lenoury, Inspector-General of the Artillery, echoed Charpentier in 1836: 'There is a danger that the lack of promotion will discourage and alienate NCOs whose support is so essential for the government and whose influence on the troops was so conclusively demonstrated in the 1830 revolution.'[38]

General La Mortière recommended in 1844 that NCOs promoted to second-lieutenant be required to change regiments to prevent them conspiring with the NCOs to oust other officers: 'When a regime falls, we have witnessed military conspiracies in which officers promoted through the ranks join, secretly or otherwise, with their ex-colleagues in the regiment to harass and even denounce other officers in the hope of taking their place or of avenging punishment.'[39]

The revolutionary inclinations of the NCOs made them a particularly favoured target for republican propaganda throughout the July Monarchy. General Danrémont, commander of the 8th Military Division at Marseille, noted in April 1833 that republican efforts to undermine military discipline centred on the NCOs and soldiers.[40] 'NCOs and soldiers are especially vulnerable to republican propaganda.' The Prefect of the Bouches-du-Rhône, Thomas, reported in March 1834, that republicans were active among NCOs in the Marseille garrison:[41] 'Shrewd agents have introduced republican pamphlets to many soldiers. They entice off-duty soldiers into public houses and try to undermine their loyalty. A pamphlet signed "Richard" contains a self-styled protest by Paris NCOs reprinted from the *Tribune*. They have convinced several of our NCOs that Paris NCOs had made a collective declaration that they would never open fire on the people. They were told that the entire Paris garrison was therefore going to be transferred but that replacement regiments would take the same stand. These efforts have been directed especially at NCOs from the 13th Infantry Regiment.' In April 1834 the commander of the 11th Military Division at Bordeaux reported, 'They [the republicans] have of late attempted to establish contacts with NCOs in this garrison to win them over to their demagogic ideas. But so far there is no evidence that these criminal plans have met with success.'[42] 'NCOs are the favourite targets of conspirators,' reported General Pajol in May from Paris. 'They follow them on Sundays and holidays, take up with them, and buy them drinks.'[43] He reported again in June that republicans had not been discouraged by their setback in April: 'The enemies of our government and of the King, republicans and Carlists, continue their intrigues to draw our soldiers, especially the NCOs, into their camp. They will fail for the army leadership is vigilant.'[44] Thiers noted that NCOs touched off the 1830 disorders in the army: 'Trouble broke out in the army after several unfortunate incidents made NCOs realize they could reach officer rank by denouncing their superiors.'[45]

In April 1834 pamphlets appeared in regiments all over France calling on NCOs to throw out their officers.[46] Saint-Menaud, public prosecutor under the Restoration, wrote to the Société des Droits de l'Homme at Dijon in March 1834 that republicans were certainly strong enough to overthrow the government as they had the support of many NCOs: 'With NCOs from several regiments already on our side, we are assured of victory.'[47] After 1834, when republican activity in the army became more conspiratorial, many secret societies would only accept NCOs. In 1835 a secret society in the 11th and 17th Infantry Regiments at Toulouse was opened only to 'militaires gradés',[48] while Sergeant Rebière, arrested in 1836 as the leader of all republicans in the army, confessed that 400 NCOs belonged to secret societies.[49] Colonel Vaudrey, who led Louis Napoleon's attempted *coup d'état* in October 1836, reported that the future emperor had confidence in the success of his plot because he had the support of many NCOs: 'I pointed out that one regiment was not sufficient to ensure the success of such a conspiracy. But the prince replied that he would find support throughout the garrison and especially among NCOs.'[50]

In 1837, the colonel of the 60th Infantry Regiment reported trouble in his regiment with 'a good number of NCOs with many years of service behind them (the 60th has many Corsicans) and easily influenced'.[51] An address delivered at a republican meeting in September 1836 reveals that republicans counted on NCOs to lead the revolution:[52]

> Citizen NCOs, I have been asked by many of your friends in several garrisons, soldiers like yourselves, to appeal to your loyalty, so that you will join with us to overthrow the government on the day which will change the future of France. Tell us we can count on you, but keep what you have just heard strictly secret, for we know how to deal with traitors.

Of those soldiers cited by name in reports to the War Minister for republican activity under the July Monarchy, 18 per cent were sergeant-majors, 51 per cent were sergeants, 14 per cent were corporals and only 17 per cent were privates. The vast majority of military republicans were NCOs.[53]

NCOs continued to lead efforts to spread republicanism in the army after 1830. They stood to gain by indiscipline and confusion in the army and therefore were attracted to the opposition, as in 1830. For this reason, republican success in the army depended greatly on governmental instability.

Chapter 4

Casimir Périer and the politics of stability

The unstable revolutionary foundations of the July Monarchy undermined the government's ability to impose order. The government formed on 1 August united men who had nothing in common but their opposition to the Bourbons. Both the cabinet and the famous 221 deputies who had formed the liberal majority under the Bourbons were heterogeneous groups of liberals and conservatives with irreconcilable political differences. Consequently, Paris was unable to formulate a coherent approach to the nation's political, social and economic problems.

The economic crisis and the almost total absence of governmental control aggravated the disruptive effects of the revolution. Rioting increased and local officials who feared that Paris would not endorse a hard line hesitated to enforce order. Thus, the revolution soon became more powerful than the government.

Ceding to conservative pleas for firm government, Louis-Philippe, who nevertheless assiduously courted the Left, finally asked the prominent liberal banker, Laffitte, to form a cabinet. On 2 November he appointed Marshal Maison (later replaced by General Sebastiani) as Minister of Foreign Affairs, Dupont de l'Eure as Justice Minister and Montalivet as Interior Minister. Mérilhou entered the Ministry of Public Instruction and Argôut the Naval Ministry, while Gérard, who was succeeded by Soult on 17 November, remained in the War Ministry. This compromise cabinet of liberal and conservative members and the *laisser-aller* philosophy of Laffitte were not destined to restore confidence in the government. The Chief Minister, whose favourite phrase was 'tout s'arrangera', believed that his liberal philosophy obliged him to govern as little as possible – Carrel called Laffitte's administration 'government by neglect'. Consequently, the nation continued to suspect its leaders.

The army too suffered from the absence of a firm hand. General Gérard, a leftist sympathizer, was no more conscientious than Laffitte and failed to exercise a stabilizing influence on the regiments. He merely issued inspector generals with cartes blanches to re-establish discipline in Castellane's case or to purge the army of pro-

Bourbon officers in General Rouget's. Consequently, discipline was very unevenly enforced, if at all. General Rouget, who nurtured a grudge for his dismissal in 1824, seriously undermined discipline by encouraging political denunciations. Other inspectors certainly followed his lead: forty-four out of sixty-four infantry regiments and five out of six dragoon regiments changed their colonels. La Motte Rouge, who was himself suspended for a brief period, reported the complete breakdown of discipline following the revolution, especially after General Rouget's irresponsible September inspection: 'Order and authority were rendered impossible. Insubordination grew alarmingly in the days following the revolution and especially during this inspection. Men whom the rest of the corps had rightly dismissed as good-for-nothing, played the victim and complained they had not been given their due because they held liberal views.'[1]

TABLE 5   *Imperial veterans reactivated in 1830**

	Reactivated 1831	In active service 1841	Promotion with	Promotion without
Infantry				
Colonels	7	5	3	2
Lieut.-colonels	6	4	3	1
Majors	43	20	15	5
Captains	176	55	11	44
Lieutenants	269	74	64	10
2nd lieutenants	312	126	110	16
Total	813	284	206	78
Cavalry				
Colonels	6	4	2	2
Lieut.-colonels	11	7	7	—
Majors	30	18	12	6
Captains	97	35	15	20
Lieutenants	158	67	63	4
2nd lieutenants	153	81	75	6
Total	455	212	174	38

* Devalez de Caffol, *Statistique militaire*, Paris, 1843, 5ᵉ tableau A[5].

General Gérard was also criticized for filling officer vacancies with ex-royal guardsmen and Napoleonic *demi-soldes* reinstated with full seniority. A 28 August ordinance reserved half of the vacated positions for imperial veterans. As a result, 813 retired officers rejoined the infantry and 455 the cavalry, although only nine artillerymen came out of retirement. This had a long-term effect on promotion for in 1841, 36 per cent of these infantry officers and 47 per cent of these cavalrymen were still in active service.

Carrel complained that trouble in many regiments stemmed from competition for promotion:[2]

> The regiments are not prepared to tolerate men who
> denounced, harassed and oppressed them under the last
> regime. Nor do they want to compete for promotion with
> reinstated Royal Guard officers. Lastly, they fear the return of
> Imperial veterans with crushing seniority. That is the key to the
> trouble which has disrupted several regiments.

Canrobert also deplored the indiscipline occasioned by the reinstatement of the *demi-soldes*:[3]

> They touched off insurrections in a number of regiments and
> momentarily destroyed all discipline. Several reinstated generals
> did not believe it to be in the government's interest to act
> decisively against these attempted mutinies. To shirk one's
> duty only encourages insubordination.

Indiscipline plagued many regiments following the revolution. Baron Sers, who took over the prefecture of the Moselle in late August, deplored the indiscipline in the Metz garrison: 'The soldiers were running wild.' Soldiers in several regiments had thrown out their officers and roamed the streets in drunken bands waving tricoloured flags. Officers felt powerless to stop them as both the municipal government and top army officers were sympathetic to the Left. The mayor was an avowed republican while General Barrois, the new commander of the 3rd Military Division, had voted for the death of the Duc d'Enghien. General Soyé, the garrison commander, was afraid to oppose mobs who claimed to be acting in the name of the revolution: 'He was imbued with the idea that the people were sovereign.' General Duchand, commander of Metz's two artillery regiments, ostentatiously wore an imperial legion of honour ribbon and publicly called for a Napoleonic restoration. 'The colonels felt the need for strong support. They bemoaned the generals' lack of resolve and obsequiousness in the presence of left-wing leaders.'[4]

Several officers in the 10th Infantry Regiment en route from Lyon to Avignon were arrested when they attempted to proclaim a republic. 'This is an example', wrote Canrobert, 'of how out of touch with reality everyone was at that moment . . . The revolution and the reigning state of mind had severely weakened any notion of convention and discipline.'[5]

Worsening social conditions in the east following the revolution especially favoured the opposition. Republicanism flourished in the east's large commercial middle class which was attached to the liberal principles and patriotism of the Left. After the 1830 revolution, the population of the large eastern garrison towns soared. Between 1830 and 1840 the population of Strasbourg increased by 20,586 people while Nancy and Besançon experienced a similar influx from the countryside. The population of Metz increased by 81 per cent in this period and that of Lyon by 76 per cent between 1830 and 1836 alone. This sudden influx brought with it problems of unemployment, overcrowding and bad housing. The social unrest which accompanied this population growth strengthened government opponents in these large garrison towns. The army soon felt the effects of the militant political climate in the east. General Brayer reported in October that republicans at Strasbourg had infiltrated the garrison,[6] while NCOs in the 7th Cuirassiers and 4th Dragoons at Thionville repeatedly insulted their superior officers.[7] The 31st Infantry Regiment in Paris reported that NCOs refused to obey orders and insubordination in the 36th Infantry at Nîmes was so bad that the regiment was transferred to Dijon.[8] Trouble was reported among Strasbourg artillery regiments in November[9] and in December Captain Lacombe of the 1st Hussars was accused of belonging to the Paris republican party.[10] The mayor of Soumières accused NCOs in the 2nd Light Infantry Regiment of insulting the king.[11]

This social unrest was accompanied by a progressive deterioration of the political situation. The split in opposition ranks became apparent in the first hours of the revolution, as republicans led by Lafayette flocked to the Hôtel de Ville leaving parliament in liberal hands. But the republicans were too few and too disorganized to steer the revolution, and, following the Orléanist initiative, fell in behind Louis-Philippe, who was proclaimed king on 9 August.

This fragile alliance soon began to strain as Cavaignac, Trélat and the militant Amis du Peuple called for the enfranchisement of the lower middle classes, an elected judiciary, the election of army officers and NCOs, free universal education, the abolition of the wine tax and an end to state support of the Church.[12] The working classes were largely ignored by this group who attracted students and young professional men.[13] Their foreign policy was a restatement of the revolutionary 'war on kings' which would liberate Europe from her oppressive aristocracy and reflect glory on France.[14]

Although the Amis du Peuple confined their activity to Paris, they had many provincial sympathizers, especially in the east. 'By drawing a line from Metz to Montpellier', the tribune announced in August 1833, 'you have a republican map of France.'[15] But virtually every French town counted some republican sympathizers. And this map would exclude Paris and other quite large republican centres like Toulouse and Perpignan and many smaller ones including Rennes, Nantes and Montauban.[16]

Patriotism, above all, motivated provincial republicans, who commanded some fifty newspapers by 1833.[17] In the wake of the revolution, patriotic 'associations nationales' sprang up throughout France, especially on the eastern frontiers, to repulse the invasion they believed imminent. Provincial republicans feted Polish officers after their 1831 revolution was crushed by the Czar, organized to pay government fines imposed on republican journals and agitated against the fortification of Paris which they claimed would only serve to facilitate repression of insurrections. Yet, only in 1833 after government harassment had virtually silenced the Amis du Peuple did the Paris Droits de l'Homme attempt to co-ordinate republican activities throughout France.

In 1831 indiscipline and political opposition began to fuse in the army. In the south, republican activity was reported in the 37th Infantry and the 4th Light Infantry Regiment in Marseille,[18] and soldiers were arrested for making anti-government speeches in the 48th Infantry Regiment at Bordeaux and the 55th Regiment at Tarbes.[19] Two NCOs in the 2nd Light Infantry Regiment were arrested after the colonel complained of the regiment's 'mauvais esprit' and several NCOs in the 9th Light Infantry Regiment at Montpellier joined an anti-government demonstration.[20] Insubordination and desertions were reported in the 12th Infantry Regiment as both republicans and Carlists tried to disrupt the national service call-up and induce soldiers to desert.[21] In March Hussards from the 4th Regiment led by a 2nd Lieutenant ordered the father superior to vacate his seminary at Le Mans, probably taking their cue from revolutionaries who had sacked a number of Paris churches – including Saint-Germain l'Auxerrois one month earlier.[22] Republicans were also active in the 46th Regiment at Tours and the 50th at Nantes.[23] Republican canvassing continued in the east in the 17th Light Infantry at Belfort,[24] and several Paris regiments, including the 13th, 52nd and 60th Infantry Regiments, reported that some among their NCOs and soldiers supported the republican cause.[25]

This was the situation in the army when Casimir Périer agreed to form a Cabinet on 11 March. The nation, too, was discontented.

Revolutionaries had forced Louis-Philippe to scratch the fleurs-de-
lys from his coat of arms, while the impotence of Laffitte's *laisser-
aller* philosophy in the face of revolution had driven the press to
distort its valid criticisms of the government. Fearing revolution,
some 150,000 well-to-do Parisians left their homes, leaving behind
many closed shops and unemployed to aggravate the economic
crisis. Pressured by conservative attacks on Laffitte – 'La France
demande à être gouvernée et sent qu'elle ne l'est pas' – and by a
war-hungry public, Louis-Philippe dismissed his chief minister
only four months after his appointment.

The decisive Casimir Périer immediately set about stabilizing the
country. He named a conservative Cabinet, excluding showpiece
liberals such as Dupont de l'Eure and Mérilhou, and demanded that
it publicly support his proposals. He instituted regular Cabinet
meetings, insisted that all correspondence pass through his hands
before reaching the king and that he sign all royal proclamations,
before publication in the *Moniteur*. He also advised Louis-Philippe to
move from the Palais Royal, the traditional residence of the
Duc d'Orléans, to the Tuileries to bolster the prestige of the monarchy and took steps to order bureaucratic chaos.

The army also began to feel the effects of strong government.
Liberal mayors of garrison towns were replaced and generals
sympathetic to the Left cashiered. In Metz, for instance, the republican mayor lost his job and General Barrois was quietly retired
and his position given to General Delort. In April military pensions,
which had been a major source of discontent in the Restoration
army, were raised to a level double or nearly double the Restoration
figures (see Table 6). Discipline companies were set up in Algeria
to take political dissidents and particularly troublesome regiments
were also sent there. On 13 April Casimir Périer informed Soult
that he opposed the notoriously republican Metz National Guard's
plan to give a banquet for NCOs in the garrison.[26] In 1831 he
instructed inspecting generals to dismiss political dissidents who
complained about their superiors. General Rouget, who had been
very sympathetic to military 'liberals' in 1830, dismissed or jailed
every potential troublemaker in 1831; he cashiered three officers
in the 56th Infantry Regiment at Grenoble, and in May jailed a
captain and a lieutenant in the 35th Infantry Regiment with the
comment: 'They continued the sort of agitation I wanted to end.
Some, whose political opinions are hardly in keeping with their
position, would perhaps still plot with the Grenoble bourgeoisie.'[27]
In an extraordinary inspection of the 66th Infantry Regiment at
Lyon, General Hulot dismissed six officers.

In June the government moved against the popular 'associations nationales' which covered forty-one departments by March. Founded after the revolution under the leadership of Armand Carrel, Béranger and Salverte, these associations had vowed to 'guarantee the country's independence and the definitive exclusion of the elder branch of the Bourbons'. Their cry for a war of European liberation and their strong following in the east, where many regiments were stationed, made them especially attractive to officers and NCOs.

TABLE 6   *Pensions for Restoration and after Périer reform*

	Restoration	April 1831
Lieutenant général	3,000	4,000
Maréchal de camp	2,000	3,000
Colonel	1,200	2,400
Lieut. colonel	1,000	1,800
Chef de bataillon	900	1,500
Capitaine	600	1,200
Lieutenant	450	800
Sous-lieutenant	350	600
Sergent-major	182.50	300
Sergent	136.87	250
Simple soldat	91.25	200

On 15 June the order of the day in the 7th and 19th Military Divisions at Lyon and Clermont-Ferrand warned officers that membership in political associations was incompatible with their duties:[28]

> I have been informed . . . that some of you belong to
> organizations where the uniform and the sword should never
> appear. We must remain above politics. I can understand how
> inexperienced officers could go astray in these difficult times.
> In becoming soldiers, you have not ceased to be citizens. You
> can prove this by respecting property, by supporting order
> and by enforcing the law . . . But to use your influence as
> soldiers to spread and even to impose one doctrine or one form
> of government, to take part in political agitation, when we
> must remain above politics, is to misinterpret your duty.

After issuing several warnings, War Minister Soult dismissed several officers in the Metz garrison and a student officer at the

Ecole d'Application for belonging to the Association de la Moselle. In September, however, Charpentier, deputy for La Moselle and himself a member of the association, accused the War Ministry of retiring the officers illegally: 'No government has ever treated the army so overbearingly, despotically and illegally. I doubt whether Bonaparte himself went so far.'[29] The liberal deputy Tracy seconded Charpentier's demand that the officers be reinstated.

Soult's defence of his action sums up government policy towards political activity in the army and is proof of his own determination to reassert military discipline and to dissociate the army once and for all from politics.[30]

> As for the societies the officers joined, I respect their feelings and was convinced their motives were honourable. However, they were soldiers, and as such it was my duty to supervise their conduct. Only in this way can the minister answer for the army to the king and country . . . No soldier, whatever his rank, can be permitted to join a non-military organization. I knew that societies were forming; I weighed my decision. Only those who, after repeated warnings, refused to leave the society were told: 'All right, go home and think about it for a while.'

Supporting Soult, General Bugeaud attacked the double standard of liberal deputies and insisted that the army must never become involved in politics: 'Duty and nothing else must be the army's watchword. What would your reaction be if officers organized for a rival cause? If, for example, Carlists organized political associations . . . officers who joined such groups would have to be dismissed.'[31]

Yet, although the government took steps to re-establish discipline, political activity increased in the regiments. A second-lieutenant in the 53rd Infantry Regiment at Metz wrote articles for the liberal *Journal du Commerce*, which later became *La Constitutionelle*,[32] while NCOs in the 18th Infantry Regiment at Bitche were reported collecting money for the poor – a move which the government believed to have been instigated by republicans.[33] Activity continued in the south as police had to be called in to subdue riotous soldiers in the 55th Regiment at Tarbes. In May soldiers in the 6th Infantry Regiment at Montpellier were associating with local republicans, prompting the War Minister to move the regiment to another garrison,[34] while the 42nd Infantry Regiment was transferred from Grenoble after three officers were jailed for political activity.[35] NCOs in the 66th Infantry Regiment were cited for insubordination.

This dissent reached a peak at the end of May, as republicans launched a campaign to plant 'liberty trees' all across France. The 15th Light Infantry Regiment called out on 23 May to break up a republican tree-planting demonstration in Tarascon refused to disperse the dissidents and instead turned on a Carlist counter-demonstration with drawn sabres, wounding twenty demonstrators. The Tarascon affair had repercussions throughout the army and the country: for many it embodied the army's refusal to endorse Périer's politics of stability.

Rebellion increased in the east, especially in the Metz and Strasbourg garrisons. A Strasbourg republican wrote to a friend in Paris that the army would turn the revolution into a republican victory: 'We have at least 300 republicans here. We joined with some workers for the riot, convinced that the troops, especially the artillery, were behind us. We knew no one would fire on the people. They will rally to us when the Republic is proclaimed.'[36] Republicans attempted to force a confrontation with authorities in the Bouches-du-Rhône with further tree-plantings. The commander of the National Guard and the colonel of the 2nd Infantry Regiment informed the mayor of Aix-en-Provence that they could not count on their troops to disperse a planned republican demonstration, as they were conspiring to imitate the example set by the 15th Regiment:[37]

> The colonel of the 2nd Infantry Regiment dares not take it
> upon himself to answer for the conduct of his 400 men. I have
> just learned from reliable sources that most of the NCOs in his
> regiment have been won over by the anarchists. I am told the
> same is true of several officers who, when asked in the cafés
> what they would do if ordered to clamp down, said they would
> not hesitate to follow the example of their brothers at Tarascon.

General Rouget reported that officers in the 66th Regiment would lead a regimental mutiny if ordered to break up demonstrations: 'At the time of the Tarascon affair, officers in the 66th Infantry Regiment boldly declared that in similar circumstances the troops should be incited to revolt to crush what they call the Juste Milieu.'[38] The Prefect at Montauban complained to the Minister of the Interior that the 55th Regiment which, after repeated trouble, had been moved from Tarbes and which had received a number of soldiers 'reprieved' by the discipline councils which were reluctant to enforce a strict discipline could not be counted on to crush a popular insurrection: 'This is the regiment', he wrote, 'which caused trouble in Bordeaux and one other town a few years ago. It is not reliable, and I shall probably ask that it be replaced by a more devoted, more dependable regiment.'[39]

On 26 June the Prefect of the Bouches-du-Rhône wrote that republicans had indoctrinated troops in the Marseille garrison and Rouget reported that several officers at Grenoble were masons.[40] Insubordination was reported in the 13th Light Infantry Regiment,[41] and republicans encouraged soldiers and NCOs in Toulouse to revolt against their officers.[42] The situation was so critical that the Minister of the Interior sent a circular to all Prefects instructing them to take special precautions against infiltration of local garrisons.[43] A lieutenant in the 52nd Infantry Regiment at Paris was arrested for republican activity and trouble continued in the east as the Prefect of the Bas-Rhin reported that soldiers in the 5th battery of the 6th Artillery stationed at Drusenheim were plotting with local republicans.[44] General Delort reported that a conspiracy to overthrow the government had been uncovered in the 7th Dragoons at Epinal[45] – this plot was closely linked to the Lunéville insurrection three years later. Republican activity continued to gain momentum in the 66th Regiment, the 21st and 37th Infantry Regiments at Marseille, the 56th at Grenoble and the Toulouse, Bordeaux and Toulon garrisons. Although the 15th Light Infantry Regiment was sent to Algeria, soldiers of the 6th Chasseurs and 23rd Infantry Regiment, who replaced it in Tarascon, soon began to frequent republican cafés.

Legitimists also began to organize after their 1830 defeat. This revival took two forms. One group – led in parliament by Berryer and in the press by Chateaubriand and Genoude, editor of the *Gazette de France* – prepared an alliance with the Left to mobilize grassroots support against the common Orléans enemy, confident that a republican victory and the bogey of anarchy would rally France behind them.

Republican resistance to Carlist overtures crumbled as the government gained strength – 'If we do not have the same heaven', the saying went, 'we have the same hell' – and Carlist gold soon began flowing into republican coffers: Genoude helped found the leftist journal *Nation* in 1831, while Chateaubriand and the *Gazette de France* contributed to the government fine imposed in the same year on the *Tribune*.

In the south, republicans and legitimists met at the banqueting table as white journalists echoed red support of the Polish insurgents and called for universal suffrage and liberal reforms designed to embarrass a government which still paid lip service to revolution.

A second group led by the Duchess de Berry, Comte Ferdinand de Bertier and General Bourmont planned to combine a popular uprising in the Vendée, a royalist stronghold since 1789, with a military rebellion.

Hoping to rally officers who had resigned in 1830 rather than serve the July Monarchy, they drew up a programme promising financial and moral incentives. They proposed:

1. To release from the army all who were unwilling to support their cause.
2. To pension all wounded men and their wives.
3. To promote and decorate the African army.
4. To introduce a new recruitment law abolishing conscription above task strength and raising pay.[46]

Bertier was confident the army was eager to avenge its 1830 defeat:[47]

> Officers who resigned after the July days [he wrote to the Duchess de Berry] could play the same role in our party as the *demi-soldes* among the Bonapartists. Of those who stayed in the army, many have felt humiliated by the victory of the streets and would welcome the army's revenge on the people of Paris. The threat of purges created a serious malaise among officers and NCOs.

The Duchess replied in December that the loyalty of officers who had resigned after the revolution should be ensured by healthy incentives – the conspirators, she said, should pay senior officers two-thirds of their salary, while lieutenants and captains should be paid in full.[48]

A military committee was established to contact retired officers and to determine the political orientation of the regiments. Carlist sympathizers were encouraged to enlist in the National Guard and conscripts awaiting military service were urged to hold themselves back for a chouan uprising.

By January 1831 the west and the south of the country had been divided into six strategic divisions, each commanded by a royalist general under the supreme command of General Bourmont. Bertier claimed that, outside the artillery, only two regiments in these areas remained to be won over, although little ground had been gained in the north and east.

The uprising in the west was to be followed by a declaration of a provisional government which would court mass support by slashing taxes.

In July police reported that two ex-Royal Guard officers, Bermont and Mauduit, had been arrested at Aix-en-Provence after encouraging desertion among ex-Guards in Lyon's 66th Infantry Regiment.[49] The two men had apparently stressed the inferiority of the line regiment. 'You are not as well off here as in the Royal

Guard', they told NCOs. 'Your uniforms are not so handsome and your pay is lower. But we must hope that all this will soon change.'[50]

Royalist activity, spearheaded by ex-Guard officers, was also reported in the Bordeaux, Avignon and Marseille garrisons.[51]

However, the Carlists were most successful in Paris. A government investigation into the arrest of three Swiss chouans near Rennes and twenty others at Le Mans revealed that legitimists had recruited widely among ex-Swiss Guards in Rueil, outside Paris.

The public prosecutor at Versailles noted that the Swiss, whose regiments had been abolished, were idle and impoverished and easily won over by the hundred franc enlistment bonus offered by the Carlists: 'They have little to live on. They do not work . . . They feel nothing but hatred for a government which dismissed them from its service. They dream only of civil war.'[52]

Royalist activity continued into the autumn, but without much success either in Brittany or in the south.

Republican activity, however, mushroomed throughout France in the autumn of 1831, but government attention was focused on Lyon where silkworkers demanding higher wages threatened violence. The presence in the garrison of the 66th Infantry Regiment, formed after the July revolution from the remnants of the Royal Guard, also worried officials. Most officers and men had tasted defeat on the barricades in 1830. Consequently, the 66th was demoralized and reluctant to confront Lyon workers.

The position of the army in this politically explosive town had been difficult since July 1830. In August the government named ex-Napoleonic General Bachelu, a *demi-solde* retired by Clermont-Tonnerre in 1824, to command the 19th Military Division. A liberal opposition leader in his native Jura in the last years of the Restoration, Bachelu actively courted the Lyon Left. In January 1831 he published a pamphlet criticizing the government for retaining ex-Restoration officials and failing to punish adequately Charles X's ministers. He also demanded immediate electoral reform and decried the July Monarchy's peace at any price foreign policy.[53]

Elected deputy for the Jura, Bachelu resigned from the army in March 1831 and was replaced at Lyon by General Rouget. Discipline, already weakened under Bachelu, further deteriorated under Rouget, the son of a locksmith and a notorious liberal. The republican-dominated National Guard gave banquets for the garrison and the vocal liberalism of both commanders undermined officers who attempted to keep the troops firmly in hand.

In October General Rouget reported that republican and Carlist agents were active in the garrison and he feared that both groups had solicited foreign backing to co-ordinate popular uprisings in Lyon and the Midi which would draw the army away from the frontiers and invite an invasion: 'Our enemies want to keep the army occupied far from the neglected frontiers. They are trying to undermine discipline and this could lead to trouble.'[54]

By November, the Prefect, Bouvier-Dumolard, complained that revolution was imminent. Most workers were paid only 18 sous a day while tax reform had tripled their annual contributions.[55] The police force was too small and ineffective and Paris ignored repeated requests for a budget increase. Consequently, the Prefect was forced to give his annual 6,000 franc entertainment allowance for its upkeep. Both the examining magistrate and local juries were reluctant to convict political misdemeanours.[56] The town's five newspapers supported the opposition and Paris refused to fund a sixth favourable to the government. The garrison, which consisted of only one infantry and one cavalry regiment, was too small and the National Guard unreliable.[57] Furthermore, relations were strained between the Prefect and General Rouget since the former had asked for the 66th's transfer. 'This report', wrote Bouvier-Dumolard, 'deeply wounded General Rouget.'[58]

On 20 November General Roguet strongly refuted the Prefect's allegations: 'The morale of the 66th is still very high and everything you hear to the contrary is completely false.'[59] He confidently declined to attend a security meeting on 20 November of the Prefect, Mayor and Police Chief and even forbade the garrison commander, General Saint-Geniès, to be present.[60]

'Police reports predict trouble tomorrow', Rouget wrote on 20 November, 'but I repeat, these are police reports . . . I believe that reports of the agitators' plans are exaggerated and I think that you need not worry. In any case, the slightest disturbance will be dealt with instantly.'[61] After his dismissal, he claimed that he had not been informed of the security meeting.[62]

When Lyon workers threw up barricades on 21 November, army morale was dangerously low. The Prefect complained that the soldiers were called out only several hours after the fighting began and that many who were billeted with civilians stayed at home.[63] In the afternoon, part of the 66th refused to fight and cavalry was ineffective in Lyon's narrow, sloping streets. Repression was also hampered by the lack of artillery. Rouget sent for help from nearby garrisons, but his message was intercepted at the barricades. On the 22nd, the army abandoned the city after suffering over 900 desertions. Rouget confessed that the troops lacked resolve: 'in several quarters, the troops willingly handed over their weapons, others absolutely refused to fight; most seemed, despite the leadership and tenacity of the officers, disposed to join the insurgents.'[64]

The government quickly rushed 18,000 troops to Lyon led by the Duc d'Orléans and Marshal Soult and so restored order. The size of the garrison was subsequently increased and the War Minister ordered barracks for 20,000 men built. The police force was strengthened and 100,000 francs given for poor relief.[65] On 8 December Rouget was relieved and replaced by General Hulot.

These disorders in the army set the stage for the debate on the army reorganization bill and shaped the final provisions of the 1832 Soult law.

Chapter 5

The Soult law

Sandwiched between the Saint-Cyr law of 1818 and Niel's dazzling if futile effort to reform the army in 1867, the Soult law of 1832 has been sadly neglected by historians. Not only is the law a crucial piece of military legislation, but by studying its history one can trace the conservatism of the July Monarchy under the Périer ministry.

Theories of military organization traditionally split France into two political camps. Until 1870, conservatives favoured a small, tightly organized professional army insulated against political ferment. Liberals, however, influenced by Revolutionary notions of military organization, fought to broaden conscription and organize a trained reserve.

The issues raised by laws on military organization in this period are therefore central to the political and ideological questions which then divided France. Far from being a minor bill, the Soult law, introduced only a few months after Casimir Périer replaced the liberal Laffitte as chief minister, was to be a major test of the government's ability to seize the parliamentary initiative from the liberals, still drunk with the success of 1830.

This chapter sets out to define both the military significance of the Soult law and the political climate which shaped it.

Most historians have assumed that the Soult law merely duplicated the 1818 Saint-Cyr law. Among them was Monteilhet: 'Except, perhaps, for a year of service, the 1832 law only reproduces the 1818–1824 law . . . Why look for a legal innovation when neither ideas nor facts have changed?'[1]

Bertier de Sauvigny maintains that the 1818 law governed the army until 1872. 'Until 1872', wrote Bertier de Sauvigny, 'the army lived by the principles laid down by Gouvion-Saint-Cyr in 1818.'[2] Bernard Schnapper makes the same point: 'After the July revolution, the law of 21 March 1832, which charted military recruitment for forty years, did not modify the principles of Gouvion-Saint-Cyr.'[3] A closer examination of the 1832 law, however, reveals that it did differ in fact and in concept from the 1818 law.

The July Monarchy, hastily constructed on revolutionary

foundations, was eager to surround itself with stable institutions. The army bill, introduced in 1831, was a major test of the Périer ministry's ability to snuff out indiscipline in the ranks and give the July Monarchy the conservative orientation for which it was hesitantly groping.

Presented to the Chamber of Deputies by the Minister of War, Marshal Soult, on 17 August 1831, the Soult law retained many provisions of the 1818 Saint-Cyr law. Though Soult paid tribute to Saint-Cyr and the 1818 law, he stressed the need to modify it.[4]

> Gentlemen, the law of 10 March 1818 has already undergone a thirteen year trial. Carried out, for the most part, with an impartiality which makes it less burdensome, the law has become, so to speak, part of the national way of life. This trial, proof of the wisdom and skill of the illustrious captain [Saint-Cyr], the law's author, has also revealed some loopholes which escaped his notice. The bill which the king has ordered put before you . . . is designed to retain those provisions which have stood the test of time and to incorporate others which long experience has shown to be indispensable.

Prepared by a governmental commission under Marshal Count Jourdan, the new laws on recruitment and advancement were not intended to change radically the 1818 'charter of the army', which was considered the legal guarantee of a national army. Soult's 1831 proposal contained several provisions which would have further popularized the army. Although he did not try to resurrect departmental legions, abolished by the Bourbons in 1820, the policy of conscription, which had horrified Chateaubriand, was sanctioned without discussion. In introducing the law, Soult declared: 'The first part states that the army recruits principally by conscription which you will regulate. Voluntary enlistments, always variable, will be only a secondary means.'[5] Conscription was now accepted as the rule and article 69 of the 1830 charter accorded the Chamber the right to vote the size of the annual call-up. By 1831, all citizens were liable for the draft. Neither the Restoration nor the July Monarchy included military service among the 'duties' of citizenship, however. Conservatives still looked upon conscription as an 'impôt de sang', but justified national service by the pragmatic need for an army which voluntary enlistment alone was unable to furnish. Soult stated this concisely: 'It will be positively demonstrated that voluntary enlistments are and always will be inadequate to keep the army up to strength.'[6]

Conscription was passed without argument, along with the principle of direct legislative control over the size of the annual contingent and the effective strength of the army. This could have been a victory for the liberal principle of civilian control of the army, but the Chamber never used its power to build a large national army. The narrow electorate of 170,000 upper middle-class voters feared the political unreliability of a large, essentially lower-class army. Had parliament's representative base been broader, 1832 might have opened a new era in civil-military relations. After the dismissal of Laffitte in March 1831, however, the July Monarchy paid only lip-service to democratic principles, and the right to control the size of the army both through the annual draft quota and yearly military budget remained in the hands of a conservative Chamber.

Guizot, however, reflects the commitment of many deputies to the ideal of legislative control of the annual call-up. In reply to the Landes deputy General Lamarque who proposed a measure to fix permanent army strength at 500,000 men, Guizot said: 'The real tax is paid in men, and you must not waive the right to vote it annually . . . It is the Chamber's prerogative written by you into the 1830 charter as a national right.'[7] Lamarque countered that to subordinate the military to civilian control would compromise both the security of the state and the stability of the army: 'States, like individuals, need stability. You must see how dangerous it would be to leave a military question unsettled when it needs above all unassailable stability.'[8] General Pelet, deputy for Loir-et-Cher, agreed with Guizot; a fixed army could have its advantages, 'but it contradicts the charter.' Soult, seconding Pelet, pointed out that the changing financial situation also affected the size of the army. The liberal arguments of Guizot, Pelet and Soult prevailed over the General's Bonapartist inclinations and he withdrew his amendment before it came to the vote. In practice, however, the Chamber voted a draft of 80,000 each year. This fixed the maximum strength of the army at 500,000 men, though it never reached this figure. In January 1830, Bourbon military strength stood at 223,073 officers and men, including the Royal Guard. After the numerous resignations, desertions and dismissals which followed the July Revolution, the Orléans regime inherited a depleted force of 183,311 officers and men. By April 1831 army strength was up to 304,060 and remained at this level until the reorganization of 1834. It slumped to 275,597 in 1839 but with the renewed threat of war escalated to 348,311 in 1843.[9]

Passed on 21 March 1832, the Soult law raised several of the issues already discussed in 1818. The new legislation continued the system of paid replacements and the 'conseil de révision', a body which heard appeals from conscripts and subsequently designated the 'dispensés'. Many deputies, including Teste, a deputy for the Gard, felt that military service should be a privilege reserved for French citizens:[10]

> The government's bill is based on the French idea that the army must be a national one. It is not only a question of the defence of the country and its interests. It is also a question of defending national institutions. For this reason it is both moral and politically expedient to insist that the French army be exclusively French.

The desire to keep the French army nationally pure was inherent in article 13 of the 1830 charter: 'No foreign soldier may serve the state unless permitted by law.' This amendment was adopted without discussion. Subsequently, article 2 of the Soult law also stipulated: 'No one will be permitted to serve in the French forces if he is not French.' The provision may have been designed to exclude from the French army large groups of mercenary soldiers such as the Swiss Guards and Hohenlohe regiment of the Bourbons, although this reasoning was never spelt out in any of the debates on the 1832 bill. Emmanuel Poulle, a deputy from the Var, supported by a number of other frontier deputies, complained that border areas had absorbed a large number of foreigners who enjoyed all the benefits of French law and citizenship, but claimed foreign nationality when called on for military service. Destutt de Tracy, a deputy from the Allier, argued that they formed a potential fifth column within the army. 'Is it advisable, is it politically wise to enlist men who will always be foreigners at heart and who might go over to our enemies?'

Colonel Lamy placed the finishing touches on the argument by asserting that conscription was not after all an 'impôt de sang'. 'Conscription is an obligation, a duty ... admission to our army is still a national privilege.'[11] Lamy's statement shows that some members of the Chamber intended to reconstruct the post-Bourbon army in the image of the broad-based republican and imperial armies which had conquered Europe. But as the initial flush of revolutionary excitement began to wear off and the conservative Casimir Périer firmly grasped the reins of government, the Revolutionary 'nation in arms' proposals of the original bill were abandoned in favour of a short term of service in a professional army. The astute Marshal Soult, sensing this change in the government's political mood, quickly threw his support behind the modified version of his law.

The practice of replacement underwent some slight but interesting modifications in 1832. In 1818 a conscript was permitted to buy himself out of the draft by hiring a replacement. This system provided military exemption for those whose wealth dictated that their talents could be better employed elsewhere. The Saint-Cyr law set the replacements' age limit at thirty, stipulated that they meet the army's physical standards and that they should not come from the same conscript class as the men they contracted to replace.

This system did not prove satisfactory. The army objected that replacements were physically and morally weak and, dubbing them 'les vendus', compared them to prostitutes. Replacement companies formed to assemble all eligible men for sale after the annual lottery. Agents with prostitutes on each arm hovered around the barracks to entice those who were about to be discharged to 're-enlist' as replacements. The companies conspired to raise the price of replacement and were notoriously dishonest. They attracted clients, however, for they provided a second replacement if the first one deserted within a year. According to both the 1818 and 1832 laws, if the replacement deserted within a year the conscript was required either to serve out the unfinished term of service himself or hire a second replacement. Larabit, deputy for the Yonne, bitterly attacked these companies: 'Everywhere replacement companies enlist corrupt and immoral young men.' He claimed that these companies had even sent circulars to the local priests asking them to recommend young men whose 'corrupt morals will be set right by military discipline'.[12]

The Soult law took steps to eliminate these abuses in replacement. Article 19 reiterated the physical requirements for replacements and added that they could neither be married nor widowers with children. Nor were those who had been discharged from the army for disciplinary infractions allowed to sign on as replacements. Article 20 required the prospective replacement to provide a certificate from the mayor of his commune stating the length of his residence there, that he enjoyed all civil rights and that he had never been imprisoned for a major crime. In the event that the replacement was a soldier re-enlisting as a replacement, article 21 required a statement of good conduct from his commanding officer.

Though small, these changes in the 1818 law are nevertheless significant. In requiring mayoral certification, the government required that the replacement give proof of an upright life and of his respect for the law. In theory, this restriction relieved Marmont's fear that the system would give the army, one-fourth of whose soldiers were replacements, over to undisciplined vagabonds. With this provision, the July Monarchy sought to give replacement a more democratic veneer by requiring that all replacements furnish proof that they were good citizens. This was a deceptive tactic, however, for replacement by its very nature was undemocratic. All the law really did was to provide the army with replacements who would be reasonably amenable to discipline. Far from sending good citizens into the army, the new law sought to send it potentially good soldiers. These replacements would be doubly suitable to military life. The mayoral certificate guaranteed their reasonably good conduct, while the lack of a suitable civilian alternative to military life had driven them into the army in the first instance. Consequently, the army could count on most replacements becoming permanent members of a stable professional force.

This system had a decisive effect on the social development of the army. Under the Bourbons, many aristocratic families had sent their sons into the army. After 1830, most of these legitimist officers resigned. The upper bourgeoisie, however, the traditional political base of the July Monarchy, did not fill this gap by sending their sons in sufficient number into the army. Consequently, the officer corps assumed a definite lower middle-class character. Castellane complained in 1846 that the officer corps was coming to be dominated by sons of artisans and farmers, while the military schools were filled with sons of officers and government employees. He feared that the army was treading the same path as the Church which traditionally opened the priesthood to the lower classes and was assuming a decidedly republican character.[13] The practice of replacement, together with the absence of aristocratic or upper and middle-class officers, therefore narrowed the social base of the French army. France was to have the lowest-class officer corps in Europe, drawn mainly from lower middle-class elements. The German, Hillebrand, was surprised that French officers were not 'classé' as in Germany, while R. H. Roberts blamed the French defeat in 1870 on the educational inferiority of her officers.[14]

The final and most important issues of the recruitment law concerned the duration of service and the reserve. These two topics in fact overlap. By exploring the motivation behind these measures and their subsequent alteration, we can see how the new law departed from Saint-Cyr's legislation.

According to article 29 of the 1832 law, all those who had drawn a 'mauvais numéro' in the draft lottery reported for induction. The army took those, in the order drawn, whom it needed or was financially able to absorb, sending the rest home on indefinite 'congé' or leave. Monteilhet reckons that of 80,000 men called up each year under the 1832 law 65,000 were left after the revision council had issued exemptions. Of this number, only 33,000 men at the most were actually inducted.[15] The rest were sent home to await call-up in case of a national emergency. Conservatives wished to form the reserve solely from those untrained men liable for call-up only by royal ordinance. The dynastic Left, however, believed that the advantages of a trained reserve were obvious. It ensured military flexibility and provided the army with a trained force which could be rapidly assembled in the event of an emergency. As a civilian force, it embodied the political theory of the 'nation in arms' and for this reason was opposed by conservatives. But in their attempt to ensure its internal stability, conservatives left the army open to defeat by a numerically superior enemy. The absence of a trained reserve was the real failing of the Soult law and largely accounted for the 1870 defeat. In 1866, the French army stood at 288,000 men from whom garrisons had to be furnished for Algeria, Mexico and Rome. The estimated Prussian strength after Sadowa, inclusive of their trained Landwehr and Landsturm, was one million men.[16] Worse than limiting the size of the army, however, the law entrenched in post-Revolutionary France the tradition of a small professional army unsupported by an adequate reserve.

In 1818, Saint-Cyr had acted partly on liberal principles and partly in the Bonapartist tradition of 'la guerre absolue', which necessitated a large, flexible force augmented by a trained reserve. As many of the Napoleonic veterans retired under the Restoration and July Monarchy, they were replaced by young officers raised in the traditions of a small, long term of service professional army. These officers, in positions of influence by 1866, resisted War Minister Niel's efforts to remodel the army along Prussian lines. Even after 1870, when faced with the proven impotence of a small professional army, many officers raised in the traditions of the Soult law waxed nostalgic when talking of the old, pre-1870 force. General Thoumas, an 1844 graduate of the Metz artillery school, praised the 'anti-bourgeois' spirit of the army under the July Monarchy:[17]

> Before 1854 each regiment was like a family where authority was more or less paternal . . . But every regiment shared a military and, if you put it this way, anti-bourgeois spirit. This feeling was maintained by a life apart from the population and by the little contact NCOs and soldiers had with their families.

The Duc d'Aumâle claimed that a long term of service ensured the formation of a 'national' army: 'The length of service enabled the formation of knowledgeable, dependable and devoted NCOs who today are a thing of the past. It was a brave, unified, smart, impartial, temperate, intelligent and national army.'[18]

The idea that the army was élite and yet national is confusing. D'Aumâle's conception of nationalism obviously differs from the

Revolutionary idea of the 'nation in arms', i.e. of every citizen's right to bear arms for the defence of his country. The professional army was 'national' in that it desired glory, the international dignity of France and the internal stability of the country. The Count de Mun, for example, subscribed to the conservative definition, believing that if France followed republican military doctrine she might well have 'a nation in arms, but she would no longer have an army'.[19]

The 1832 law endowed France with a professional army and a professional military establishment. The absence of a trained reserve, however, proved the army's undoing, for it was unable to protect the stability of the government which patronized it. The debates on the reserve are crucial as, in conjunction with other measures, they committed the army to a brand of nationalism and a tradition of professionalism which were to characterize it until 1870.

Article 30 of the government proposal put before the Chamber of Deputies on 17 August 1831 reduced the term of service from eight to five years. At the end of the five years, soldiers faced a two-year reserve obligation. Soult made it apparent in his opening address that the preparatory committee headed by ex-Napoleonic Marshal Jourdan, principal architect of the recruitment law of 19 fructidor, year VI (September 1796), intended to create a short term of service army with a trained reserve. Though the committee's decision was not unanimous, the majority agreed that France needed a large army: 'That it was also in the army's interest to have a large number of young men trained; that the reduction of service to five years would no doubt make the new law more popular.'[20]

The proposal of the Jourdan commission synthesized various Revolutionary and Imperial recruitment systems. The original draft of Jourdan's 1796 law, presented on 29 nivôse, year VI called for a peacetime draft of all men between eighteen and twenty years old to serve for four years in the infantry and six in the cavalry. It also included a reserve 'armée auxiliaire' of 100,000 men to be picked by lottery. Delbrel, a deputy for the Lot, objected that a true national army required a personal commitment on the part of all citizens to serve and that the 'armée auxiliaire', by exempting 100,000 men from normal military service, undermined this idea of 'service personnel'. Delbrel collaborated with Jourdan in drawing up the final proposal which required registration of all twenty-year-old males, incorporating the youngest first as dictated by military requirements. No provision was made for a reserve.

The draft of 1798 had proved chaotic, as few cantons were administratively able to call up conscripts by date of birth. A subsequent 1799 law recognized that a system of volunteers and replacements, together with a draft lottery as prescribed in the law of 24 February 1793, would be far easier to administer. This tradition continued throughout the Empire. Valée concluded that after the 1799 law, 'military service remained obligatory, it was no longer personal'.[21] Although the proposal of the 1831 Jourdan commission was not as revolutionary as Delbrel's 'service personnel', it demonstrates Jourdan's desire to create as broad-based an army as military necessity, administrative practicality and parliament, which voted the annual draft allowance, would allow.

Soult, however, claimed affinity with the 1818 law: 'The new law retains almost all the recruitment measures of the old one [the 1818 law].' Yet the duration of service and reserve provisions of the final draft of his law resembled the professionalizing tendencies of the June 1824 law, which raised the term of service to eight years and abolished Saint-Cyr's trained reserve, more than the liberal concepts of 1818.

Lawmakers and military men had to choose between two possible reserve organizations in 1830. The first was a trained reserve of veterans like that formed in 1818 and subsequently proposed by the Jourdan committee in 1831. The second involved forming a reserve of 'congés'.

In the post-1815 French army, conscripts were frequently required to serve only a portion of their active duty and were sent home on 'congé de semestre' – six months' furlough renewable until their service obligation expired – after three and a half or four years' active service. Rather than create a standing reserve, conservatives proposed to form a service out of these congés who, after their release from active service, would be counted in the reserve for the remainder of their service obligation. They claimed that this system was superior to a standing reserve as soldiers could simply be recalled to their regiments if war broke out, eliminating the need for a separate reserve organization.

Yet the congé system had several drawbacks. In the first place, congé was given only in the infantry where soldiers were easily replaced. The cavalry and artillery, which required more highly trained men, seldom released their men until their term of service had expired. Consequently, the conservative proposal would only have provided an infantry reserve. Secondly, the conservative proposal was not in line with the realities of the French recruitment system. To provide a large reserve of congés, the army would have been required to train virtually the entire annual contingent. Yet, for financial and other reasons, the army was seldom able to utilize even half of the annual contingent and was forced to send those it

69

could not use home untrained on 'congé illimité' (unlimited leave). Therefore, rather than a reserve of trained congés, the army had only a paper reserve of untrained congés who were useless in the event of war. These men had done no military service and did not belong to a regiment, while no independent reserve organization existed to organize a general mobilization.

It is apparent that the War Ministry and military leaders raised in the Napoleonic school of large armies wanted to create a trained reserve. Soult, in a letter of November 1830 to Marshal Dermoncourt, voiced these very hopes:[22]

> Our young army would be more confident with the support of a
> reserve. It would also provide the opportunity to re-incorporate
> many brave and experienced veterans and a large number
> of excellent NCOs and soldier who face prejudice, often
> unjustly, in line regiments . . . 50,000 men chosen from the
> different arms will be sufficient for an elite reserve to support
> a regular army of 500,000 men.

One of the few surviving parliamentary commission reports (13 September 1830) strongly criticizes the untrained 1824 reserve:[23]

> It was thought possible to supplement these veterans by
> incorporating only a part of the annual 60,000-man contingent
> into the regular army, leaving the remainder at the govern-
> ment's disposal as a reserve. In this way part of the population
> was tied down while the state could make no use of them.

When the bill was reported out of committee on 12 September 1831 by Passy, deputy for the Eure, conservatives had raised the term of service to seven years and there was no provision for a trained reserve. Instead, article 3 stipulated that the annual contingent be divided into two parts, one inducted into the army according to military needs and the remainder sent home. Article 29 maintained that those who were sent home could be called up only by a royal ordinance. On the suggestion of General Lamarque, this reserve of untrained conscripts on 'congé illimité' became liable for annual training under article 30: 'Unincorporated conscripts and men sent home on six months' furlough can be called up for periodic inspections and training ordered by the War Minister.' Although this seemed a partial victory for the partisans of a trained reserve, it was in practice a defeat, as the July Monarchy, fearing the leftist inclinations of a citizen reserve, never exercised this right.[24] Articles 29 and 30 therefore created a reserve only in name. This reserve was formally recognized by a royal ordinance of 17 July 1833:

The reserve . . . is formed under article 3 of the law of 21 March 1832, of all conscripts who are not on active service whether by not having been incorporated or by being sent on leave before termination of their legal service obligation.

In introducing the revised project, Passy justified the seven years' service provision and the weak reserve in a way which was to become familiar in the course of the debates. He maintained that a five-year service provision would mean that more men would have to be called up to keep army strength at 500,000 men. Next, he claimed that soldiers should be trained for at least two years for the cavalry, artillery and engineers. If service time were reduced, Passy said, the army would 'send hopelessly inexperienced soldiers into battle'. Conservative military theoreticians always distinguished between military training and military 'education'; a civilian could be trained in the use of arms, but it took a long time to inculcate a true military spirit in him. Passy also noted that a reserve can be quickly assembled at the first sign of war:[25]

Seldom does war break out without warning. Unmistakable signs almost always announce it well in advance. When everything points to peace, the minister can easily lift the restrictions on soldiers on leave who . . . will no longer be liable for active duty.

In 1870, however, the young Third Republic discovered the impracticability of instituting a *levée en masse* after the war had been declared.

Liberal partisans of a broad-based national army deplored the lack of a trained reserve. Thus, on 4 November 1831, de Ludre, a deputy for the Meurthe, and Count de Laborde, representing the Seine, proposed a joint amendment calling for four years' active service, followed by four years' reserve duty. Laborde expounded the moral and political advantages of a trained patriotic reserve:[26]

It is this provision which will guarantee the country's independence, maintain institutional stability and assure the glory of France . . . The July revolution stood for hatred of privilege, hatred of superstition and above all hatred of foreign domination . . . 'I wish to God', Voltaire said, 'that all peasants were soldiers; they would be better citizens' . . . Such a reserve would be superior to the Landwehr and to the Landsturm . . . It would reconcile passive obedience with the rights of citizenship in such a way that liberty could never be undermined.

The liberal deputies also objected that a 500,000-man army was too small and pointed out that de Ludre's amendment would boost army strength to 650,000 including a 150,000-man reserve. Instancing Napoleon's brilliant defence of France in 1814, conservatives objected that a small, well-trained army was more efficient than a large citizen army and blamed Napoleon's defeat on betrayal. General Lamarque agreed that a well-trained army was essential, but argued that a small army could not ensure France's defence without a military genius of Napoleon's stature. Had Napoleon been able to call up a trained reserve in 1814, he could have successfully defended his country. Lamarque and de Ludre reminded Soult that in November 1830 he had called for a 960,000-man army, and stated that 640,000 men was the bare minimum 'to command the respect of neighbouring powers'.[27] De Tracy then calculated that if the upper limit was set at 500,000, the army would normally comprise less than 300,000 men: 'I wonder whether we can ensure the independence of a nation like ours with a 250,000-strong army and no reserve.'

One after another, the liberal deputies mounted the rostrum to argue the advantages of a large citizen army and to defend the four years' service proposal. Defending the amendment, General Lamarque again recalled Napoleon's successful use of large armies: 'As you know, gentlemen, we did not conquer Europe and win independence with 400,000 men without support, without reserves.' He concluded that only when the army acquired a strong reserve would it begin to reflect the goals of the 1830 revolution: 'Then and only then will the army be a complete organization in harmony with society.'[28]

Answering critics who feared that a reserve would be a financial burden, Lamarque calculated that the invasion of a single department would cost France more than ten years' reserve expenses: 'Woe to the country which counts pennies when its honour and independence are at stake.' In fact, the financial strain of a reserve appears to have been a bogus issue raised by those who objected to a reserve in principle. When resubmitting the reserve proposal in 1840, Soult assured a legislative commission that a trained reserve would not burden the budget: 'As for the expense, I repeat, we ask nothing from you. We shall operate within the army and remain within our budgetary limits.'[29] General Schneider seconded him on 18 March 1841: 'We hope, as the War Minister says, that it will be possible to keep the figure down.'[30] At the time, liberals pointed out that a reserve would be cheaper than a large active army. In reply to Soult's contention that a reserve would cost thirty million francs annually, de Ludre retorted that reservists could keep their old uniforms and equipment; the government need only furnish arms, which would cost less than six million francs. A reserve could certainly have been formed inexpensively; the financial objection to it only masked a deeper ideological difference.

Odilon Barrot, representing the Bas-Rhin, attacked those who cited the failure of Saint-Cyr's reserve in 1823 as proof of the unworkability of the system. The fault, he maintained, lay in the Bourbon government's refusal to organize and administer the reserve properly:

> Saint-Cyr's reserve was not only a military institution but a civil and national one . . . It was perhaps lacking in certain respects – in its excessive faith in the government's common interest in organizing its defence machinery. What was the result of this? That we had a nominal reserve written into law but which never materialized.

He continued that if the deputies thought the 1832 reserve was a 'fiction', as Soult claimed, a reserve composed of congés would be too.[31]

Barrot's argument was borne out by a military report of 17 December 1835, blaming the failure of Saint-Cyr's reserve on its lack of organization: 'Trained soldiers were sent home still owing a considerable amount of time, but they were not organized and consequently were useless.'[32]

In conclusion, Barrot opposed the substitution of the National Guard for a trained reserve: 'Must we adopt the committee's system,' Barrot concluded, 'which proposes to establish only the framework of a regular army based on seven years' service, and then, apart from this regular army, nothing . . . nothing but the National Guard?'[33]

Conservatives realized that the National Guard was not an adequate reserve. Reformed after the July Revolution to include men between twenty and sixty years old not called up for military service, the guard retained its revolutionary organization which permitted the lower ranks to elect their officers. After 1830, liberals supported a 'federation' programme which would have organized the guard on a national scale. Conservatives, however, feared the revolutionary inclinations of this armed citizenry and so insisted that they be organized only by local units. The National Guard law of March 1831 was therefore designed to fragment the National Guard and to limit the political rights of guardsmen. The bill did provide for the guard to be used as a military reserve as well as to ensure public order, but it stipulated that they could not be used outside the country. In the event of war, no national organization existed to mobilize and co-ordinate the actions of the individual guard units effectively, and it was therefore virtually useless as a military reserve. The prospect of a reserve fashioned from this politically conscious and armed citizenry alarmed conservatives who wanted a reliable army.

The army realized that most anti-governmental activity in its ranks was initiated by civilian agents and consequently it sought to separate its soldiers as much as possible from civilian influence by refusing to quarter troops in private homes. Revolutionary governments had continued the *ancien régime*'s practice of quartering troops with civilians, believing that it would build a national spirit, allow revolutionary soldiers to educate the peasantry and encourage class levelling. Conservatives, however, feared the detrimental effects of this revolutionary practice.

In 1825, when trouble broke out in the 51st Infantry Regiment at La Rochelle, the police were ordered especially to keep a watch on all officers and soldiers who were quartered with civilians.[34] After the colonel of the 2nd Infantry Regiment said his troops could not be counted on to put down a popular uprising in 1831, the prefect of the Bouches-du-Rhône reported that they were all quartered in private homes: 'The colonel of the 2nd Infantry Regiment, whose élite troops are all quartered with civilians, cannot assume responsibility for the conduct of these 400 men.'[35]

Realizing the danger, the army took steps to rectify this situation. In 1831 the army had barely 30,000 beds and was forced to quarter over 80,000 soldiers in private homes.[36] The following years 6,824,152.22 francs were spent, almost to double the number of beds, which gives a measure of the importance the army placed on removing soldiers from civilian influence. In a report of January 1833, the War Minister pointed out the necessity of removing troops from civilian homes, especially in republican towns like Lyon:[37]

> The need to concentrate a large number of troops at points where public order was threatened has left several garrisons without enough beds. This situation was especially critical in Lyon, for example. And as we could not quarter with civilians soldiers sent there after the troubles of November 1831, we have had to find 12,480 new beds. Similar reasons have necessitated similar action in several other towns.

When riots broke out in Lyon in 1834, the War Minister strictly forbade the quartering of troops with civilians even when the barracks were full.[38]

Republicans denounced this act as an attempt by an authoritarian government to separate the army from the nation: 'The more despotic a government, the harder it tries to isolate soldiers from civilians to ensure the military's loyalty.'[39] Yet conservatives were aware of the dangers of placing soldiers with civilians and were convinced that a trained citizen reserve would be as prone to political mischief as the National Guard.

Another obvious drawback of the National Guard as a military reserve was that the guard contained few veterans. Laborde demanded that the untrained guard be used only as a third line of defence behind the army reserve:[40] 'You do not call citizen soldiers these men who have not yet touched a rifle and who lack the training and tactical knowledge to take on similar foreign reserves, the Landwehr for example.'[41]

Lamarque objected that the National Guard would be a useless reserve: 'groups of men who for the most part will have no military training, who will not know their officers, will not be known by them, and who therefore will be useless.'[42] In December 1830 General Brenier asked that a reserve organization should replace the unorganized National Guard. A reserve, he said, 'must replace, immediately, the slow, difficult and vexatious organization of the regular battalions of the National Guard.'[43] The Duc de Broglie also opposed the reserve proposal in the Chamber of Peers: 'The idea of including our military reserve in the National Guard, the Duc de Broglie observed in the Chamber of Peers, is both questionable and dangerous. A military reserve is one thing, the National Guard is another. Contact between the two bodies can only distort both of them.'[44] General L'Etang, in a report to the War Minister in 1840, noted: 'England's newly-formed militia no more merits the name of reserve than does our National Guard'.[45]

Liberals realized that the absence of a trained reserve left the army weak and isolated from the nation. The 1831 law providing for the National Guard to be used as a reserve had satisfied no one. The army did not treat this untrained force as a reserve and liberals realized that the law ended their hopes of shattering the isolating professionalism of the army with a citizen reserve of ex-servicemen.

Contemporary historians agree that the National Guard was ill-suited for a reserve because it was composed of men without military experience and was not on a par with the Prussian Landwehr.[46] Professor Girard points out that the National Guard constituted a potentially valuable reserve, but the Périer ministry's refusal to organize, equip and train it properly lowered its effectiveness and virtually restricted it to purely local operations.[47] Monteilhet concludes that the National Guard law of 22 March 1831 left the army with only a paper reserve: 'The National Guard remained

75

a political institution. Only on paper did it become the army reserve.'[48]

The National Guard, therefore, cannot be considered the reserve either retrospectively or in the minds of those who desired a broad-based national army. The guard and the army remained two separate institutions, under the Ministry of the Interior and the War Ministry respectively.

The adjournment of the session gave conservatives time to regroup for the vote of 5 November 1831. The *Journal des Débats* for that day editorially supported the seven years' service measure and the congé reserve system:

> The soldier who leaves active service to return home always belongs to the army . . . His likings and feelings remain the same. His military training remains with him, and if war demands his services, a simple ministerial order reincorporates him into the army. If we were invaded, only a few days would be required to put a regular army of 500,000 men in the field. The congé system is therefore the best for countering invasion.

However, the argument is sophistic, for this system would provide a trained reserve only if every conscript did active service. But congés who had served for a certain period were not included in the reserve, but counted in the regimental strength until their service time was completed. The writer complained that those who served four years would be only half-trained:

> Compare this with a reserve or call-up system. At the end of four years' service, half the army goes home, only half-trained and half-free, but believing itself completely free. They will soon lose the spirit of a profession to which they no longer belong . . . and do you believe that this half-trained soldier will bother to complete his training at inspections and exercises?

The article concluded that a reserve would disarm the nation by weakening the army, sarcastically calling its supporters, mostly deputies from large cities and the 'patriotic' east, 'supporters of war'.[49]

Liberals realized that the 1832 proposal merely duplicated the law of 1824. Soult admitted that he would only have a reserve if every conscript was called for active duty: 'I acknowledge that the entire conscript contingent would first be trained and then sent home.'[50] General Sebastiani conceded that the commission's proposal contained no reserve, but claimed that the National Guard would be a good substitute. General Clauzel, however, who called for an army of 800,000 men, concluded that the Soult law failed to provide a reserve: 'I do not see a reserve either in the government's bill or in the committee's amendment.'[51] In the Chamber of Peers, General d'Ambrugeac proposed a five-year service and five-year reserve provision. He claimed that his proposal was modelled on the 1818 law, while the government's merely duplicated the 1824 law: 'This law has taken advantage of the 1824 law; it is nothing more than the 1824 law rephrased.'[52] The peers voted an amendment requiring the army to call the youngest contingent first if it was forced to recall those previously sent home on unlimited leave without training. This provision would have strengthened the reserve by making these trained men available for the reserve for a longer period after their release. However, it was reversed by the deputies, who required the army to call up the oldest contingent first. On 5 November, de Ludre's reserve amendment was defeated after Guizot declared that it sacrificed the army to the reserve.[53]

The number of military reports after 1834, when General Gérard replaced Soult as War Minister, calling for the creation of a trained reserve testify to the continued desire of many officers for such a contingent. General Pelet deplored the lack in a note to Soult soon after the bill's adoption: 'Under the current recruitment system . . . the reserve is severely handicapped . . . The only true reservists are those men trained to the service and to arms. The second group [congés] is a fictitious reserve.'[54] An infantry committee report by Durant la Salle on 21 June 1841 concluded that a reserve of congés was 'absurd': 'It was also absurd to include in an army reserve men who had not even joined their own regiments.'[55] Others suggested that all conscripts must be activated. Soult reflected in 1841 that in 1832 lawmakers thought a reserve unnecessary while the war scare made the quick formation of a regular army absolutely vital: 'The [1832] law was designed to increase the size of the contingents to mobilize all conscripts. At that time, we believed that a reserve organization was not vital. We must deal with this quickly.'[56]

The results of the Soult law have already been discussed in part. Although Monteilhet claimed that the new law did not alter the 1818 concept of the army, it upheld the reserves abolition of 1824 and reinforced the professionalizing tendencies of that law. Guizot boasted that 'its leading principles have resisted assault, survived alteration',[57] but Thoumas deplored the absence of a trained reserve as 'an absolutely crucial failing'.[58] Writing of the 1904 army bill, Kovacs says: 'Indeed, one cannot help agreeing with the authors of the project of 1904 in their conclusion that the law of

1832, by paving the way for the mercenary army of Napoleon III, sent France down the road leading to the disasters of 1870.'[59] In 1840 Louis-Philippe dismissed Thiers, realizing that his army was too small to manage an active foreign policy. As chief minister, Guizot came to realize the reserve's inadequacy: 'In the reserve I fear we shall not find an army.' Soult, too, recognized its limitations: 'The reserve would often be embarrassing.'[60] In 1841 he tried unsuccessfully to reintroduce the four years' active duty measure voted down nine years earlier. Army organization remained virtually unchanged until 1871.

Chapter 6

L'Arme Savante: Republicanism in the artillery

'It is noticeable', wrote the Minister of the Interior in 1840, 'that it is always artillery soldiers who have followed the lead given by the most radical sector of the population.'[1]

Although political activity in the army after 1815 was not strictly confined to any one arm, the artillery, which in 1835 consisted of fourteen regiments and a battalion of bridge builders, was notorious for its republican sympathies. It accounted for only 7 per cent of army strength. Yet, between 1823 and 1830, 33 per cent of the incidents of political unrest concerned the artillery. Between the July revolution and 1840, every artillery regiment was cited in reports to the War Minister for disloyalty. Given its chronic political militancy, the artillery merits special attention in a study of anti-governmental activity in the army.

Opposition to the Bourbons continued to smoulder in every arm after the Spanish campaign, but political militancy was especially acute in the artillery.

The 1st Artillery Regiment at Metz rioted in June 1824,[2] and in July 1825 police noted that soldiers from a company of ouvriers d'artillerie at Toulouse were meeting with local republicans.[3] In August 1827 the 2nd Artillery Band serenaded the liberal, Benjamin Constant, who had just been elected deputy for the Bas-Rhin.[4] In March 1828 the government expressed concern about the 'esprit' of the 5th Artillery,[5] and in March 1829 two artillerymen from the 4th at La Fère were arrested for seditious shouts.[6]

After the July revolution, republican activity began in earnest. In 1830 the 6th Regiment revolted in an attempt to throw out several officers, including its colonel, who opposed the new government.[7] 1831 reports claimed that a number of soldiers in the 6th were republicans,[8] and in 1833 a secret society was uncovered in the regiment.[9] The Prefect of the Bas-Rhin reported in 1834 that republicans believed the 6th, the 3rd and the Battalion of Bridge Builders stationed in Strasbourg sympathetic to their cause: 'The republicans say they can count on the artillery.'[10] In April, General

79

Brayer, commander of the Strasbourg garrison, expressed the belief that although the infantry was politically reliable, young officers from the Ecole Polytechnique and the Ecole d'Application at Metz were a cause for concern: 'As for the artillery, he [General Brayer] believes that he can count on it, with the exception of the young, school-trained officers.'[11] In 1835 officers of the 6th were seen at a republican meeting in Saint-Etienne,[12] and in 1838 the government again expressed doubts about the regiment's loyalty.[13]

Like the 6th, soldiers of the 4th Artillery, whose colonel led Louis Napoleon's attempted *coup d'état* in 1836, were frequently involved in republican activism. In 1833 a secret society was discovered in the regiment;[14] in the following year six officers were arrested for political activity,[15] and in 1835 the regiment was transferred from Rennes to Strasbourg after several political scraps with the 33rd Infantry Regiment.[16] In 1837, when a number of NCOs were discharged for their part in the 1836 insurrection, the regimental band, many officers and soldiers, and a number of civilians followed them to the outskirts of Douai.[17]

Strasbourg's 'affaire des pontonniers' demonstrates the solidarity of the artillery in the face of arbitrary government intervention in military affairs. When fifteen officers in the Battalion of Bridge Builders complained in October 1833 that the government had contravened the 1832 promotion law by promoting two officers from the naval artillery to the battalion, they were thrown into jail. Six were later forcibly retired. The government's action excited protests from every artillery regiment in France. In April 1834 Strasbourg republicans organized a large protest march which rallied many artillery soldiers, several of whom sported Revolutionary phrygian bonnets.[18] Several officers and soldiers of the Bridge Builders also joined the 1836 Strasbourg plot.[19]

Activity in other regiments was less spectacular, although they too were influenced by republican ideas. In 1830 the 1st Artillery subscribed to the *Globe*, the Saint-Simonist paper, and in 1833 a secret society was uncovered in that regiment.[20] Four officers in the 1st were arrested together with several Polytechnicians for belonging to the republican society, Aide-Toi, in 1834.[21] Officers in the 2nd at La Fère were arrested in 1836 for political activity,[22] while several officers in the 3rd, whose republican sympathies were well known to the government, supported Louis Napoleon's 1836 *coup d'état*.[23] After their acquittal in January 1837, their fellow officers celebrated with a banquet.[24] Secret societies were unearthed and arrests for political misdemeanours were frequent in other artillery regiments.[25]

This résumé of political activity in the artillery, although brief, clearly demonstrates that a strong liberal bias existed in this arm. The officer preparatory schools furnished the impetus for much of this activity.

The Ecole Polytechnique, which sent many of its graduates into the artillery, and the artillery's Ecole d'Application at Metz, were notorious centres of republicanism. In 1830 Polytechnicians participated in the final stages of the revolution. 'It is noticeable', said a police report of September 1831, 'that when there is trouble, a large number of students wearing black armbands are the centre of attention.'[26] In 1832 General Tholoze, the school commander, confessed that students belonged to secret republican societies: 'The students report daily to their public or secret societies to get the password. They are in touch with the most influential members of the opposition, and are privy to conspiracy plans.'[27] In the same year, students attending a banquet in honour of Lafayette shouted 'Vive Lafayette! Vive la République!' They were frequently seen in the company of republican Polish officers and at republican meetings.[28] In 1833 seven Polytechnicians were disciplined for subscribing to the *Tribune*, along with a number of students from Saint-Cyr.[29] The widely publicized 'affaire des poudres' in that year involved three Polytechnicians who were arrested for making bullets for republicans.[30]

The republican activities of these students did not stop once they reached Metz. Student officers at the Ecole d'Application made up the largest single group in the republican Association Nationale de la Moselle in 1831. 'Where there is trouble', wrote the Prefect of the Moselle in 1841, 'one is almost certain to find students from the school.' He also complained that republicans had been seen with students.[31] In February 1837 Lieutenant Laity and Lady Gordon, who were involved in Louis Napoleon's abortive Strasbourg adventure, were received at the school by a dozen students.[32]

The traditional explanations for the artillery's political opposition are by now familiar. The aristocracy shunned the artillery when firearms first appeared, preferring the 'honourable' combat of the cavalry and infantry. The artillery, therefore, at first attracted only middle-class officers who were not unwilling to challenge the established order. Second, the artillery was associated with science, technology and industry – which had set in motion vast social and economic change. Vagts sums up the aristocracy's traditional hatred of the artillery:[33]

The resentment of the nobleman against the artillery was a part of that large heritage carried over from feudal times into

modern warfare, which included the most variegated complex
of antiquated sentiments, convictions, valuations and a general
disinclination for technological progress.

For these reasons, the artillery was the arm most responsive to and
indeed most eager for social change.

On closer examination, however, these two facts alone do not
explain the rebelliousness of the artillery under the July Monarchy.

With the Revolution, the artillery acquired new prestige. As
aristocrats left France and the army, the artillery lost its stigma of
social inferiority and Revolutionary generals with inexperienced
troops became increasingly dependent on it. On 16 brumaire, year
VI (6 November 1797), the War Minister, General Scherer, placed
the artillery first in the order of march, followed by the infantry
and cavalry.[34] The Ecole Polytechnique was established in 1793
and the artillery began to furnish the army with famous generals.
Bonaparte, of course, was an artillery officer. Carnot, who reorganized the revolutionary army, was an artillery general.
Clermont-Tonnerre, archbishop of Toulouse and War Minister under
the Restoration, was a Polytechnician and held an artillery commission; Marmont, commander of the Paris garrison in July 1830,
was commissioned in the artillery; Baron d'Hautpoul, commander
of the Ecole Royale d'Etat Major under the Restoration, and the
school's inspector general Desprez were classmates at the Polytechnique and the Ecole d'Application; Generals Foy and Gouvion-
Saint-Cyr were artillery officers. Under the July Monarchy,
General Valée, an artillery general, was appointed governor-
general of Algeria, while other officers such as General Cavaignac
also staked out brilliant careers from the ranks of the artillery.

The resignation of many aristocratic officers after 1830 substantially reduced the class differentiation among the three arms which
had been assumed to be a major cause of the artillery's insubordination. The officer corps gradually assumed a definite middle-class –
if not lower middle-class – character as Castellane complained in
1846.[35] The class differentiation among the arms, while applicable
to the German army which was organized along strict class lines,
does not therefore apply to the French army.

A tradition of political opposition undoubtedly existed in the
artillery and among graduates of the Ecole Polytechnique. But to
explain the republican bias of the artillery satisfactorily, we must
look deeper into its organization and situation.

Republicans often sought to exploit regimental and personal
problems for political ends. This was especially true in the artillery,
where young officers leaving the Ecole Polytechnique and Metz's

Ecole d'Application were financially insecure. Baron Pelletier, commander of the Ecole d'Application, complained in 1837 that unavoidable debts incurred by the students were a major reason for the school's notorious republicanism.[36]

> This administration knew that four-fifths of the students at the Ecole Polytechnique come from poor families [he wrote in his inspection report] who make great sacrifices to send them there . . . On arrival at the school, most of the students face immediate and inescapable expenses of at least 400 francs. Even by frugal living, they will find it impossible to reduce this during their stay in Metz on 106 francs a month. The inability to pay this and the certainty of further debt as far as they can see often leads to troublesome indifference.

General Pelletier's contention is borne out by the archives of the Ecole Polytechnique. Of forty students cited for republican activity between 1830 and 1834, only two were sons of men wealthy enough to appear on the electoral roll. Ten were sons of minor civil servants, ten were sons of proprietors, seven of army officers, four of lawyers, four of merchants, two of engineers and two of naval officers. One student's father was a teacher, while the father of one was an elector and another, also an elector, the president of the Cour Royale at Besançon. Only the last two enjoyed real wealth. The other thirty-eight students undoubtedly faced financial problems, as almost all of them chose a military career. Of fifty-eight Polytechnicians cited for republican activity under the July Monarchy, thirty-seven joined the artillery, nine the army engineers and eight the civil service. One entered the navy and three were sent home. We can then conclude that most Polytechnicians involved in republican activity were from middle-class backgrounds and unable to build a career from family wealth or connections. The army and the civil service were therefore the most likely choices of career. In most cases their pay – a potential source of discontent – was their only source of income.

A young artillery officer's financial worries did not end with his departure from Metz. After graduating in the spring, he was given an extended leave while awaiting his orders for assignment to a regiment. General Pelletier pointed out that though the students were free to go home, few could afford to do so. Most of them were forced to await their assignment in Metz for five or six months on a salary of fifty francs a month:[37]

> This was the position of all artillery students until last July [1836] and of more than twenty until September. They are

83

free to go where they please to vent their discontent and eat
up their fifty franc half-pay . . . The students were kept on
leave, reduced to living in debt or giving private lessons to
live.

General Pelletier also pointed out the political importance of
preventing officers from accumulating debts:

Two officers implicated in the attempted mutiny at Strasbourg
are among those who have been treated in this matter.
Significantly, most of the soldiers involved in conspiracies
over the last twenty years are officers with debts they could
not have avoided.

Indeed, Parquin, one of the leaders of Louis Napoleon's 1836
coup, owed some 20,000 francs.[38]
The relationship between debt and republicanism was apparent
to others in the army. In June 1831 General Hulot held an extraordinary inspection of the 66th Infantry Regiment which was
formed after the July Revolution from the old Royal Guard and
had not fought well in the 1831 Lyon insurrection. He subsequently
suspended all officers who were in debt, equating debt with dis-
honour: 'These men lost in debt, default in conduct and in honour.'[39]
However, the army did nothing to strike at the root of the problem
and in 1835 the problem of debt and republicanism again arose in
the 62nd Infantry Regiment stationed at Marseille.[40]

A large number of officers from the 62nd Infantry Regiment
have met with local republicans on several occasions [read
a report from the War Minister] and have told them that they
would join them to lead a popular insurrection at the first
opportunity. I am also told that they took this course of
action after promises to send the 62nd to Africa were broken.
They were forced into debts which they now see no way of
discharging.

It is interesting to note that artillery regiments were stationed in
those areas of France where the cost of living was highest – the large
cities and the east.
Of the officers cited for republican activity under the July
Monarchy, almost 40 per cent were under thirty. This created a
potentially explosive situation, for these young and impoverished
officers were especially willing to embrace republicanism.
The prolonged education required of artillery officers also appears
to have affected Metz students. Upon graduation from the Ecole
Polytechnique, they received the rank of student second lieutenant

and settled down for another two years of study at Metz which they normally completed at the age of twenty-two or twenty-three. Though they received the rank and pay of a second lieutenant, they enjoyed few of the privileges. They were still forced to endure the gruelling mental and physical discipline of school life and though commissioned, they were not entitled to salutes and other military courtesies from NCOs and soldiers. While their contemporaries from Saint-Cyr and those in civilian life were enjoying the advantages and status of their positions, Metz students were still denied even the trappings of responsibility. Judging by the number of requests by the students to be allowed to receive salutes and other courtesies, this prolonged adolescence was painful to them. Their frustration over their lack of status and responsibility encouraged insubordination and their flirtations with the opposition.

Slow promotion, while an army-wide problem, was especially acute in the artillery. The smallest of the three major arms, the artillery had a smaller personnel turnover and consequently fewer opportunities for promotion. A table of army strength for 1833 (Table 7) demonstrates that the artillery comprised barely a tenth of army personnel.

TABLE 7   *Army strength in 1833*

1833	Officers	Men	Total
Infantry	9,324	268,654	277,978
Cavalry	2,766	47,650	50,416
Artillery	970	37,475	38,445
Engineers	231	7,978	8,209

Between 1831 and 1841, the artillery lost only 36·33 per cent of its officers or an average of 54·7 men a year. In the same period, the cavalry lost 50·9 or 182·9 officers a year and the infantry 55·33 per cent or 612·9 a year.[41] Artillery officers faced other promotional handicaps. At least two-thirds of all artillery officers passed through the Ecole Polytechnique and could not expect the same career advantages to follow from their élitist education as could the relatively rare Saint-Cyrians in the infantry and cavalry. Of 179 artillery second lieutenants listed in the 1834 *Annuaire*, for example, fifty had been promoted through the ranks. The remainder were Polytechnicians. Saint-Cyrians counted for less than one-third of cavalry officers and one fourth of infantry officers.

TABLE 8 *Men promoted to second lieutenant between 1831 and 1841 from Polytechnique or Saint-Cyr:* *

	School	Ranks
Artillery	449	211
Infantry	960	3,758
Cavalry	300	1,099

* Devalez de Caffol, op. cit., tableaux 17 and 18.

Also, between 1815 and 1854 an artillery officer had virtually no chance to distinguish himself in the field. Ambitious infantry and cavalry officers could look for rapid promotion in Algeria, but the nature of guerilla warfare and General Bugeaud's tactics, which called for small, mobile 'flying columns' designed for long range patrols rather than large scale operations, dictated that the artillery would be used only in defence. Consequently, only 4 per cent of officers stationed in Algeria in January 1840 belonged to the artillery and those who were sent there could look forward to an uneventful stay (see Table 9).

TABLE 9 *Strength of Algerian army on 1 January 1840* *

	Officers	Men	Total
Infantry	1,066	38,843	39,909
Cavalry	337	6,082	6,419
Artillery	67	2,893	2,960
Engineers	56	2,537	2,593

* AHG, Fonds Préval 1948.

Ambitious artillery and engineering officers, like Cavaignac, La Moricière, Duvivier and Marey-Monge who joined the Zouaves and Chasseurs d'Afrique in Algeria, were forced to transfer to other arms or face the prospect of an unprofitable career. 12.25 per cent of the Polytechnicians who joined the artillery between 1831 and 1841 resigned from service as opposed to 8·67 per cent of the Saint-Cyrians who joined the cavalry and only 5·94 per cent who joined the infantry in the same period, indicating that discontent was more widespread in the artillery.[42]

Slow promotion was also a problem for artillery NCOs and

soldiers. Although promotion in the infantry and cavalry was slow, one or two years might pass with no promotions at all in the artillery. An inspection report of 1836 pointed out that artillery NCOs had had no promotions for two years and might be encouraged to join the opposition camp:[43]

> No artillery NCO was promoted in 1834 or 1835. There is a danger that the lack of promotion will discourage and create dissatisfaction among NCOs whose loyalty is crucial for the government and whose considerable influence on the soldiers' morale was demonstrated so conclusively during the 1830 revolution.

Another important consideration in the study of republicanism in the artillery is the location of garrisons. Political opposition in the army depended largely on civilian agents for its propagation; it was rare in areas where the republican party was weak, but frequent in garrison towns where the party was strong. The Prefect of the Bouches-du-Rhône drew notice to this in 1834: 'Republicans, most of whom are working-class people, meet in the inns and public houses where they take the soldiers. This is not only the case in Marseille, but in every garrison town where these societies exist.'[44]

Of 15 artillery units in 1835, three were stationed in Strasbourg, two in Metz, two in Toulouse and one each in Paris, Lyon, Besançon, Rennes, Douai, La Fère, Valence and Bourges. Strasbourg, Metz, Toulouse, Paris, Lyon and Besançon were all republican strongholds and local republicans were active in the garrisons. The remaining four cities boasted smaller republican societies. Almost three-quarters of the artillery regiments were stationed in traditionally republican areas – this is proportionally higher than the other arms – and every regiment was in continual contact with civilian republican societies.

In addition, artillery regiments, on account of the limited number of practice ranges, remained in one station for four to six years, longer than infantry and cavalry regiments.[45] This is important for two reasons. In the first case, republicans had plenty of time to canvass in the regiments. Second, as the regiments were recruited locally, they were composed almost entirely of local soldiers, and republicans found it easier to recruit among people from their region.

The army was not blind to the disadvantages of a prolonged garrison stay in a republican area. In June 1833 the Minister of the Interior, Thiers, warned that the danger of republican influence on soldiers in Paris was so great that the army should 'avoid giving too many temporary leaves and change the regiments assigned to the

Paris garrison as frequently as possible'.[46] An inspection report for 1834 claimed that two companies of ouvriers d'artillerie stationed at Grenoble had been there too long and should be moved: 'The 3rd and the 7th Labour Companies have been in Grenoble for several years. I think it would be advisable to transfer them so that their military spirit is not weakened by lengthy contact with the same civilian population.'[47] 'It is generally recognized and conclusively demonstrated', wrote General Pajol, commander of the first military division, to the War Minister in 1835, 'that a prolonged stay in the capital of any one regiment has grave disadvantages. It is preferable ... that regiments stationed in Paris be replaced every year.'[48]

A long stay in Strasbourg was particularly damaging to military discipline. Dependent on Germany for much of its trade, the town had a large liberal, commercial middle class. Unlike French cafés, Alsatian *brasseries* attracted all classes of people who mixed freely. In Strasbourg, soldiers were more likely to mix with this liberal middle class than to confront fist-happy workers who resented the army. The gregarious *brasserie* afforded republicans the opportunity to establish contacts in the garrison.[49]

> Garrisons should be rotated occasionally [the Inspector General of the Artillery, General Lenoury, pointed out in 1834]. The drawbacks of a lengthy stay are especially noticeable in Strasbourg. NCOs and artillerymen there find it easy to make contacts which are as harmful to discipline as they are opposed to the military spirit. Even officers fall into habits little becoming to gentlemen. This is especially the case in Strasbourg where the different social classes, which elsewhere keep apart, mingle in the *brasseries*. This observation, which may seem superficial, is, however, not without interest in the light of the government's discouragement of close contacts [between soldiers and civilians] which weaken the regimental *esprit de corps*. Take the Bridge Builders: it is certainly regrettable that this battalion has remained here for sixteen years. This is one reason why regiments which have spent a certain number of years in Strasbourg must be transferred.

In 1837 he again noted the military disadvantages of Strasbourg: 'The 3rd Artillery Regiment has been in Strasbourg for five years. Every officer familiar with this garrison knows that within a very few years a soldier makes contacts with the local inhabitants, especially the *brasserie* habitués, which inevitably lead to disorder and neglect of duty.'[50]

Combined with a long garrison stay, the policy of regional

recruitment created a dangerous homogeneity among artillery soldiers. In 1840 the War Minister, General Cubières, spelled out the advantages to the army of regional recruitment. Not only was it physically easier for recruits to reach their regiments, but new soldiers were less likely to desert because of homesickness: 'I would like young recruits sent to regiments stationed in their own regions,' he ordered. 'They adapt to army life more easily and are less likely to desert than if they were sent immediately to distant regiments.'[51]

Yet local recruitment had its disadvantages. Republicans could canvass more easily among local recruits, while soldiers from a particular region, like Alsace, could adopt an opposition political doctrine as a sign of regional independence and pride. After the 'affaire des pontonniers', Colonel Boursaroque obtained permission from the War Minister to close his battalion, which was permanently stationed in Strasbourg, to Alsatians who made up one-third of his force: 'Good soldiers in every other way, . . . they are led into serious breaches of discipline by civilians.'[52] In 1831 the bureau of military operations expressed fear that the 1st Infantry Regiment at Paris, whose ranks were dominated by local soldiers, would be won over by Parisian republicans: 'The agitators seem to count on complicity in the garrison. I am especially anxious about the 1st Infantry Regiment which has many Parisians in its ranks. It might be wise to move it from the capital.'[53] General Lenoury voiced this same fear in 1833 after an inspection of the 5th Artillery Regiment at Toulouse: 'The 5th Artillery Regiment has been in Toulouse for several years. It is almost entirely composed of southerners. This homogeneity perhaps could cause problems . . . It would be best to transfer it to another school.'[54] In June 1833 the colonel of the 15th Infantry at Grenoble hoped to avoid Lyon because too many of his soldiers came from that city. 'This regiment cannot be sent to Lyon because it contains 500 or 600 soldiers from the department of the Rhône, most of them from Lyon.'[55]

As many regiments were stationed in Protestant areas such as Strasbourg, Metz and Toulouse, many soldiers in the artillery were Protestants. Religious differences frequently carried over into politics in the Midi and the east, as Protestants often chose republicanism as a means of politically expressing their traditional religious non-conformity. Many also hoped that a republic would end the social inequality forced on them by Catholic France. Protestants frequently ran their own schools and were usually better educated than their Catholic counterparts. Although it is impossible to ascertain the religious make-up of the regiments, artillery regiments by virtue of their locations probably took in a higher proportion of Protestants.

Most of those soldiers who were engaged in political activity in the army, especially in the artillery, were volunteers. In 1835 one-twentieth of the army consisted of volunteers.[56] Yet no less than 65 per cent of the soldiers disciplined for political activity were volunteers,[57] and inspection reports frequently complain of these men. 'Volunteers are always in the front ranks of the trouble-makers', the Inspector General wrote in 1834.[58] He underlined this view in 1836: 'The disadvantages of replacement and voluntary enlistment are the same in the artillery as in the rest of the army. They threatened to undermine this élite corps.'[59]

As professional soldiers, these men were deeply concerned with regimental issues which directly influenced their careers. Conscripts, on the other hand, thought of themselves as civilians able to return home after three or four years' service and were consequently less interested in military issues.

The proportion of replacements and volunteers appears to have been higher in the artillery, largely because it was a relatively sedentary arm and because many regiments were stationed in the east which traditionally furnished large numbers of volunteers. A resident of an artillery garrison could volunteer for the artillery knowing that he would remain close to home for a long time.[60]

> Men from these two categories today make up almost half of the total strength of the artillery [complained General Lenoury in 1836]. One group is greedy, the other undisciplined and generally without morals . . . The ministry and parliament have received numerous complaints about abuses of replacement and voluntary enlistment. These abuses affect the whole of the army. But the artillery presents other problems which, as I have tried to point out, are inherent in the new make-up of its personnel.

Education was another contributory factor in the artillery's republicanism. Because of its technical nature, the artillery had a definite policy of recruiting soldiers with above-average intelligence and education. These soldiers, who were more conscious of political and social problems and less content with the *status quo*, were commonly thought more open to republicanism or socialist influence. Sergeant Boichot, an infantryman and a candidate for political office in the Second Republic, pointed this out: 'Soldiers in the special arms, usually better educated than their counterparts in the infantry and cavalry, support social reform. Infantrymen and cavalrymen only complain, for the most part, of things which affect them personally.'[61]

It is generally recognized [wrote General Lenoury in 1833]
that in the French artillery, as in the rest of the European
artillery corps, the preliminary studies required for admittance,
by encouraging an inquiring and analytical mind, sometimes
take officers a little too far. Criticism is more common there
than in other corps. The Inspector General, who has often
commented on this opposition mania, has noticed this year a
definite improvement in attitude, owing to increased confidence
in the government or to a move to sounder ideas.[62]

Soldiers arrested for political activity were frequently reported to
be well educated.[63]

Education, therefore, was an important factor in military
republicanism and definitely contributed to the chronic political
activity of Polytechnicians and student officers at the Ecole d'Application. The Metz inspection report of 1838, which believed republicanism to be abating among students, pointed out the link between
education and republicanism. 'The political issues which so influenced the most recent classes have lost their impetus. But the
main cause of the moral disorder, attributable to the education
received at the Ecole Polytechnique, is still unchanged.'[64]

If the relationship between education and political opposition
in the army is indisputable, as even contemporaries realized,
certainly the artillery as the most intelligent arm could claim to be
the most republican.

TABLE 10   *Conscript literacy rates – 1831–5*

Bas-Rhin	91·3
Meuse	88·5
Doubs	88·2
Haute-Marne	86·0
Jura	84·8
Seine	84·7
Haut-Rhin	81·4
Ardennes	80·0
Marne	79·1
Hautes-Alpes	78·9
Meurthe	78·4
Haute-Saône	77·8
Vosges	77·1
Moselle	77·1
Aube	77·0

Furthermore, as most artillery corps were stationed in the east and the large cities, most of their recruits came from these areas. A table of literacy rates for conscription between 1831 and 1835 reveals that Paris and the east were the most literate areas in France: regiments stationed in these areas drew on the educational élite of France, and the artillery, because of its longer garrison stays, recruited a larger proportion of these men. On a purely numerical basis then, the artillery qualifies as the 'arme savante'.

Regiments of any arm stationed in the east and in cities with active republican societies were affected to some extent by republican propaganda. However, the combination of a long garrison stay in a republican area, regional homogeneity, a high proportion of volunteers and replacements, financial problems, many intelligent, and probably Protestant soldiers, and its dependence on schools, especially the Ecole Polytechnique, increased the incidence of republican opposition in the artillery.

Chapter 7

The Droits de l'Homme

Casimir Périer and his rigorously conservative 'système de 13 mars' forced the Left to break with the government. By 1832 the army had successfully liberated Belgium from the Dutch and removed the threat of a European war. The economy also began to return to normal as the tax yield increased and businessmen and shopkeepers regained confidence in the government. Throughout France and in foreign capitals, the name Périer was equated with stability. Consequently, riots and other civil disturbances tapered off in the first months of 1832.

This was a year of transition for the Left. It could no longer feed on governmental instability, but was not sufficiently organized to challenge the Périer ministry. Left-wing leaders were split into three factions. Moderates led by Armand Carrel supported a programme of political reform which included press freedom, wider franchise and an aggressive foreign policy. A second group under Marrast and the elder Garnier-Pages advocated a mixed programme of political and social reform in the belief that the revolution should benefit the working class as well as the middle classes. A third and more radical group led by Ledru-Rollin, Arago and Cavaignac demanded more equitable taxation, a reformed penal code and the election of all public officials from judges and jailers to army officers and NCOs. These reforms, they believed, could only be effected under a republic. They preached a Rousseauian doctrine of 'natural rights' as opposed to the political right of Carrel: if parliament did not reflect the will of the people, the people should rise up and bring parliament down.

The army, too, experienced a brief lull in opposition activity early in 1832. Military reports for the first half of the year contain little more than requests for surveillance on several officers suspected of republican or Carlist activity. On 15 May officers of the 34th Infantry Regiment and artillery officers in the Toulouse garrison whistled when the king's name was mentioned during a play.[1] This one incident gives the measure of the general level of activity.

However, this brief calm was shattered by the cholera epidemic which swept France in the spring, killing Casimir Périer. The death of the dynamic leader on 16 May gave the Left new energy. Opposition papers redoubled their attacks on the government, while thirty-three liberal deputies meeting at Laffitte's house severely criticized the administration's record. Once again, the revolutionaries appeared to have seized the initiative and on 5 June, following the funeral cortège of General Lamarque, they rioted. The 40,000-man Paris garrison only put down the rebellion after two solid days of fighting.

The army, however, did not rise in support of the Left, although in November 1831 over 900 soldiers in Lyon had deserted during riots there. In the only reported incident, Commandant Fauchier of the 12th Light Infantry apparently assured an insurgent that his battalion would not fire on the demonstrators. And indeed, the the battalion stood by while one man was killed and five wounded in an attack on a ten-man municipal guard post. After a brief investigation, however, the War Minister concluded that the incident was fictitious.[2]

June 1832 ushered in a triple victory for the government. The republicans were defeated in Paris, the Duchess de Berry's Vendéan uprising was put down and the Duc de Reichstadt, Napoleon's son and heir, died in Vienna. The Left realized that if it were successfully to challenge the increasingly confident government, it had to increase its grassroots support both in the capital and the provinces. Concerted republican efforts, quite unlike all previous canvassing, slowly crystallized army opposition to assume a definite political character.

In the second half of 1832, much republican activity was reported in the east. In August, no less than thirty-four officers and soldiers of the 4th Lancers at Thionville were tried for political opposition, while six NCOs in the 20th Infantry Regiment at Dijon, 'hostile to the government', were sent to Africa.[3] Lieutenant Lebrun of the 53rd Infantry Regiment at Dôle refused to drink a toast to the king and then spoke out his grievance: 'What use have we for the king now? We must drink to liberty and the great days of July.'[4]

Elsewhere, soldiers in the 5th Infantry Regiment at Lille were sent to Africa for their political activity and republican officers and soldiers were reported in the 23rd at Lyon and the 16th Infantry Regiment at Paris.[5]

Carlists rarely attempted to indoctrinate the army after the Duchesse de Berry's abortive 1832 uprising in the west. In June a soldier in the 65th Infantry Regiment at Metz was arrested with legitimist pamphlets and in September the Prefect of the Rhône claimed that a few officers of the 23rd Infantry Regiment had been seen at a legitimist meeting in Lyon.[6] But Carlists continued to provoke desertions among young recruits in the west. In June 1833 General Bigarré, commander of the 13th Military Division at Rennes, reported that most of the 170 absentee conscripts in the Ille-et-Vilaine and the 262 in Morbihan had been encouraged to desert by pro-Bourbon priests.[7] By February 1834 the number had been reduced slightly to 152 and 221 respectively as the chouan bands still operating in the west increasingly turned to brigandage and abandoned their political goals.

Government repression had curtailed the activities of the Amis du Peuple and in November 1832, Cavaignac took over the direction of the Droits de l'Homme. To sidestep article 291 of the penal code forbidding associations of over twenty members, he instructed that the society break into small cells. These took revolutionary names such as Robespierre, Blanqui, Marat etc. By February 1833, the Droits de l'Homme claimed to have 4,000 members, mostly Paris students, although workers were well represented.[8] Unlike the Amis du Peuple, however, Cavaignac also set up a central committee to contact provincial republicans. Local groups were encouraged to write frequently to Paris and were assigned a party official to look after their interests.[9]

Cavaignac met only limited success in the provinces. Local republicans, like those in the Jura, often preferred to remain independent of Paris.[10] Many moderate leftists, including Carrel and Marrast, objected to the neo-Jacobin programme of the new group which called for, among other things, a strong elected executive, a National Guard including all Frenchmen, universal suffrage and the creation of a federation of European states.[11]

With Paris providing the direction, activity in the army grew at an alarming rate as republicans put their new tactics into practice.

The Prefect of the Bouches-du-Rhône reported in 1834 that the Droits de l'Homme was attempting to arm each of its members with a rifle and twenty-five cartridges and to attract more soldiers into its ranks:[12]

> The goals of the association are well defined. But here are two points overlooked in the statutes: 1. Every member must have a rifle and 25 cartridges. 2. Each branch must try to attract soldiers to its meetings to enlist them in the rebellious republican party.

To accomplish their first task, republicans either established clandestine arms factories, such as the one in which four Polytechnicians were arrested in the 1833 'affaire des poudres', or purchased cartridges from soldiers. This practice was especially common in Paris. By April 1833 the rapidly deteriorating situation forced General Pajol to demand that speedy measures be taken to stop soldiers selling cartridges to enemies of the government.[13] From then on, any soldier who sold his equipment was severely punished. Exactly a year later, Saint-Cyrians rioted when several students were arrested on suspicion of selling seven barrels of gunpowder to republicans.[14]

The second phase of the programme was two-fold: soldiers were either paid to desert and fight against the government or encouraged to join the Droits de l'Homme. Republicans had clearly established a financially viable organization which was often backed by Carlists who hoped to turn republican unrest to their own advantage. The first incident was reported in Montpellier in April 1833;[15] other garrisons were soon affected – notably Toulon, where republicans went to work in regiments about to be shipped to Algeria.[16]

By the end of 1833, many regiments, especially in Dijon, Lyon and Marseille, reported that republicans were causing an increasing number of desertions.[17] In October 1834 a deserter from the 20th Infantry Regiment in Dijon was arrested in Lyon. He confessed that in April of that year, republicans had paid nine men from his company to desert and had then taken them to Lyon, where they were fed, clothed and given five francs a day – an enormous sum for soldiers who cleared only five centimes a day – on the condition that they would fight for the insurgents: 'We were told that an insurrection to overthrow Louis-Philippe would break out at Lyon.'[18] He was placed with a silkworker named Favre, but could not tell where his fellow deserters were as they were lodged separately and were strictly forbidden to divulge their addresses. This high degree of organization made it possible for the republicans to provoke a confrontation with the government at the first opportunity.

Paris republicans were especially successful in attracting soldiers into their party. Officers and soldiers in the 8th, 38th and 58th Infantry Regiments, the 5th Lancers and the 8th Chasseurs were arrested in the spring of 1833 for belonging to the Droits de l'Homme.[19] In June, the Minister of the Interior announced that republicans had formed a special organization, the Association Patriotique Militaire, to co-ordinate efforts to win military converts.[20] To remove the army from the source of the trouble, he suggested that Paris regiments be changed as frequently as possible and soldiers refused leave to visit the capital: 'The recent arrest of a sergeant-major in the 58th Infantry Regiment on political charges seems to prove that the propagandists are active and have met with some success.'[21] General Pajol, however, assured the War Minister that these fears were exaggerated: 'Some regiments have been approached by subversives, but this has happened rarely and has been without success.'[22] But despite General Pajol's reassurances, NCOs in the 3rd Dragoons were arrested for joining the Droits de l'Homme in August.[23]

In Paris republicans made headway by exploiting regimental rivalries and discontent in the hope of sparking off trouble in the garrison. In March 1832, for example, the 35th Infantry Regiment had distinguished itself by its harsh treatment of a republican demonstration in Grenoble. Liberals complained that the regiment had spilled the people's blood and compelled General Saint-Claire to transfer it to Lyon. However, Périer praised the regiment's discipline and returned it to Grenoble with a victory parade. The 35th was subsequently brought to Paris as a reward for its loyalty. But once it was in the capital, republicans began to incite other regiments to avenge the people of Grenoble and provoked duels and fights with soldiers of the 35th. The Minister of the Interior noted, 'They are inciting it to excesses which might force the government to send it to Africa. And if this happened, they would try to make it rebel on the way.'[24] Finally, a group of about 300 carabineers, lancers and artillerymen, incited by ex-captain Kersausie, attacked soldiers of the 35th, wounding seven and killing one. A quarrel also broke out between the 1st Carabineers, which was known for its Carlist sympathies, and the 42nd Infantry Regiment. When the 1st was transferred to another garrison, the newly arrived 2nd Carabineers took up the quarrel.

The Paris troubles had their counterpart in the east, as a series of politically motivated fights and duels broke out in the Wissembourg, Regnisheim and Strasbourg garrisons. Obviously worried by the republican offensive in the army, military officials set up a local 'service d'observation' to obstruct republican attempts to contact soldiers in their off-duty hours.[25]

Republicans met with success in several provincial towns, especially in the east. Thirty officers in the 49th Infantry Regiment at Strasbourg belonged to the Droits de l'Homme, together with many officers and NCOs in the town's artillery regiments.[26] Republicans also infiltrated the 4th Lancers at Thionville, the 20th and 52nd Infantry Regiments at Dijon, the 26th at Regnisheim, the 11th Dragoons at Epinal, the 4th, 9th and 10th Cuirassiers at Lunéville, the 2nd Chasseurs at Sedan, the 13th Light Infantry Regiment at Metz, and twenty-five NCOs in Metz's 3rd Engineers were accused of belonging to the Droits de l'Homme.

In the north, soldiers in the 25th Infantry Regiment at Cambrai were arrested as republicans, as were four officers in the 65th Infantry Regiment at Avesnes, near Lille, and several NCOs in the

3rd Infantry Regiment at Amiens. Republican activity mushroomed in Lyon, while one officer and a sergeant in the 2nd Infantry Regiment were arrested for belonging to the comité révolutionnaire de Lyon.[27] General Durrier warned officers to keep an eye on 'les allures politiques de la troupe' and ordered that a special watch be put on soldiers during their off-duty hours.[28] Seventeen NCOs in the 15th Infantry Regiment at Grenoble were arrested for belonging to the Droits de l'Homme.[29]

Republicans were also active in several cities in the south. In an article for the *Sémaphore de Marseille*, Maréchal de Logis Vaucher claimed that the 13th and 24th Infantry Regiments were full of Saint Simonists and the Prefect confirmed that opposition groups had strong followings in the garrison.[30] Republicans were arrested in the 17th Light Infantry Regiment at Carcassonne, the 30th at Nîmes and in the Montpellier garrison.

Subscriptions to opposition newspapers also increased. A lieutenant in the 6th Hussars at Limoges was reported for subscribing to the *Tribune*,[31] as were soldiers in the 24th Infantry Regiment in Marseille, the 22nd in Paris, the 39th Infantry Regiment in Douai, the 45th at Lille, the 50th and 56th at Nantes and several Strasbourg regiments.[32] Several students in Saint-Cyr and the Ecole Polytechnique were also reported for the same offence. Several soldiers wrote letters to the *Tribune* criticizing army attempts to ban political discussion in the army. Corporal Roberts wrote that many NCOs in the 24th Regiment read the *Tribune*, often aloud to their illiterate comrades: 'Your newspaper has recently attracted the interest of some NCOs and soldiers of the 24th who heartily agree with your opinions.'[33]

For the first time republicans attempted to co-ordinate their propaganda efforts on a nation-wide scale in the summer of 1833 with a pamphlet entitled *A l'Armée* which appeared simultaneously in Paris, Strasbourg, Nantes, Lyon, Meaux, Montpellier, Thionville, and other towns. The pamphlet, a reprint of a June speech in the Chamber of Deputies by ex-Napoleonic Colonel Briqueville, criticized the 1832 law for weakening the army. By restricting the size and composition of the army to ensure its political loyalty, the government was undermining its wartime effectiveness: 'He wants to fill it with men [who would be] more manageable at home and less eager for foreign war . . . If, under the new plan, the army was more effective at home, it would, on the other hand, be less effective in war.' He also deplored the lack of a trained reserve and criticized Soult's reserve of congés as 'a useless reserve'. He blasted governmental favouritism and intervention in military affairs and praised the French army as the last bastion of national honour:[34]

Military honours have fallen prey to corruption by civilians. A pure life dedicated to serving the nation is seldom a passport to favour and power . . . How, in these circumstances, can one hope to foster military virtues, impartiality and loyalty? Each time that the nation has been oppressed, each time that its feelings have been violated, national honour has taken refuge in the army. Today, as during the Terror and the Restoration, the army will not fail to rise to this glory and privilege.

Republicans also sponsored banquets for officers and NCOs in many towns. In direct opposition to the government, officers in the 19th Light Infantry Regiment attended a banquet given by the notoriously republican Metz National Guard.[35] Republicans gave a banquet for NCOs of the 2nd Engineers in Montpellier and the 31st Infantry and 6th Dragoons in Tours. Such banquets, often sponsored by the National Guard, were a commonplace occurrence in Montpellier, Nîmes, Metz and other garrison towns.

In July police informers reported that a large number of soldiers in Paris were masons. In a letter to Soult, the Minister of the Interior pointed out that in masonic lodges, many infiltrated by republicans and liberal Polish refugees, 'impassioned support of republican ideas has replaced that of philanthropic principles'.[36] General Pajol wrote that every association, whatever its stated purpose, had a political goal:[37]

In this political climate, one has to recognize that all these meetings, whatever name they go under, today have a more or less overt political orientation, contrary to the principles of constitutional government. NCOs are exposed to dangerous influences. Moreover, it conflicts with the spirit of the army, which can only serve one flag.

Masons were subsequently found in the 8th, 42nd and 58th Infantry Regiments. 'NCOs are exposed to the proposals of the agitators', Argôut warned Soult, 'who are always hanging about outside the barracks. They take them to taverns and wine shops and, after standing them drinks and meals, they often offer them money.'[38] Republican activity continued to gain momentum all over the country until they boasted strong followings in several important garrison towns and were at last in a position to challenge the government.

Chapter 8

Lunéville, 1834

1834 marked a crucial year for French republicans. As the July Monarchy tightened its grip on the political situation and the economy gained strength daily, many turned against the republicans' revolutionary programme. The opposition, therefore, led by Cavaignac, mounted one last offensive. Late in 1832 the Droits de l'Homme had launched a campaign to win over the army and to build a network of provincial cells. This effort, the most organized to date, culminated in 1834 as republicans made the final preparations for a co-ordinated military uprising in the east.

Simultaneously, republican activity increased all over the country. Paris was no exception: in January NCOs in the 22nd Infantry Regiment attended the funeral of the republican leader, Tissot.[1] Republicans were arrested in the 5th, 32nd, 58th and 61st Infantry Regiments, while twenty-three officers in the garrison attended a republican banquet.[2] In April police reported that eight officers and several NCOs in the 38th Infantry Regiment were republicans and that five officers in the 1st Artillery had formed a republican society in their regiment. They claimed that many students at the Ecole Polytechnique belonged to the Droits de l'Homme and that a lieutenant in the 61st Infantry Regiment had refused to lead his troops against the people.[3] Seventeen NCOs in the 36th Regiment were sent to Algeria for republican activity.[4]

In the north, activity was reported in the 2nd Chasseurs in Cambrai and the 45th Infantry Regiment at Lille.[5] Le Mans republicans gave a banquet for officers of the 10th Dragoons,[6] as republicans stepped up activity in the 56th at Nantes and six officers in the 4th Artillery at Rennes were sent home after openly criticizing the government.[7]

Republicans were also active in the south, especially in Marseille. In March the Prefect claimed that the Droits de l'Homme had no less than twenty-six sections in Marseille and that republicans were still active in the garrison.[8] In April republican influence in the 13th Infantry, whose left-wing bias dated from the 1815 massacre by white terrorists at Nîmes, was so strong that the Prefect requested the regiment's reassignment: 'The attempts to win over NCOs are more intensive than ever. They are ordered by the central committee. I sincerely urge that the 13th be recalled from Marseille. It has been there for two years. That is easily too long.'[9] Republicans continued canvassing in the Toulon garrison and for the first time penetrated the Aurillac garrison, while eight NCOs in the 17th Light Infantry at Perpignan were sent to Africa after assuring local republicans that they would not fire on the people.[10]

Supported by a liberal population, however, republicans were most influential in eastern garrisons, especially Strasbourg and Metz. In April the Minister of the Interior reported that several officers in the 49th Infantry Regiment at Strasbourg were members of the Droits de l'Homme[11] and activity was reported in the 1st Light Infantry Regiment at Strasbourg and the 13th at Metz. A company of pontonniers was moved from Strasbourg to Auxonne in the wake of a series of politically motivated fights with the 19th Light Infantry. Their departure provoked a large public demonstration.[12]

Mounting opposition activity induced the War Minister to order the commanding general of the 3rd Military Division to arrest any soldier in the Droits de l'Homme.[13] Republicans were arrested in the garrisons at Besançon, Colmar, Neufbrisach, Sedan and Verdun, while several officers and NCOs from the 20th and 52nd Infantry Regiments were sent to Africa for joining the Droits de l'Homme in Dijon. On 3 April the Minister of the Interior confirmed that republicans had initiated an all-out effort to infiltrate the army in the east: 'Anarchist agents are working to undermine the army', he wrote, 'especially at Belfort, Colmar and in the 5th Military Division in general.'[14]

This militancy climaxed with the Lunéville rebellion – the high point of republican activity in the army and the only spontaneous military revolt of the July Monarchy.

Like all republican activity in the army until 1834, the seeds of the Lunéville rebellion were sown by local republicans. In 1831 Mathieu, a member of the Carbonari and editor of the republican *Sentinelle des Vosges* at Epinal, met several NCOs in the 7th Dragoons stationed in that town – Mascarène, Hane, Crozel, Renard, Chaband and Quary. After several weeks of casual meetings in local cafés, he proposed that they organize a society. Though Mathieu at first spoke of a social group, he encouraged soldiers to voice their grievances and soon succeeded in giving this society a strong political orientation.

This procedure follows the typical pattern of republican infiltration and was well known to government officials. In November 1835, after the discovery of a secret society in the 12th Infantry

Regiment at Dijon, the Prefect of the Côte-d'Or reported that republicans frequently formed social groups which gradually assumed a political character:[15]

> In loyal units, these meetings at first put on a show of pleasure and regimental fraternity, before going on to speak of political trends . . . cautiously broaching matters pertinent to the regiment, to the army, and then to the government itself.
> When a large part of the army is committed to some degree, having taken a vow of supreme loyalty to the group, they aim at co-ordinated rebellion.

Sergeant Quary of the 7th, whose arrest on 13 April 1834 uncovered the plot, confirmed that Mathieu had transformed the social group into a republican cell with the goal of establishing 'a purely democratic government in France'.

In November 1832 the 7th was transferred to Lyon and replaced by the 11th Dragoons. Mascarène was placed in the 11th Dragoons as a police agent and returned to Epinal, where he accepted Mathieu's invitation in the summer of 1833 to join a Carbonari vente.[16]

The Carbonari was an influential secret society under the Restoration, for it attracted virtually all opponents of the monarchy. After 1830 its importance was diminished by dynamic republican societies like the Amis du Peuple and, after 1832, the Droits de l'Homme. But its influence remained strong in the provinces, which the Paris-based republican societies initially neglected. Carbonari organization depended on a national 'vente directrice' in Paris, which ranked between the European 'vente suprême' and the provincial 'ventes intermédiaires'. Mathieu was the head of the Epinal vente which corresponded with several lower 'ventes ordinaires'.

Towards the end of 1833, republicans opened a successful recruitment campaign in regiments in and around Epinal – the 1st Cuirassiers at Nancy and the 5th at Toul, the 11th Dragoons at Epinal and the 4th, 9th and the 10th Cuirassiers at Lunéville. In December the Paris committee of the Droits de l'Homme informed Mathieu that they wanted to strengthen links with the provinces: 'There is one thing which, until now, was lacking in the organization of the French republican party – contact between patriots in the departments and the Parisian political societies, an association between the provinces and the capital.'[17]

As republican activity mushroomed, some officials became worried by Mascarène's role as police agent, and in November General Hulot requested permission to clamp down on his activity:[18]

> Mascarène has never passed on any significant information about the Carbonari movement. He is a great nuisance and a

danger for his regiment. I would ask that he be sent to Africa. This NCO [seconded General Venevelle, commander of the Vosges subdivision], if not a positive danger, does give cause for concern . . . He persists in his behaviour. He sees only people hostile to the government and he goes to their meetings. It is rumoured that he is their secretary. Mascarène's transfer is absolutely vital.

The government, however, insisted that Mascarène continue his work. The army was forbidden to nip the plot in the bud as an attempt to arrest guilty NCOs would have exposed Mascarène and deprived the government of an invaluable informer. And officials were powerless to arrest Mathieu, who had not broken the law.

The plot therefore continued to grow, unhindered by the authorities.

In February 1834 Mathieu and Coevilier, another Epinal republican, applied for passports and travelled to Lyon via Châlons, Besançon and Nancy to co-ordinate plans for a nation-wide uprising. A letter of 23 February from General Venevelle to Hulot shows that the army was informed of Mathieu's movements and realized the danger of a large-scale republican rebellion:[19]

They travel from town to town to inventory their men, arms and munitions. With this aim he will visit in the first town [Nancy] a certain M. Thomas, a law student and editor of the *Patriot*, and at Châlons a M. Macant, a lawyer. Mathieu holds that the rebellion will break out at Lyon and that a large number of patriots will make their way there singly to support the uprising, which will cover several departments, so nullifying government action. He is also counting on troop desertions. After the republican government is proclaimed there, he says he will immediately return here to organize the new departmental administration, and that the arrest of the general and the colonel will be his first task at Epinal because, he claims, these leaders taken, the regiment will be intimidated and no longer present an obstacle to the patriots.

Mathieu is exceedingly sorry that Mascarène will not be with him in Lyon to establish the new contacts with the 7th Dragoons. Indeed, I believe that if we wanted to send him there, he could be of use now. I am sure that the republicans are organizing a large-scale conspiracy.

Tension began to mount in March as a revolution appeared inevitable. On 7 March the Minister of the Interior relayed a report from the Prefect of the Bas-Rhin which confirmed that provincial republicans hoped to co-ordinate a nation-wide revolution, but concluded that 'like all departmental republicans, they will only follow Paris's lead'.[20] A letter of 17 March to the War Minister reported that Mathieu was planning a spring uprising and had contacted an officer in the notoriously republican 20th Infantry Regiment at Dijon, a lawyer named Demontry, a Doctor Lortel at Lyon and a Besançon architect named Convert, whose brother was a captain in the National Guard. On 28 March Sergeant Hane of the 1st Dragoons and one of the original members of Mathieu's society, wrote to a friend that revolution was imminent: 'I believe that the crisis is nigh. A people may sleep, but they will awaken. But to shake them from their lassitude, we need the fusillade and the tocsin . . . Vengeance! Liberty! We hasten to avenge the first martyrs [of 1830].'[21]

By March Mathieu had organized a chapter of the Droits de l'Homme in Epinal, including two officers in the 4th Cuirassiers, and had warned sympathetic NCOs in the 11th Dragoons to prepare their troops to march on Lyon at the first sign of trouble. On 1 April Quary obtained leave from the 7th Dragoons at Lyon and travelled to Epinal and Lunéville to carry Mathieu's instructions to Chaumont in the 10th Cuirassiers, Clement Thomas in the 9th and Geslin Bernard in the 4th. On 13 April the Prefect of the Vosges reported that six NCOs in the 11th Dragoons had been spotted at a Carbonari meeting.[22] Under the pretext of seeing friends, Thomas made several trips to Nancy and Toul to keep other regiments abreast of the latest plans.[23] Sergeant Stiller of the 9th Cuirassiers asked for leave to visit his family in Nancy and took the occasion to co-ordinate movements with the 1st Cuirassiers, Dugaillon, co-editor of the *Patriote*, and Doctor Bechet, who had visited NCOs at Lunéville on several occasions.

On 13 April Colonel Laporte of the 11th Dragoons arrested Quary, who had been visiting NCOs in the east. Quary confessed that twelve NCOs in the 7th Dragoons at Lyon were plotting with soldiers at Nancy and Lunéville to overthrow the government and claimed that de Ludre, deputy for the Meurthe, and the liberal General Clauzel were involved in the plot.[24] Sergeant Stiller confirmed that Doctor Bechet had given the same assurance to NCOs at Lunéville: 'He saw M. de Ludre and we can count on him.'[25] Colonel Laporte informed Colonel Clomadeux of the 9th Cuirassiers at Lunéville, who called Thomas in for questioning on 14 April. Thomas, however, professed ignorance of any plot and Colonel Clomadeux let the matter drop. His 'blind confidence' was later criticized by the War Minister.[26]

In March the government had moved to outlaw the Droits de l'Homme by extending the ban on associations to include those with fewer than twenty members. The law exasperated Lyon mutualists who had been agitating for higher wages since their uprising in November 1831 and who had walked out unsuccessfully in February 1834. Rioting broke out in Lyon on 9 April which the army only put down after a bitter five-day battle. In Paris news of the riots touched off two days of fighting which ended on 14 April with the widely publicized massacre of civilians in the rue Transmonian.

Reports of uprisings in Paris, Lyon and Saint-Etienne and an article in the *National* claiming that the 52nd Infantry Regiment at Belfort had rebelled and proclaimed a republic spurred Thomas on. Although he had received no instructions from Mathieu, he decided to act and on the evening of 16 April called a meeting of forty NCOs in the 4th, 9th and 10th Cuirassiers on the Champs de Mars, the garrison parade ground and the scene of several previous meetings. General Hulot claimed that 'the majority of the NCOs in the three regiments had a hand in the conspiracy'.[27]

Thomas drew the men up by regiment and delivered a ringing indictment of the government. He urged them to raise the garrison and ride to Nancy to join other mutinous regiments and march on Paris. Sergeant Denvers later testified that Thomas intended to proclaim a republic once the capital fell: 'He intended to proclaim a republic because the government did not wish to and indeed could not bring happiness to France.' Sergeant Caille of the 4th Cuirassiers seconded Denvers' testimony: 'The conspiracy aimed to overthrow the government and establish a republic.'[28] 'I called this meeting', Thomas confessed, 'to spark an insurrection hoping for a military revolution which would overthrow the government . . . The government does not want and could not achieve the happiness of France.'[29]

The meeting broke up with the NCOs resolved to carry out their plan at midnight.

But as the conspirators left the Champs de Mars, they met two officers of the 10th – Lieutenant Noel, a native of the Vosges, and Lieutenant Vautravers – who had been warned of the meeting and had rushed immediately to the parade ground to discourage the project.

Soon arguments and fighting broke out among soldiers of the 4th and 9th and those of the 10th who, at the sight of their officers, refused to go through with the plot. At this point, witnesses agree that Thomas became frightened and decided to call off the insurrection. This, Noel insisted, was why he did not report the incident.

He shook hands with Thomas and promised not to divulge the plot, as the NCOs feared they would be sent to Algeria. Bernard, however, objected to the cancellation and convinced part of the group to keep the midnight rendezvous: 'We all left determined to carry through the rebellion at midnight.'[30]

However, the plot was finally broken up by the actions of a local woman, Thérèse Arbot, the girl-friend of a twenty-one-year-old volunteer from Verdun, Sergeant Roberts, also in the 10th. As the couple were walking outside the Champs de Mars, she noticed the assembly and asked Roberts what was going on. He replied jokingly: 'They are going to see their mistresses. Be quiet, you will find out later.'

The plot was therefore known to the colonel, to two lieutenants and many NCOs and soldiers who were not actively involved in it. Yet whether through disbelief or pure negligence, no official action was taken until Thérèse Arbot ran to warn General Gustler at 9 p.m. The General immediately called the three colonels, ordered the stables and harness rooms locked and put out fifty pickets per regiment commanded by officers.

The conspirators were arrested as they filtered back to their barracks.

Lunéville marked a crucial failure for republicans in the east and compelled them to realize they were not strong enough to challenge the government. Most eastern towns like Epinal and Strasbourg were commercial rather than industrial centres and eastern republicans could not call on the traditionally revolutionary working class which Paris and Lyon republicans had at their disposal. Only the army could spark off a revolution in the east and for this reason republican activity in the eastern garrisons was especially high. Republicans in Paris and Lyon could hope to defeat the army as they had done in the capital in 1830 and in Lyon in 1831. But in the east, they had to goad the army into revolt or face certain defeat.

Despite news of the Paris and Lyon insurrections, Mathieu and other eastern republicans realized that the army there had remained faithful to the government, as the *National* reported on 12 April: 'The soldiers [at Lyon] showed a steadfastness throughout the five-hour fight which must deflate the criminal hopes of those who reportedly counted on them.' Lacking the support of the working class, they lay low as the insurrections were quickly and quietly snuffed out.

Left to their own devices, the NCOs proved less than competent revolutionaries. Thomas' noisy meeting on the Champs de Mars put paid to secrecy and led directly to his arrest. Nor did he plan to arrest officers and government officials who might oppose him.

The naïvety and shapelessness of the conspiracy condemned it to failure from the start and testified that republicans in the provinces were far less organized than the government believed.

A study of the motives behind the rebellion reveals other fatal shortcomings in the republican campaign to subvert the army.

On the surface, the Lunéville NCOs appeared to be dedicated republicans. De Regnier testified that many in the garrison feared being sent to Paris or Lyon to put down popular uprisings. And General Hulot reported that Thomas had told the NCOs on the Champs de Mars that loyalty to the government meant disloyalty to the people: 'It is a question of whether we would fight against the people, is how they put it.'[31] Thomas confirmed this was indeed the main arrow in the republican bow: 'They [the republicans] only said that for the past four years, the army had fought only against honest citizens.'[32]

Republicans hoped to undermine military discipline to deprive the government of its main repressive force and ensure the triumph of a civil insurrection. Republican military propaganda in this period aimed to convince soldiers not to fire on insurgents. One pamphlet which appeared in several garrisons in the spring decried France's humiliating defeat at the hands of the Holy Alliance and claimed that it could be avenged only by a republic:[33]

Rebuild the walls of Hunigue! Tear up the treaties of 1815, infamous treaties forced on France over the dead bodies of our fathers . . . AVENGE WATERLOO! The Dijon garrison will never fire on the people! . . . the soldiers are armed, equipped, fed, paid for by the people – the army is drawn from the people – the army is the people – the army is a family . . . The Dijon garrison will never commit parricide . . . Woe be to any officer base enough to give the order to fire! . . . The Dijon garrison remembers what Napoleon said: 'Within fifty years, Europe will be either Cossack or republican.' And for us, men, the voice of Napoleon is the voice of God! NOT COSSACK . . . cries the Dijon garrison in a single voice! . . . The republic . . . is the only form of government commensurate with the dignity of man. The Republic! . . . And, if it must be, WAR!'

A song entitled *Bon Sens*, which appeared in several garrisons, contained the refrain, 'But on the people, Oh! I will never fire!'[34]

Another pamphlet, 'Protestation des sous-officiers', urged soldiers to revolt against the doctrine of 'passive obedience': a soldier's first loyalty was to the people and his duty was to defend the country not the government:[35]

Today, each government places a shameful burden on the uniform [it read]. It refuses to let the idea of liberty take root in the ranks because it needs these men to smother this idea in the hearts of others . . . We refuse to be slaves any longer.

We are told: a soldier must not have any opinion. We say, however, that he must, because a man without an opinion is indifferent to right and wrong. We say that he must be involved in politics.

We are also told that we must support those who pay us. Well, who does pay us? It is not the king with his own savings. It is the people, the nation that pays us. WE ARE NOT THE KING'S SOLDIERS! WE ARE THE NATION'S SOLDIERS!

No one has the right to order us to fire or to have us fired on in the streets by our fellow citizens. That is not our job, nor our place. Our job is to defend the fatherland, our place is at the frontier.

However, ideology only papered over the more concrete attractions of a republic for the NCOs. NCOs were interested primarily in improving their own social position and were attracted by the republican promise of faster promotion under a republic. Republicans proposed to model the army on the National Guard, with soldiers electing sergeants and officers to the rank of lieutenant-colonel. A pamphlet found in the Strasbourg barracks of the battalion of pontonniers urged the adoption of this programme to eliminate promotional abuses. 'Then, soldiers of France, you will rise to the rank of general faster than you become an NCO today.'[36] 'Protestations des sous-officiers' also decried slow promotion.

Discontent over slow promotion was brought to a head by the army reorganization of 9 March 1834. With the July revolution and the subsequent war scare, the army in 1831 increased its total manpower from 168,000 to 304,060, creating two new squadrons per regiment in the cavalry and an extra 'demi-bataillon' in the infantry. But in 1834, as the international situation cooled off, the government disbanded the 6th Squadron and demi-battalions and reduced army strength to 275,500.[37] Career officers and NCOs saw in this measure the end of their hopes of promotion, and officers and NCOs in the demi-battalions were forced to accept a reduction in rank and pay.

This reorganization, together with fears that the government might reduce military pensions, sent a wave of discontent through the army.[38]

Three things combined almost instantaneously to cause concern among soldiers [reported General Pajol on 1 April].

Troop reductions which dimmed the promotion hopes of officers and NCOs, the possibility of a smaller pension, which would have hurt everyone, and the obligatory six months' furloughs for infantry officers. Nevertheless . . . despite some worry about its future, army morale remains high.

The Minister of the Interior confirmed on 21 March that republicans had exploited military discontent over the reorganization: 'The republicans [at Epinal]', he wrote to Soult, 'gathered at a banquet where they stressed that they hoped to take advantage of the discontent they expected to follow from the troop reductions and the din raised over the revision of the pension law.'[39] Fifteen days later, the Prefect of the Rhône confirmed that NCOs were angered by the troop reductions:[40]

Lyon police reports now mention only the discontent among NCOs over the new measures the War Minister was forced to take. This discontent is given forceful expression even in public. They have worked hard this week [he again wrote on 4 April] to contact army officers and NCOs, and have tried to exploit the discontent resulting from the new ordinances . . . It seems that a small number of NCOs have been indoctrinated.

The Prefect of the Bouches-du-Rhône reported that the promotion crisis had seriously damaged morale in the Marseille garrison:[41]

The latest ordinance on troop reductions has served as a pretext for malcontents to turn officers against the government. The suppression of the fourth demi-battalion, which leaves many NCOs without regimental positions, has hindered promotion. Several first-class captains who were earning 2,400 francs a year will lose their rank and earn only 2,000 francs. Republicans are trying to take advantage of these circumstances to indoctrinate officers.

In April the demi-battalion of the 52nd Infantry Regiment at Belfort, led by a second-lieutenant, threatened to mutiny. Discontent was so widespread that the War Minister sent a circular to all colonels instructing them to assure their men that the troop reductions would not endanger their careers.

The troop reductions left many Lunéville NCOs bitter. 'Thomas told me', testified Lieutenant Noel, 'that discontent was rife among NCOs following the disbanding of the 6th squadron.'[42] Sergeant Gueréchaux of the 4th Cuirassiers confirmed Lieutenant Noel's testimony: 'I only remember hearing Sergeant Thomas say that, since the disbanding of the 6th squadron, NCOs had no chance for promotion.'[43] Sergeant Tricotel, who was arrested after riding to Nancy to raise the 1st Cuirassiers, made the same point: 'Since we learned of the disbanding of the 6th squadron, the NCOs have been dissatisfied.'[44]

Ambitious NCOs especially resented the troop reductions. A 6 May report to the War Minister concluded that republicans exploited ambition: 'The leaders sent their emissaries, full of extravagant promises, to the very ambitious NCOs.'[45] In a letter to the War Minister, the colonel of the 4th Cuirassiers agreed that ambitious NCOs had sparked the Lunéville affair:[46]

> The instigators have presented the disbanding of the 6th
> squadron as a government effort to kill promotion in the army.
> This tactic was not unsuccessful among young ambitious
> NCOs, above all those from Saumur [the cavalry school].
> Almost all those arrested are in this category, and I have
> noticed that it is often these young students who are the most
> militant and the most dangerous.

This exposes the roots of the republican failure to win over the army. Republican promises of free trade and wider franchise meant nothing to lower- and lower middle-class soldiers. They were therefore forced to exploit military discontent. Yet this entailed no ideological commitment on the soldiers' part and without a dedication to the republican cause they quickly gave way before the authority of government and military discipline.

A study of the backgrounds of the Lunéville conspirators reveals the link between republicanism, ambition and class in the army.

The army was one traditional means of social advancement for the lower middle class attracted by the Napoleonic promise of 'a career open to talent'. Republicans, who tended to be middle-class, geared their propaganda to these lower middle-class NCOs. Of those soldiers arrested for republican activity under the July Monarchy, 40 per cent were artisans before joining the army, 16 per cent merchants or shop assistants, 11 per cent students, 10 per cent farmers, 8 per cent day labourers, 6 per cent ex-soldiers or seamen, 5 per cent professional men, and 4 per cent listed themselves simply as property owners.[47]

Most of the Lunéville conspirators also came from lower middle-class backgrounds. The largest portion, including Thomas, were small property holders. The second largest group were clerks; four, including Bernard, were students, two were bakers, one a tailor, one a Lyon silkworker, one a watchmaker and one a dyer. Birth, a lawyer, and Lecoindre, a surveyor, together with Bernard, appear to be the exceptions.

Ambitious young men joining the army could hope to finish their career as superior officers, possibly as captains and almost certainly as senior NCOs. Regimental questions, especially the slow rate of promotion, were therefore burning issues. Most NCOs involved in the Lunéville conspiracy were young volunteers with three to six years' service who planned to make the army their career. A survey of NCOs arrested for political activity during the July Monarchy (see Table 11) reflects the same pattern:

TABLE 11 *Percentage of NCOs arrested for political activity during the July Monarchy*

*Condition of service**	
Volunteer	63
Replacement	10
Conscript	25
Récompensé national	2
Age†	
18–19	0·3
20–21	7
22–23	25
24–25	32
26–27	14
28–29	9
30–35	11
Over 36	1·7
Years of service‡	
0–6 months	3
6 months–2 years	3
2	10
3	21
4	22
5	11
6	11
7–10	10
Over 10	9

* See appendix IVa.
† Appendix IVc.   ‡ Appendix IVd.

Only ten of the fifty-six NCOs arrested at Lunéville had joined the army after the July revolution, further indicating that the rebellion was a product of discontent with the conditions of service rather than frustration at the failure of a republican revolution.

Inspection reports confirm that, as career soldiers, volunteers were more indisciplined than conscripts. The Inspector of the 1st Infantry Regiment in 1836 noted that 'a number of serious offences have been committed by soldiers, most of them replacements and volunteers.' The Inspector of the 2nd Infantry made the same observation in 1838: 'Voluntary enlistment has brought the regiment few good men. In general, these men are indisciplined and unruly.'[48]

Bernard, the most rabid of the Lunéville conspirators, is a typical example. Born in 1809 in Montbéliard (Doubs), he was the son of a prosperous wine merchant who was able to send him to Paris to study. Two of his elder brothers were Paris bankers, while the third was a naval captain. His sister married a government official in Strasbourg. Although Bernard volunteered in 1828 hoping to make a career as an officer, he had not received his commission by 1834 when the reduction of troop strength placed it virtually out of his reach. In March he was introduced into Thomas' plot by Tricotel and soon came to the conclusion that only a revolution could save his career. The Paris Prefect of Police reported that Bernard believed he would have been commissioned within four years had the colonel not blocked his promotion: 'Seeing that he had been passed over for promotion several times, he welcomed the proposals made to him and allowed himself to be led astray.'[49]

The promotion issue was heightened by the war fever sweeping France. Soldiers realized that war would bring promotion and De Regnier confirmed that republicans were promising war: 'Allusions were made to a republic, and as soldiers want war at any price, some answered: "We are for a republic, if it will bring us war."'[50] Furthermore, many of the conspirators had not been promoted in over two years (see Table 12).

The conspirators were not unaware that many soldiers received their last promotion after the revolution and subsequent war scare.

Although the Lunéville rebellion failed, republicanism had clearly made its mark on the army. But to what extent?

Major Bonnet, commissioned by the War Minister to investigate the plot, concluded that NCOs did not have enough influence over the soldiers to carry out a successful rebellion: 'The NCOs could not raise their regiment. Their influence on the soldiers is much less than was imagined.'[51]

This statement highlights a key republican miscalculation in the campaign to win over the army. NCOs, traditionally viewed as the most revolutionary group in the French army, successfully provoked the 1830 rebellion because the fall of the government had under-mined officer authority. But by 1834 officers were backed by a determined government and few soldiers or NCOs were willing to defy their officers to follow rebellious sergeants. Republicans, however, canvassed almost exclusively among NCOs, believing they held the key to successful military revolution. Lunéville demon-strated that an NCO-led rebellion was doomed to failure in a period of relative political stability.

TABLE 12 *Time since last promotion of NCOs arrested for political activity**

Years	Lunéville %	July monarchy %
0–1	4	17
1	33	26
2	17	25
3	25	16
4	8	8
Over 5	13	8

* See appendix IVe.

Republican claims to have involved other regiments in the rebellion also appear exaggerated. Tricotel admitted that the 1st Cuirassiers at Nancy seemed surprised at his suggestion of an uprising and categorically refused to take part. Even the Lunéville conspirators were far from being paragons of revolutionary fervour. On the afternoon of 17 April, it took only an order to turn back the thirty drunken soldiers of the 4th Cuirassiers who set out to rescue Bernard.

This pinpoints another republican failure. Although republicans won over a certain number of NCOs, they failed to win over many officers.

Lunéville demonstrated that, in the final analysis, discipline prevailed over revolution. Republicans realized that officers were the greatest threat to the success of an NCO revolution. For this reason, Mathieu planned to arrest senior officers at Epinal to prevent them from intimidating their subalterns.[52] But in March he was forced to promise Lunéville NCOs who refused to act unless led by a general that General Clauzel would command the rebel-lion. Had the Lunéville conspiracy been officer-led, NCOs could have justified themselves on the pretext of obeying orders. Like Sergeant Commissaire's lieutenant, who cautioned him to be less vocal in his opinions, republican officers usually kept their opinions to themselves.[53]

The ringleaders of the abortive rebellion were eventually tried by the Court of Peers, which handled all national security cases under the law on associations. De Ludre was arrested, but later released because of lack of evidence. Laportaire was sentenced to three years in prison, while Mathieu, Caillé and De Regnier were jailed for five years. Stiller and Tricotel received ten-year sentences and Bernard twenty years. Thomas was sentenced to deportation. However, he soon escaped from Sainte-Pélagie prison to England, where he lived until 1848. Louis Napoleon exiled him after the 1851 *coup d'état*, but he returned to France in 1871 as commanding general of the National Guards of the Seine. He was executed by the Communards in the same year. Every sentence, with the exception of Thomas's, was commuted by the general amnesty of 1837.

In addition to the seven soldiers tried by the court, the army arrested fifty-six NCOs for their part in the plot – an attempt, General Hulot claimed, by the colonels of the three Lunéville regiments to get rid of unpopular NCOs: 'A number of colonels have asked to be rid of NCOs suspect for their political opinions and connections without being known members of secret societies.'[54] On 18 April he asked permission to send several NCOs to Algeria, even though they were not guilty: 'The comings and goings of republican agents in the three towns [Lunéville, Nancy, Epinal] would indicate a co-ordinated insurrection. May I send to Africa some of those NCOs arrested as a security risk but cleared for lack of evidence?'[55] On 22 April Soult replied affirmatively.

However, the court ruled that all those not tried were innocent and should return to their regiments. Yet the army refused to reinstate them, arguing that their presence would undermine discipline. The colonel refused Sergeants (now privates) Chaumont and Denvers, who had refused to join the plotters, readmission to the 10th Cuirassiers: 'I shall always believe that they took an active part in the Lunéville affair and therefore that their presence in the regiment can only be harmful and dangerous.' Hulot complained that discipline would suffer if these men were pardoned:[56]

> We can have no illusions about the feelings which these
> perverse men will take with them to the regiments where they
> are assigned as privates. Their behaviour will only improve
> with their moral attitudes. Bad examples that they will set,
> their bitter, continual complaints . . . can only exert a bad
> influence wherever they serve. It would perhaps be less
> dangerous to discharge them from the army.

However, the Peers insisted that innocent soldiers be reinstated in their original regiments with their former rank. The Inspector General of the Cavalry confirmed this order on 14 August. On 3 September the War Minister compromised and the soldiers returned to their regiments to earn back their stripes: 'Their stripes will be returned as soon as circumstances permit, provided that they prove themselves worthy by good conduct.'[57] In practice, however, this gave the colonels an excuse to withhold promotion indefinitely.

By October government officials were pressing the army to reinstate the sergeants. Baron Pasquier criticized the army's refusal to reinstate these men in a letter of 4 November to the War Minister:[58]

> The Court of Peers committee therefore has completely exonerated these NCOs [he reminded General Gérard]. The President of the Court and M. le Grand have sent several official requests to the War Minister that these soldiers who, far from meriting punishment, should be compensated for their arrest, be reinstated in their regiment and rank.

He also criticized the idea that reinstatement would undermine discipline and argued that discipline would suffer more if men were unjustly punished: 'In my opinion, these compensations will honour and strengthen discipline. The confidence of the troops would be far more shaken by an obstinate and undeserved show of severity towards their innocent comrades, treated as guilty men.' Lingay, secretary of the Peers' commission, was of the same opinion: 'To persist in their punishment would be disastrous.'[59]

The army was at last forced to relent and reinstated the men in their old rank. Such political pressure was uncommon under the July Monarchy, as the government seldom interfered in military matters, in the belief that non-interference was the best way to guarantee the loyalty and stability of the army. When a large Carbonari organization was discovered in the Toulouse garrison in 1836, the Minister of the Interior wrote to the Prefect of the Haute-Garonne that he was not to interfere in the investigation: 'If the Toulouse garrison is, as it seems, thick with Carbonari supporters, you will not interfere personally . . . The soldiers have their own courts.'[60]

Several NCOs released by the Peers, however, continued their political activity. In 1836 Farolet was arrested with several republican pamphlets on him and sent to Africa. Hatton continued to attend frequent republican meetings and was dismissed in the same year after fifteen years' service.

Several factors contributed to the decline of republicanism both in France and in the army after 1834. Although the March 1834

law against associations fused moderate liberals and the radical
left at a time when troop reductions were bringing latent discontent
in the army to the surface, the government was strong enough to
contain the revolutionary threat.

Furthermore, political associations were broken up and republican
leaders – including Cavaignac and Marrast – were jailed or exiled.
With Lafayette's death in May 1834 followed by Carrel's in 1836 in
a duel, the republican leadership fell to pieces. The party was so
discredited that no republican deputies were returned in the June
1834 elections.

Republicans therefore went underground and were organized
into secret societies by hard-core revolutionaries like Barbès and
Blanqui, in whose hands republicanism became a doctrine of
revolution and social reform. This alienated moderate liberals who
joined Laffitte, Arago and Dupont de l'Eure to work for parliamentary reform.

Two 1834 military reforms also help to explain the return of
political tranquillity to the army. In this year, pensions – a major
cause of complaint under the Restoration, especially during the
economic recession – were increased to a level double and sometimes
triple the Restoration figures (Table 13). They were no longer

TABLE 13   *Pensions*

| | *Restoration* | 1831 | 1834 | |
			Infantry	*Artillery*
Lieutenant général	3,000	4,000	7,500	7,500
Maréchal de camp	2,000	3,000	5,000	5,000
Colonel	1,200	2,400	2,500	3,375
Lieut. colonel	1,000	1,800	2,150	2,850
Chef de bataillon	900	1,500	1,800	2,450
Capitaine	600	1,200	1,000	1,300
Lieutenant	450	800	780	1,020
Sous-lieutenant	350	600	720	1,020

given on the basis of campaigns fought, as, on this reasoning,
twenty years of peace would guarantee most officers only a minimum
pension. Officers were now paid a flat sum according to their arm.
This increased the security of the officer corps, which no longer
felt that a peaceful foreign policy would affect retirement pay.
Although the pro-war plank in the republican party platform was
still attractive, war was no longer essential for an officer's well-
being.

The second law, protecting officers from the arbitrary or politically motivated dismissals so common under the Revolution, Empire and Restoration, was passed on 19 May. It stipulated that officers could only be dismissed by a commission composed of their peers. The War Minister no longer had the right to dismiss his subordinates, though he could suspend an officer for three years. The law was crucial, for it guaranteed the stability and continuity of the army under any regime.

Chapter 9

Professional revolutionaries and secret societies, 1835–7

Defeated on the barricades, deprived of leadership and outlawed, republicans were forced to alter their tactics in the face of mounting government repression. Radical republicans, Barbès and Blanqui, took over the party leadership and soon began to organize secret societies on the Carbonari model. These new tactics had repercussions in the army. Civilian canvassing, which flourished through 1834, was declining sharply by 1835 as arrests and tougher police measures in the wake of the April riots curtailed political activity.

In May the government mopped up pockets of republican sympathizers in the Paris garrison, arresting NCOs in the 32nd, 35th and 36th Infantry Regiments and the 5th Lancers.[1] The following month, the government replaced the entire garrison after civilian and military officials reported that the April defeats had not ended republican activity in the army.

In the north, soldiers of the 5th Infantry Regiment were reported with republicans at Saint Omer.[2] Republicans continued to be active in the 6th Light Infantry Regiment at Nantes, the 29th at Rennes and the 58th at Rochefort.[3]

Polish refugees, who had been scattered throughout France by the government in 1832 to deprive Paris republicans of potential sympathizers, occasionally joined politically orientated masonic lodges or spearheaded republican efforts to infiltrate garrisons in towns with no organized republican party. In May, for instance, two refugees were arrested handing out republican journals to soldiers in Laval.[4]

Republican activity was still greatest, however, in the south and east. A number of soldiers were arrested in the 11th Infantry Regiment at Montpellier[5] and republican activity was reported in the garrisons at Pau and Perpignan.[6]

The most troublesome regiment in the Midi was the 24th Infantry. Moved from Marseille to Corsica after republican activity there reached critical proportions, officers and NCOs continued to read republican journals to illiterate soldiers and, against army orders, to keep up an active correspondence with their editors. The army, in an extraordinary inspection, finally dismissed three republican officers and so restored order.

In the east, Metz and Strasbourg maintained their reputations as activist centres. The Strasbourg Prefect complained that republicans were entering the barracks to hand out journals and pamphlets. Alarmed by the increase in subversive literature, the War Minister banned newspapers in the army, thus formalizing the army's traditional prejudice against newspapers.

Republicans immediately exploited this issue as an example of the government's desire to separate the army from the people. Corporal Roberts of the 24th Infantry Regiment protested in a letter to the *Tribune* that the doctrine of passive obedience which required a soldier to abstain from political activity undermined the ideal of a citizen soldier: 'This political control on the soldier is a disgrace and puts the army back to the time when it was composed only of the King's soldiers . . . The time has come to renounce the role of automaton.'[7] Under increasing pressure, the War Minister eventually relented and permitted soldiers to read newspapers in the barracks provided they were not critical of the government.[8] He later authorized each regiment to set up a reading room where soldiers had access to approved periodicals such as *Le Moniteur* and *Le Spectateur Militaire*.

By the end of the year, however, republican activity had virtually ceased, suggesting that the government had finally silenced opposition.

Little activity was reported in the army in the opening months of 1835. In the south, republican activity continued in the Pau garrison and for the first time penetrated the Bayonne garrison.[9] In June the Prefect of the Bouches-du-Rhône expressed the fear that the high cost of living might force officers in the 62nd Infantry Regiment into the republican camp.[10] Other garrisons also recorded complaints over rising costs. In September he requested that the 62nd be sent to Algeria, claiming that many officers would seize the first opportunity to 'play a nasty trick'.[11] Again, however, the republican threat failed to materialize, and a report of 5 October declared the Prefect's concern unwarranted.

Republicans were again reported active in the 17th Light Infantry at Perpignan, the 11th Chasseurs at Marseille[12] and the 26th Infantry Regiment at Montpellier.[13] Nantes and Saint-Etienne continued to witness republican activity,[14] while politically motivated scraps erupted between the 37th Infantry Regiment and the 4th Artillery at Rennes.[15]

In the north, soldiers in the Sedan garrison were reported to be attending republican meetings in Belgium, while Paris police noted that newspaper subscriptions were increasing in the garrison, especially in the 1st Carabineers and the 5th Light Infantry.[16] Canvassing was again reported at Strasbourg and Metz, and General Gustler reported that republicans had infiltrated newly arrived regiments in Lunéville.[17] In August a republican officer in the 61st Infantry Regiment at Besançon was arrested after placing a light in his window which suspicious local police believed to be a signal.[18]

Republicans, who appeared to be recovering from their April defeats, received a disastrous setback when Fieschi, an ex-NCO, attempted to assassinate the king with his multi-barrelled 'machine infernale'. This assassination attempt, which resulted in the death of several innocent spectators and the subsequent justification of regicide by many left-wing journals, rallied a horrified public to the monarchy.

Lawmakers capitalized on this sudden surge of anti-republican feeling to pass a series of measures known as the September laws. The first law curbed the freedom of the press by threatening to close down any paper which was irresponsibly critical of the government. Thirty left-wing journals disappeared immediately, while others were forced to moderate the tone of their articles. To deal with the problem of excessively lenient juries and to ensure the conviction of many republicans previously acquitted by local juries, a second law provided for secret jury ballots and stipulated that only seven of twelve votes were needed for conviction. The third and final law set up a *cour d'assises* to deal with political subversion.

The September laws and the July condemnation by the Peers of the leaders of the April 1834 riots confirmed the government's April 1834 victory and completed Casimir Périer's conservative programme.

Frenchmen everywhere appeared weary of republican excesses: Carrel lamented the people's loss of faith in the republican party, most of whose leaders were locked away in the Sainte-Pélagie prison, while Béranger was forced to admit that the country was 'disgusted' by his party: 'Everyone considers the Republic of Sainte-Pélagie worn out.'

The opposition was routed and France at last appeared to have achieved stability.

As republican spirits ebbed, Barbès and Blanqui stepped into the party leadership and began to organize the secret Société des Familles to replace the defunct Droits de l'Homme. These men realized that open insurrection would result only in further defeat and intensified government repression. They planned to organize a republican *coup d'état* by building up a tightly knit secret society which, on a given signal, could seize key government bureaux. These revolutionary élitists depended heavily on the success of their recruitment in the army. Military personnel provided the society with well-disciplined members as well as with arms.

The first indications that the new republican tactics were working in the army came in the summer of 1835. The 14th Infantry Regiment had witnessed some political activity in 1833 and when in June 1835 the colonel at Tours suspected four NCOs of republican sympathies, he quickly sent them to Algeria. However, this proved to be only the tip of the iceberg. In July the republican *Courrier d'Indre et Loire* published a list of those who had given money for the 'prévenus d'avril' – republicans arrested during the April 1834 riots and tried by the Court of Peers. The list included thirty NCOs in the 14th. Furthermore, the journal claimed that the majority of NCOs in that regiment were ardent republicans. Several of these NCOs led by one Sergeant Maillac met local republicans on the night of 15 July and decided to mutiny before they too were sent to Algeria. But the attempt fizzled out when the troops refused to rally to the mutineers, proving once again that republicans had miscalculated the revolutionary influence of NCOs.

A subsequent investigation revealed that several NCOs in the 14th had formed a secret republican society in which the members swore 'hatred of kings, fidelity to the principles of the Droits de l'Homme, and an unlimited dedication to liberty'. The society had been organized by Sergeant Pesqui, a native of Marseille living in Paris in 1830. A dedicated republican who had fought on the barricades in July, Pesqui had been rewarded by the new government with the rank of sergeant as a 'récompensé national'.

The idea of giving military positions as a reward for participating in the 1830 revolution was first suggested by a retired cavalry captain named Gauthier. In a letter of August 1830 to General Gérard, he suggested that agitation would continue in Paris until those who had fought in the revolution were rewarded. He suggested that the army hold six captaincies, fourteen lieutenancies and thirty second-lieutenancies for such men.[19] Conservatives welcomed the idea as a means to rid Paris of its turbulent citizens. Scattered throughout France and under the iron thumb of military discipline, they argued, they could no longer threaten governmental stability. The army, however, balked at the idea of turning whole companies over to men without military experience and whose political beliefs might jeopardize stability. A compromise was therefore hammered out, whereby two positions for second-lieutenants and four for sergeants were held open in each regiment.

This solution to Paris's revolutionary turmoil soon proved un-satisfactory. Republican activity did not decrease significantly in the capital, while the army was forced to contend with a fifth column in its ranks. The government had in fact provided republicans with a bridgehead into the army. The *récompensés* maintained their contacts with opposition leaders and refused to be intimidated by military discipline. By 1833, therefore, many regiments had dismissed these politically disruptive elements. The government, however, feared these men would drift back to Paris to swell the ranks of the Left and so pressed the army to retain them. Pesqui's dismissal in 1833 was quashed by the Inspector General, as was that of Sergeant Hane, who was involved in the Lunéville conspiracy. Complaints continued to reach the War Minister throughout 1833 and 1834 as *récompensés* attended republican banquets and meetings. After a republican crowd fêted the demi-battalion of the 52nd Infantry Regiment at Belfort under Lieutenant Demay, a *récompensé*, and urged it to join the Lyon revolutionaries, Soult sent a circular to all regiments asking the number of *récompensés* in each regiment, especially those still wearing the distinctive July decoration given for bravery on the barricades in 1830. Several colonels replied that these decorations, which the army deplored as a symbol of republican sympathy and as a reward for fighting against the army, were no longer worn.

After 1834 and the arrest of many opposition leaders, the *récompensés* proved especially valuable to republicans who had previously depended on local parties to establish contacts in their garrisons. Local republican groups were now outlawed, disorganized and forced underground. The impetus for republican activity in the garrison could no longer come primarily from external agents. To maintain their influence in the army, republicans were forced to organize internal secret societies around agents planted in the army specifically for that purpose.

In 1834 and 1835 *récompensés* formed the nucleus of these societies while other dedicated republicans were encouraged to enlist. Secret societies now began to spring up in several garrisons formerly free of republican activity – at Poitiers, a secret society was dis-covered in the 19th Infantry Regiment led by two *récompensés*.

Pesqui began to organize his society in the summer of 1834 while the 14th was stationed at Orléans, a town with no active republican party. Letters found on him after his arrest revealed that he corres-ponded with republican leaders in Paris and Marseille. Building his group around a nucleus of eight or nine NCOs, he became president of the society. Sergeant Maillac, who had been a primary school teacher before entering the army, became vice-president.

Pesqui was soon able to attract other members by promising them comradeship to relieve the boredom of garrison duty. Army investigators in December judged that of fifty-six NCOs arrested for belonging to this society, only twenty-five were out-and-out republicans. The rest sought only social intercourse.

After a secret society was discovered in his regiment in 1836, the Colonel of the 20th Infantry Regiment at Paris described how military republicans gradually drew apolitical soldiers into their camp:[20]

> How cleverly they exploit the passionate youth of these young
> men who, at the age of eighteen or twenty, leave home to
> serve the state without ever having heard the word politics.
> They are seduced by promises and promotion hopes and quickly
> identified as dangerous, they suffer the consequences of beliefs
> they are not aware they subscribe to. Punishments rain down
> on them, fear leads them astray and at last they conspire,
> believing that there is no going back.

This statement underlines, once again, the reasons behind the failure of secret societies in the army. Republicans needed politically committed soldiers to staff their military secret societies. But as few soldiers were attracted to the republican programme, they were forced to exploit regimental issues to build up a following.

If opposition activity in the army had been politically inspired, it would have been carried out by young men who joined the army immediately after the 1830 revolution, when a wave of patriotism swept over France and war with Europe appeared inevitable. These young patriots would eventually have rebelled at the conservatism of the July Monarchy. The Minister of the Interior claimed this was the case in October 1835: 'The events of July have brought the army a mass of ardent young men who dream of the heroic follies of the Empire.'[21] However, most of these potential republican sympathizers steered clear of political activity: two-thirds of the soldiers and NCOs arrested as republican activists after 1830 had enlisted before the July revolution while less than 20 per cent of the NCOs arrested at Lunéville had joined the army after July 1830.[22] This suggests that politically active soldiers were attracted by republican promises of promotion. Other evidence which corroborates the idea that most soldiers were apolitical and influenced almost exclusively by regimental issues is found in a list of those arrested for republican activity. This reveals that many politically active soldiers came from areas where the republican party was weak or virtually non-existent.[23] Lunéville demonstrated that soldiers who merely hoped to further their careers seldom chose revolution over

discipline. Recruitment problems intensified after 1834 when republicans began to demand complete political dedication from their
military members.

The gradual transition in these military societies from a social to a
political orientation is apparent in other cases. The Société Philanthropique des Francs Amis, discovered in the ouvriers d'artillerie
and the 12th Infantry Regiment at Auxonne in the autumn of
1835, though espousing vague philanthropic principles, was not
political in character. Organized by Lieutenant Demay, a *récompensé* in the 52nd Infantry Regiment at Dijon who was dismissed
in 1834 for his political opinions,[24] its articles specifically stated that
it was to be non-political.[25] However, officials suspected that
Demay, like Mathieu in 1831, hoped eventually to give it a political
orientation. Yet subsequent investigation revealed that the society
was indeed purely social, and that those involved were good soldiers
(the president was the son of a general). They received a relatively
mild sentence of fifteen days in prison. However, General Merlin,
commander of the 18th Military Division at Dijon, noted that
article 4 of the group's laws called on all members to swear loyalty
to France, 'whatever form her government may take'. He believed
that republicans planned to convince soldiers that patriotism was
irreconcilable with the July Monarchy. 'There is reason to believe
that the founders of the Auxonne society, by requiring an oath of
loyalty to France, whatever form her government may take, were
planning to use eventual recruits for their guilty designs.'[26]

Military authorities soon realized that republicans were joining
the army to organize secret societies. Two soldiers who ended a
two-year retirement to join the 66th Regiment were exposed as
republicans, while one soldier was arrested in the 45th Regiment
at Versailles with Carbonari-styled diplomas and orders to form a
regimental secret society called La Meurtrière. An NCO in the
18th Light Infantry Regiment, Sergeant Pitancier, was accused of
enlisting to organize a secret society: 'Pitancier came from the Paris
society of the Droits de l'Homme with instructions to spread republican propaganda in the army. He enlisted only for this purpose.'[27]

In Toulouse, a secret society, La Guerrière, which included
thirty-five NCOs, was discovered in the 11th Infantry Regiment.
At the same time, a second society, La Compagnie Franche, was
unearthed in the 17th Infantry Regiment stationed at Collonne,
near Toulouse. Members of this society were required to swear
loyalty to the republican cause and death to traitors:[28]

I swear on my honour to use every means in my power to help

establish a republican government. I swear a deadly hatred for monarchical government. I undertake to slit open the heart of any traitor to the association. I will devote all my energies to the nation's happiness and glory.

Accused NCOs denied making contact with local republicans, but the army refused to believe that soldiers had organized the group without outside aid: 'It is difficult to believe that identical societies could spring up individually . . . A more rational explanation is that they were organized by the same party and knew it.'[29] The army clearly found it difficult to believe that republican activity, though centrally directed, was now often organized from within the regiment.

The purchase of cartridges from soldiers also continued and was reported in the 23rd Infantry Regiment at Pau, the 27th at Grenoble, the 31st at Soissons, the 36th at Dijon, the 40th at Nantes and the 3rd Light Infantry at Thionville.

But regimental secret societies seldom remained secret for long and by the end of 1836 some republicans began to recognize the futility of their efforts. In October Sergeant Rebière of the 20th Infantry Regiment wrote to tell republicans at Rouen he could no longer perform his political mission in the army. His letter reveals that republicans in the army were discouraged by constant harassment from their superiors and demonstrates that the desire for career stability influenced even dedicated republican soldiers:[30]

As a result of the frequent political charges made against me [he wrote], I was so persecuted that I would have ended up by losing my mind! The meetings I went to were misconstrued; they seldom had a purpose. I cannot understand how I earned such a reputation as a political activist. I was wrongly called leader of the military patriots . . . It is in my interest to stay out of such affairs. All I want now is my discharge, for there is so much bad feeling against me that I am convinced they will eventually break me. So kindly tell the patriots they must not count on my leadership and that I want to hear no more of it.

Sergeant Rebière testified that there were approximately 400 republican NCOs in the army – a small proportion of the total. He was reprieved for his confession, but was sent to Algeria two months later, after two men in his company were discovered selling cartridges to civilians.

Corporal Doncieux of the 1st Light Infantry Regiment also wrote to fellow republicans in October that he was discouraged and was leaving the army:[31]

> I have long believed that every soldier who loves his country
> must stay in the army to sow the seeds of propaganda, so that
> one day we should arrive at the breach with the weapons our
> oppressors meant to use against us. I made this my duty,
> despite the harassment I have suffered for so long. But today
> I want only to be discharged.

The army continued to uncover scattered secret societies in the
early months of 1837. *Récompensés* were arrested in the 21st Infantry
Regiment at Châlons and the 2nd Infantry in Paris for attempting
to organize secret societies.[32] Other societies were unearthed in
Lyon's 3rd Light Infantry Regiment, the 67th Infantry at Grenoble
and the 15th Light Infantry at Perpignan.[33] After a secret society
was discovered in the 60th Infantry at Paris in April, the Minister
of the Interior claimed that it was composed primarily of Corsicans
whose republicanism was merely a manifestation of their independence and pride: 'The 60th seems to have a large number of
Corsicans who are vindictive and easily won over.'[34]

In July the Prefect of the Ardennes reported that two retired
captains who sought reinstatement in the army intended to organize
a secret society. And in September the colonel of the 1st Hussards
feared that many recent Paris volunteers in his regiment were
republican agents:[35]

> It would have been wise to keep Paris conscripts away from
> this regiment, but this was not done. Nor should volunteers
> from the capital have been sent there, for it seems certain that
> some of these men came with instructions to infiltrate the
> regiment. At least, their backgrounds pointed to this possibility.

Nevertheless, the letters of resignation, coupled with the drop in
republican activity in and outside the army, indicate that republicans were seriously discouraged by 1836. The leaders of the Société
des Familles made a crucial tactical miscalculation in believing that
secret societies could be a means to power in themselves. They
could only hope to succeed if backed by a street revolution. But the
defeats of 1832 and 1834 had taught workers the futility of challeng-
ing the government at the barricades. Republican influence in the
army was strongest in the months following the July revolution when
civil disorder seriously threatened governmental stability. Republicans were forced to organize after the advent of the Périer ministry,
when increasing government stability diminished spontaneous
support in the street. But each organizational step was a retreat and
indicated that the revolutionary tide was ebbing.

By the autumn of 1836 the government was firmly in control and
the republicans' days were numbered.

Chapter 10

Strasbourg, 1836

The government at last appeared to be firmly in control of the
political situation when it was shaken by a challenge from Louis
Napoleon Bonaparte. The attempted *coup d'état* in October 1836 by
the nephew of Napoleon I momentarily rallied dispirited Strasbourg
liberals against the July Monarchy.

The Strasbourg affair, the only Bonapartist military insurrection
after the death of the emperor in 1821, provides an opportunity to
contrast republican and Bonapartist military opposition and to
assess the position of the Bonapartists after 1830.

Louis Napoleon Bonaparte was the second son of Louis, King of
Holland. Born in 1808, he was only seven years old when he and his
mother, Hortense, were forced to leave France in the political
upheaval which followed Waterloo. Their exile was made official
a few months later with a law of January 1816 banning all Bona-
partes from France. Hortense settled in the Château d'Arenenberg
at Thurgau, Switzerland, where she engaged a French republican,
the Abbé Bernard, to tutor her son. When Hortense took a house in
Augsburg in Bavaria in 1819, Bernard was replaced by Philippe Le
Bas, son of a regicide deputy of the Convention. The young Louis
Napoleon attended the local gymnasium as a day boy while studying
privately under Le Bas' direction. This arrangement lasted until
Louis Napoleon's education was completed in 1827.

Educated by liberal tutors and surrounded at Arenenberg by relics
of the Empire, Louis Napoleon was both steeped in radicalism and
conscious of his position as a potential heir to the French Imperial
throne. Hortense constantly reminded the young prince that he and
his elder brother, Napoleon Louis, who lived with his father in
Florence, must be prepared to take up the Bonapartist standard:[1]

> Because of your name you will always be something either in
> Europe or in the New World – never lose hope. Always be on
> the look-out for favourable opportunities. If France escapes
> you for good, Italy, Germany, Russia or England would still
> give you resources in the future. Everywhere one can conceive

of turns of fortune which can raise the heir of a great and
famous name to the clouds . . . You and your brother are, after
the King of Rome, the heirs of Napoleon.

Italy, which Louis Napoleon visited frequently after 1823, and
where he met Italian liberals like Francesco Arese, also played an
important part in his development. It was to Italy he returned after
the French Chamber of Deputies had dashed his hopes of entering
France in September 1830 by re-enacting the banishment law of
1816.

The death of Pope Pius VIII in November 1830 and the belief
that France's July revolution was the first phase in a liberal revolution which would sweep Europe encouraged Italian liberals. But
suspicious Roman authorities accused Louis Napoleon of plotting
with these revolutionaries to revolt and establish a regency for the
Duc de Reichstadt. Expelled from Rome, Louis Napoleon drifted
to Florence to join his brother. By February 1831 parts of central
Italy were in revolt and the two brothers rushed to join the revolutionaries. But the revolt was quickly crushed and in the same month
Napoleon Louis died of measles at Forli. Louis Napoleon, however,
narrowly escaped arrest and made his way in disguise across northern
Italy to France with a British passport furnished by his mother.

In Paris Louis Napoleon petitioned the king to be allowed to
serve in the French army, while in a secret meeting Hortense
begged to be allowed to live in France. Louis-Philippe replied that
both must swear allegiance to the July Monarchy. They refused.
Consequently, shaken by a Bonapartist demonstration in the Place
Vendôme on 5 May, the government hurried them to England.

However, Louis Napoleon's six-week stay in Paris had left its
mark on him. He had met republican leaders, who had convinced
him that opposition to the regime was extensive but as yet lacked a
popular leader. The death the following year of 'l'Aiglon' in Vienna
elevated Louis Napoleon to Imperial pretender and in the wake of
their setback in June 1832 during the funeral of General Lamarque
some republicans looked to Louis Napoleon to spearhead their cause.
In a letter in July to the young prince, Lafayette claimed that the
government was on the brink of collapse and that France was ripe for
a Napoleonic restoration: 'Seize the first opportunity to return to
France, because the government cannot maintain control and your
name is the only popular one.'[2]

Louis Napoleon immediately began to prepare the ground for an
Imperial restoration. In 1832 he published a brochure entitled
Rêveries politiques which set the Empire up as heir to the liberal
traditions of the Revolution. And in 1835 he brought out a *Manuel*

d'artillerie which he sent to many French officers with a friendly covering letter assuring them of his esteem and inviting criticism of the book. If the gift were acknowledged, he initiated an active correspondence with the recipient and sent him extra copies to distribute among his friends. In this way Louis Napoleon hoped to make his name familiar in the French army.[3]

In 1834 he began to lay plans for a military *coup d'état*. Eastern France with its large garrisons and patriotic population appeared the ideal point from which to launch his *coup d'état*. Thus, in 1834 he began to visit the spas in Baden where many officers in France's eastern garrisons vacationed. One visitor reported that at a banquet given there in August 1834 for Louis Napoleon, the many French officers present enthusiastically toasted the Empire: 'They vied for the most compromising toasts, the rashest vows. Agents provocateurs could not have done better.'[4] It was also in Baden that Louis Napoleon met Colonel Vaudrey, an ex-Napoleonic officer and commander of Strasbourg's 4th Artillery Regiment who later agreed to lead his *coup d'état*.

Convinced that the army was eager for a Napoleonic restoration, Louis Napoleon moved to Kehl in August 1836 and began final preparations for the October insurrection. There he assembled a group of dedicated conspirators including Colonel Vaudrey; Parquin, a retired cavalry major and a commandant in the Paris municipal guard; Geslin, a retired officer living in Paris; De Querelles, a lieutenant in the 7th Light Infantry Regiment at Nancy; Lieutenant Laity of the Strasbourg pontonniers; Persigny, an ex-cavalry NCO, and de Bruc, a retired officer known for his legitimist sympathies who hoped to turn the conspiracy to the advantage of his own party. These men were instructed to visit officers and NCOs in eastern garrisons and win their support for the uprising.

Meanwhile, Louis Napoleon invited officers to visit him at Kehl. In August he approached Captain Raindre of the 16th Light Infantry Regiment stationed at Strasbourg, but the captain, though at first flattered by the attentions of the prince, refused to join the conspirators and subsequently reported the plot to General Voirol, commander of the 5th Military Division, who in turn alerted the War Minister.

The government, however, brushed the warning aside, believing the young pretender was not well enough known to rally the army. But by October officers in the 3rd Cuirassiers at Haguenau, the 6th Cuirassiers at Neufbrisach, the 7th Light Infantry at Nancy the 46th Infantry Regiment, the 3rd and 4th Artillery Regiments, and the battalion of bridge builders at Strasbourg had been contacted by the conspirators.[5] Most of these men subsequently denied their complicity. And in fact few of them had reacted positively to these overtures, preferring to await the outcome of the conspiracy. The government, eager to minimize the affair's importance, elected not to prosecute these officers.

At five o'clock on the morning of 30 October, Louis Napoleon – accompanied by Vaudrey, Parquin in general's uniform, De Querelles and de Bruc – appeared at the barracks of the 4th Artillery Regiment. Vaudrey assembled his men and announced that a revolution had toppled the July Monarchy, and the regiment was to unite behind Louis Napoleon.

The prince then praised the 4th Artillery as the regiment of his uncle and told them, 'Yours is the honour of being the first to shake off the shameful yoke of the *juste milieu* which would enslave us to the Holy Alliance . . . I am of the people and a soldier.' Then, according to officials, he promised everyone who joined him promotion: 'Today everyone remains in his place. Tomorrow, all the NCOs will be officers, and the officers will rise one grade.'[6]

Vaudrey distributed money and cartridges among the troops, who then marched to raise the 46th Infantry Regiment. Men were also dispatched to arrest the Prefect, General Voirol and Maréchal de Camp Lalande, head of the subdivision of the Bas-Rhin. A fourth group seized a press to print proclamations of the Empire.

The 46th Regiment, however, refused to join the conspirators. Louis Napoleon's pleas to the troops fell on deaf ears and, isolated in the barracks courtyard while most of his followers waited in the street, he was shouted down and quickly arrested by Lieutenant-Colonel Taladier of the 46th.

The insurrection was effectively contained by 8 a.m.

On the night of the 30th, a second plot to overthrow the government was discovered in Vendôme's 1st Hussars. Corporal Bruyant, a twenty-two-year-old volunteer from the Seine-et-Oise who had been a jeweller before joining the army, attempted to convince fellow soldiers to mutiny, lock up all officers and NCOs, take the National Guard's two cannons and ride on Paris to proclaim a republic. Reported to his commanding officer, he shot the NCO sent to arrest him, plunged his horse into the Loir and escaped. He returned to the barracks at 2 a.m., however, and submitted to arrest.

The government initially believed that the Bruyant affair was connected with the Strasbourg *coup*. But the police chief dismissed Bruyant as a 'hairbrain' and reported that no civilians had been involved. The conspiracy seems to have been a purely local one. Of the ten soldiers subsequently tried for conspiracy, six were acquitted and sent to Africa, and two sentenced to five years imprisonment, while Bruyant and Thiéry, a private from Auxonne, were sentenced to death.[7]

Strasbourg demonstrated that ideologically Bonapartists and republicans shared much common political ground. Rank-and-file leftists believed the Empire embodied the greatest accomplishments of the Revolution – the abolition of feudal society, modern administration and tax structures, anti-clericalism, and, above all, patriotism and military glory. Republicans could therefore rally to the Imperial pretender with a clear conscience. Lieutenant Laity confessed that he joined the plotters after Louis Napoleon identified with his republican ideals: 'I asked if his designs were democratic and republican; I am a democrat and a republican. On hearing his reply, I accepted.' Louis Napoleon played on republican sympathies by addressing his appeal to the 'Soldats de la République! Soldats de l'Empire!' and by claiming that he was both 'peuple et soldat'.[8] Ponteil summed up the fusion of the Bonapartist and republican Left under the July Monarchy: 'They were Bonapartist through hatred of the Bourbons, through disdain for the cautious *juste milieu*, through nostalgia for glory, but no less republican for all that.'[9]

TABLE 14* *Promotion of officers accused of republican activity during the July Monarchy*

Commissioned through:	%	
Ranks	57	
School	30	
Saint-Cyr		47
Ecole Polytechnique		53
Récompensé national	13	

* See appendices Va–f. These figures are based on names taken principally from AHG series E[5] and can be regarded as only a sample.

The fusion of doctrine in the Strasbourg *coup* is confirmed by the fact that of the nine officers arrested for joining Louis Napoleon's conspiracy, seven were young graduates of the notoriously republican Ecole Polytechnique. However, the schools had no monopoly on political opposition in the army after 1830 and many officers promoted through the ranks rallied to the republican banner after 1830 (see Table 14).

Imperial memories probably influenced the older officers who engaged in anti-governmental activity after 1830. Although the average age of left-wing officers was higher than that of opposition NCOs, a large part were young officers, as a chart of those accused of republican activity under the July Monarchy reveals (see Tables 15–18).

TABLE 15 *Age of officers accused of republican activity during the July Monarchy*

Age	%
18–20	1
21–25	11
26–30	26
31–35	18
36–40	18
41–45	12
46–50	10
Over 50	4

TABLE 16 *Years of service of officers accused of republican activity during the July Monarchy*

	%
0–2	3
2–5	13
6–10	21
11–15	17
16–20	17
21–25	13
26–30	11
Over 30	5

TABLE 17 *Initial service of officers accused of republican activity during the July Monarchy was accomplished under:*

	%
Republic	4
Empire	26
Restoration	57
July Monarchy	13

TABLE 18 *Rank of officers accused of republican activity during the July Monarchy*

	%
Sous-lieutenant	33
Lieutenant	37
Capitaine	19
Chef de bataillon	5
Lieut. colonel	3
Colonel	3

Like republicans, Louis Napoleon appealed to the army's patriotism. Captain Raindre testified that the pretender believed Louis-Philippe's abandonment of European national revolutions had caused widespread dissatisfaction in the army:[10]

> He [Louis Napoleon] spoke of army dissatisfaction over the government's policy of peace at any price, over its abandonment of every national cause – the Poles, the Italians and, last of all, the Spaniards, who saw the French army represented by foreign mercenaries [the Foreign Legion].

De Bruc also complained to Captain Dufaur at Neufbrisach about the pacifism of the July Monarchy: 'We spoke of war. He said that there were no more wars, that the great man was dead.'[11]

Like republicans, Bonapartists also exploited military discontent over slow promotion. Several officers and NCOs testified that the insurgents had offered them promotion. Among them, Captain Geslin saw his promised promotion as long overdue: 'I have served for thirty-nine years; I have served since the year IX of the Republic, and it would have been only just.'[12] A chart of officers cited for republican activity after 1830 reveals that despite the large number of promotions which resulted from the July revolution, promotion for most was agonizingly slow.

The fact that many officers accused of republican activity came from areas where opposition support was weak also indicates that they were influenced by regimental rather than political issues.[13]

However, the Lunéville affair showed that hopes of war and promotion were not balanced by ideological commitment to strengthen the insurgents against initial failure.

Despite tactical similarities, Strasbourg revealed a major conceptual difference in the Bonapartist and republican view of the revolutionary role of the army. Most republicans counted on a

civilian rather than a military revolution to bring them to power.
Their military activities, directed almost exclusively at NCOs, were
geared to weaken the army by undermining discipline in the hope
of provoking a military mutiny. Louis Napoleon, on the other hand,
put his hopes in a military *coup d'état* and shunned social revolution.

TABLE 19* *Years required by officers accused of republican activity during
the July Monarchy to reach their rank*

Years	Sous-Lt.	Lt.	Cpt.	Chef de bn.	Lt.-Col.	Col.
	%	%	%	%	%	%
0–2	—	—	—	—	—	—
3–5	9	13	—	—	—	—
6–10	10	17	2	—	—	—
11–15	5	10	4	—	—	—
16–20	—	5	9	—	—	1
Over 20	2	2	5	2	1	1
Over 30	—	—	—	—	2	—

* Appendix Vf.

Rather than weaken the army by appealing to NCOs, he sought to
win officers to his cause. Republicans had to convince NCOs and
soldiers that republican ideals took precedence over military discipline and authority. But an officer-led revolt turned military
discipline to its advantage, for NCOs and soldiers could justify their
revolutionary conduct as merely following orders. Sergeant Marcot
of the 4th Artillery made this clear when he was broken for his part
in the *coup d'état*: 'I don't meddle in politics', he testified. 'I don't
know anything about it. They said terrible things about me: I
have been punished, I have been in prison, and I have just been
discharged . . . I only follow instructions. My colonel gave me an
order, I had to carry it out.'[14] Louis Napoleon did not disrupt the
military hierarchy and therefore hoped to attract officers who feared
republican plans for an elected officer corps modelled on the National
Guard.

The Strasbourg revolt failed for a variety of reasons. For most
officers the Empire was only a memory. They might have supported
Napoleon, but hesitated to rally to his relatively unknown nephew.
When Louis Napoleon encouraged ex-Napoleonic general Excelmans
to join his insurrection, the general replied that he revered the

Emperor, but not his family. Louis Napoleon depended unsuccessfully on the magic of his name to win support.

Furthermore, Louis Napoleon seriously miscalculated the state of opinion in France and in the army: he believed that the climate was similar to that preceding the July revolution, confident that he was the man to turn discontent to action. 'This prince', wrote General Voirol to the War Minister, 'is convinced that he has a large following in France, and that, if there is a new crisis, all the Emperor's partisans will rally to him. He even claims that a military insurrection is imminent.'[15] The July Monarchy, however, was firmly in control of the political situation by 1836.

An intensification of anti-governmental activity usually accompanied a period of political and economic instability. By 1836, the economy was sound and the opposition had been defeated on the barricades in 1832 in Paris and Lyon in 1834 and discredited politically. The 1834 laws gave officers career guarantees and in most cases substantially increased their pensions. And so, far from teetering on the edge of revolt, both the army and the civilian population were enjoying an interlude of stability.

Louis Napoleon also failed to consider the fundamental political inertia of the overwhelming majority of officers.

Baron Sers, Prefect at Metz, castigated officer indecision in the face of trouble when in June 1832 officers there hesitated to act decisively against rioters supporting the Paris demonstrations at the funeral of General Lamarque: 'You cannot imagine how ignorant the officers are when it comes to trouble', he complained. 'They never know when to act or what to do.'[16]

When the Strasbourg revolt broke out, many officers simply disappeared, only to re-emerge after the insurgents had been arrested. This opportunism was underlined by Captain Franqueville, General Voirol's aide-de-camp: 'He himself was unsure of the role he should play, and weighed the insurrection's chances of success. Like every soldier faced with a *coup d'état*, he tried to sit on the fence to the very end, and then to declare for the strongest faction.'[17]

This opportunism often left NCOs leaderless in time of trouble. 'The whole story must be told', said Sergeant Marcot. 'The officers were too severe: they were courageous enough when it was all over, writing reports and breaking NCOs. But if they had been on the scene earlier and not been I don't know where, that would not have been necessary.'[18] Strasbourg demonstrated that most officers and NCOs simply abstained from political activity. After 1830 the opposition was unable to overcome the army's desire for stability which both the 1832 and 1834 laws mirrored.

The Strasbourg affair did produce short-term political consequences. Eager to play down the importance of the attempted *coup*
and resolved not to turn Louis Napoleon into a political martyr
or alternatively to avoid an embarrassing acquittal, the government
promptly shipped him to the United States. But as some of the
remaining prisoners were civilians, officials were forced to try
them in the public Strasbourg Court of Assize rather than by court-
martial. When the twelve-day trial in January before an Alsatian
jury ended in unanimous acquittal, Strasbourg exploded with joy –
the conspirators were fêted in the town and officers in the 3rd
Artillery gave a banquet in their honour. The police chief for the
Bas-Rhin attributed the verdict to republican corruption of the
jury: 'The acquittal can be attributed only to the campaign for the
accused. Lies and bribes were rife. It seems no stone was left
unturned.'[19]

The trial only served to draw attention to the presence of a new
Bonapartist pretender – 8,000 hastily printed copies of Louis
Napoleon's biography were sold in January alone. Inhabitants of
Strasbourg began to provoke duels and fights with the soldiers of
the 46th Infantry who had foiled the coup.[20] And in March, eight
NCOs of the 4th Artillery now at Douai, dismissed for joining the
plotters, were given a rousing send-off by the regimental band and
followed to the town's outskirts by a large number of sympathetic
civilians and officers and soldiers of the 4th Artillery and 33rd
Infantry Regiments.[21]

Alarmed by the publicity surrounding the Strasbourg trial and
its failure to punish disloyal officers, the government introduced
the law of separation (*loi de disjonction*). This stipulated that in the
event of joint participation by civilians and soldiers in certain crimes,
each would be tried in his respective civilian or military court. Two
other articles revived an 1810 law repealed in 1832, making knowledge and non-revelation of a conspiracy against the state or the
king a crime and setting aside the Ile Bourbon as a prison for
deportees.

The law mirrored the government's desire for a stable army,
but opponents of Molé and Guizot led by Thiers and Odilon
Barrot succeeded on 7 March in narrowly defeating the proposal
by 211 votes to 209 after a week of debate. The defeat of the separation law served to undermine the Molé-Guizot alliance which split
the following month.

Strasbourg marked an important turning point in military opposition. Republicans had rallied to Louis Napoleon in 1836 because
they realized their own hopes of a revolution were temporarily
stymied. Republicans in the east believed that in Bonapartism

they had at last found a formula to rally the army. Louis Napoleon's defeat was therefore also a republican defeat. But it was a republican defeat in another sense. With the emergence of Louis Napoleon, Bonapartism appeared as a political movement in its own right. The army could now equate patriotism with Bonapartism as well as with republicanism. Strasbourg signalled the beginning of a divorce between republicanism and Bonapartism which eventually led to the 1851 anti-republican *coup d'état.*

Chapter 11

Conclusion

Louis Napoleon's arrest and the suppression of regimental secret societies virtually ended military dissent, although opposition activity continued on a very limited scale.

Secret societies were discovered in Grenoble's 8th Infantry Regiment in 1838 and among artillery NCOs at the Metz Ecole de Pyrotechnie in 1839. A few political arrests were still reported, especially of soldiers accused of selling cartridges to republicans, while opposition journals appeared sporadically in Paris and eastern garrisons. A handful of republican diehards enlisted with the avowed aim of killing the king.

In 1840 Louis Napoleon failed to convince soldiers in the Boulogne garrison to join his second attempted *coup d'état*. And although some soldiers joined nationwide pro-war demonstrations in 1840, officials were quick to point out that these demonstrations were not anti-governmental.

The decline of republicanism in France and in the army after 1834 is attributable to the republican defeats of that year, to the Algerian conquest which promised promotion for ambitious officers, and to military reforms which guaranteed a soldier's personal security and the army's stability and continuity under any regime. 'The charter, the 1832 and 1834 laws and subsequent ordinances', declared the *Moniteur de l'Armée* in September 1841, 'have put the finishing touches to this great work. Our army's thoughtful obedience and devotion began there.'[1]

Republican political ideology, in itself, had only limited appeal for the military and had served as little more than a rallying point for discontent with the conditions of service.

The simultaneous repression of the republican movement and the reform of conditions of service brought open political dissent within the army to a near end. Less than 20 per cent of the incidents of political opposition in the army between 1830 and 1848 occurred after 1836.

Unlike 1830, the surge of political opposition in 1847 and 1848 caused not the faintest swell in the army. When the July Monarchy was overthrown in the revolution of February 1848, no open unrest had been reported in the ranks for four years. The army's June crackdown on the revolutionary movement initiated a European counter-revolution and placed the army's loyalty to the government beyond serious question for more than a century.

Ministers of War, 1815–48

Restoration

11 March 1815	Clarke
20 March 1815	Davout
9 July 1815	Gouvion-Saint-Cyr
24 September 1815	Clarke
12 September 1817	Gouvion-Saint-Cyr
19 November 1819	Latour-Maubourg
14 December 1821	Victor
19 October 1823	Damas
4 August 1824	Clermont-Tonnerre
4 January 1828	de Caux
8 August 1829	Bourmont

July Monarchy

1 August 1830	Gérard
17 November 1830	Soult
18 July 1834	Gérard
10 November 1834	Bernard
18 November 1834	Trevise
30 April 1835	Maison
19 September 1836	Bernard
31 March 1839	Cubières
12 May 1839	Schneider
1 May 1840	Cubières
29 October 1840	Soult
10 November 1845	Saint-Yon
9 May 1847	Trezel

Regiments reported for republican activity

1830

INFANTRY

line

5 Paris	31 Paris	47 Lyon
10 Lyon	33 Thionville	49 Montpellier
13 Nancy	36 Nîmes	50 Paris
19 Metz	38 Colmar	53 Paris

light

2 Soumières
4 Mâcon
15 Paris
17 Belfort

CAVALRY

Chasseurs	Cuirassiers	Dragoons	Hussards
10 Le Mans	4 Chateaudun	1 Moulins	1 Paris
11 Dôle	5 Nevers	3 Metz	5 Thionville
13 Tarascon	7 Strasbourg	4 Thionville	

ARTILLERY

1 Strasbourg
4 Paris
6 Metz
7 Strasbourg
Pontonniers Strasbourg

ENGINEERS

2 Arras

1831

INFANTRY

line

1	Paris	16	Paris	48	Bordeaux
2	Aix-en-Provence	18	Bitche	50	Nantes
5	Lille	21	Marseille	52	Paris
6	Pont Saint Esprit	23	Tarascon	53	Metz
7	Douai	35	Nîmes	55	Tarbes
12	Rennes	37	Marseille	56	Grenoble
13	Besançon	40	Lyon	60	Paris
14	Narbonne	42	Nantes	65	Metz
15	Tarascon	46	Tours		

light

4 Marseille
6 Rennes
9 Montbrison
17 Belfort
18 Nantes

CAVALRY

Chasseurs	Dragoons	Hussards
6 Tarascon	7 Epinal	4 Le Mans
8 Avignon		

ARTILLERY

6 Strasbourg
10 Toulouse
11 Vincennes

1832

INFANTRY

line

5	Lille	28	Nîmes
16	Paris	53	Dôle
20	Dijon	65	Metz
23	Lyon		

CAVALRY

Dragoons	Lancers
7 Epinal	4 Thionville
11 Lyon	

1833

INFANTRY

line

1 Dijon	21 Lyon	47 Montpellier
2 Salins (Jura)	22 Béthune	49 Strasbourg
3 Paris	24 Corsica	52 Dijon
8 Paris	25 Cambrai	58 Paris
13 Marseille	30 Nîmes	59 Toulon
14 Rochefort	31 Tours	63 Toulon
15 Grenoble	33 Rennes	67 Toulon
16 Paris	38 Paris	
20 Dijon	42 Versailles	

light

3 Amiens
5 Strasbourg
14 Paris
18 Paris

CAVALRY

Carabineers	Chasseurs	Cuirassiers
1 Versailles	10 Haguenau	3 Paris
		4 Lunéville
		6 Meaux
		9 Lunéville
		10 Lunéville

Dragoons	Hussards	Lancers
3 Paris	1 Paris	4 Thionville
6 Tours	3 Strasbourg	5 Paris
7 Lyon	4 Poitiers	
11 Epinal	6 Limoges	

ARTILLERY

3 Strasbourg
4 Rennes
6 Strasbourg
7 Toulon
11 Paris
Trains et Equipages Bourges
Pontonniers Strasbourg

ENGINEERS

1 Metz
2 Montpellier
3 Arras

1834

INFANTRY

line

2 Besançon	25 Rouen	45 Lille
5 Paris	27 Lyon	49 Strasbourg
8 Paris	29 Rennes	50 Nantes
10 Metz	31 Tours	52 Belfort
11 Montpellier	32 Paris	53 Laval
12 Dijon	33 Rennes	56 Nantes
13 Marseille	34 Montpellier	57 Périgueux
20 Dijon	35 Paris	58 Paris
22 Paris	36 Paris	61 Paris
23 Montbrison	38 Soissons	
24 Corsica	39 Douai	

light

1 Strasbourg
6 Nantes
8 Givet
9 Thionville
11 Paris
13 Metz
16 Aurillac
17 Perpignan
19 Strasbourg
20 Paris

CAVALRY

Chasseurs	Cuirassiers	Dragoons	Lancers
2 Sedan	1 Nancy	1 Neufbrisach	2 Provins
3 Besançon	4 Lunéville	3 Paris	5 Paris
9 Givet	7 Paris	4 Belfort	6 Sarreguemines
11 Béziers	9 Lunéville	5 Arras	
	10 Lunéville	7 Lyon	
		10 Le Mans	
		11 Epinal	

ARTILLERY   ENGINEERS

1 Vincennes   1 Metz
2 Lyon
4 Rennes
6 Strasbourg
12 Bourges
13 Dijon
Trains et Equipages Dijon
Pontonniers Strasbourg

1835

INFANTRY

line

3 Nantes	28 Saint-Etienne	47 Toulouse
11 Toulouse	31 Soissons	50 Nantes
12 Auxonne	36 Paris	55 Clermont
14 Tours	38 Orléans	56 Nantes
23 Tarbes	40 Nantes	61 Besançon
24 Corsica	43 Paris	62 Marseille
26 Montpellier	45 Paris	65 Nancy

light

3 Thionville
5 Paris
12 Cherbourg
17 Perpignan
18 Montpellier

CAVALRY

Carabineers	Chasseurs	Cuirassiers	Dragoons
1 Compiègne	11 Marseille	8 Abbeville	7 Belfort
			10 Tours
			11 Lunéville

Hussards
3 Niort

ARTILLERY

4 Rennes	10 Metz
5 Toulouse	Ouvriers d'Artillerie Auxonne
6 Lyon	Pontonniers Strasbourg
8 Metz	

1836

INFANTRY

line

3 Nantes	24 Corsica	50 Rouen
6 Avesnès	27 Grenoble	59 Antibes
12 Marseille	31 Soissons	60 Versailles
17 Perpignan	36 Nantes	61 Paris
19 Pyrénées-Orientales	40 Nantes	65 Nancy
20 Paris	42 Verdun	66 Avignon
22 Paris	43 Paris	
23 Pau	45 Versailles	

1836 (cont.)

light

1	Paris	15	Romans
6	Angers	17	Perpignan
10	Nîmes	19	Paris

CAVALRY

Carabineers	Chasseurs	Dragoons	Hussards
1 Verdun	13 Haguenau	6 Pau	1 Vendôme
		8 Nancy	

ARTILLERY

2	La Fère	7	Besançon
3	Strasbourg	8	Metz
4	Strasbourg		Pontonniers Strasbourg

1837

INFANTRY

line

2	Paris	20	Rennes	45	Nantes
4	Grenoble	23	Châlons	60	Paris
9	Paris	33	Douai	67	Grenoble
15	Nancy	34	Paris		
18	Aix-en-Provence	41	Paris		

light

1	Le Havre	11	Laval
3	Lyon	15	Perpignan
5	Paris	16	Paris

CAVALRY

Chasseurs	Cuirassiers	Dragoons	Hussards
1 Le Mans	2 Paris	4 Lyon	1 Vendôme
	7 Châlons	11 Paris	2 Versailles

Lancers

2 Vienne

ARTILLERY

2 La Fère
4 Douai
7 Besançon

146

1838

INFANTRY

line

1 Paris	32 Dijon	54 Mulhouse
4 Grenoble	39 Lyon	55 Orléans
8 Grenoble	43 Le Havre	
29 Paris	44 Lyon	

light

12 Arras

CAVALRY

Hussards

4 Paris

ARTILLERY

6 Lyon
13 Toulouse
Ecole Pyrotechnie Metz

1839

INFANTRY

line	light
25 Nantes	6 Lyon
40 Nantes	9 Nantes
45 Nantes	18 Versailles
64 Paris	

1840

INFANTRY

line

3 Le Havre	15 Laval	32 Lyon
4 Lille	20 Marseille	33 Lyon
8 Grenoble	31 Marseille	34 Strasbourg

CAVALRY

Chasseurs	Dragoons
12 Paris	1 Paris

ARTILLERY

4 Valence
7 Metz
Ouvriers d'Artillerie Grenoble

1841

INFANTRY

line | light
43 Parthenay | 17 Montpellier
47 Carcassonne
73 Rennes

CAVALRY | ARTILLERY

Dragoons | 4 Valence
10 Paris | 10 Bourges

1842

INFANTRY | | CAVALRY

line | light | Dragoons | Hussards
6 Dijon | 7 Givet | 9 Paris | 8 Tours
23 Paris

ARTILLERY

13 Rennes

1843

INFANTRY

light
25 Perpignan

1844

INFANTRY

line | light
5 Perpignan | 12 Verdun
14 Toulouse
28 Laval
70 Verdun

ARTILLERY

8 Toulon

Garrisons and garrison towns

Artillery garrisons

Regiment	1	2	3	4	5
1830	à organiser	Strasbourg	Besançon	La Fère	à organiser
1831	Douai	Metz	Strasbourg	Rennes	Toulouse
1832	,,	,,	,,	,,	,,
1833	,,	,,	,,	,,	,,
1834	,,	,,	,,	,,	,,
1835	Vincennes	La Fère	,,	Strasbourg	Rennes
1836	,,	,,	,,	,,	,,
1837	,,	,,	,,	Douai	,,
1838	Strasbourg	Vincennes	La Fère	,,	,,
1839	,,	,,	,,	,,	,,
1840	,,	,,	,,	,,	,,
1841	,,	,,	,,	,,	,,
1842	,,	Douai	Vincennes	La Fère	Metz
1843	,,	,,	,,	,,	,,
1844	Bourges	,,	Metz	Vincennes	La Fère
1845	,,	,,	,,	,,	,,
1846	Toulouse	Bourges	,,	,,	,,
1847	,,	,,	,,	Lyon & Alg.	Vincennes
1848	,,	Metz	Valence	Grenoble	Strasbourg

Regiment	6	7	8	9	10
1830	à organiser	Strasbourg	à organiser	Metz	—
1831	Strasbourg	Besançon	La Fère	,,	Valence
1832	,,	,,	,,	,,	,,
1833	,,	,,	,,	,,	,,
1834	,,	,,	,,	,,	,,
1835	Lyon	,,	Metz	Valence	Metz
1836	,,	,,	,,	,,	,,
1837	,,	Bourges	,,	,,	,,
1838	,,	,,	,,	,,	,,
1839	,,	,,	,,	Toulouse	,,
1840	Besançon	Metz	,,	,,	Bourges
1841	,,	,,	,,	,,	,,
1842	,,	,,	Toulouse	,,	,,
1843	,,	,,	,,	,,	,,

1844	Besançon	Metz	Toulouse	Strasbourg	Strasbourg
1845	,,	,,	,,	,,	,,
1846	Douai	Rennes	Besançon	,,	,,
1847	La Fère	,,	,,	,,	Douai
1848	Vincennes	La Fère	,,	Rennes	,,

Regiment	11	12	13	14	Pontonniers
1830	—	—	—	—	Strasbourg
1831	Vincennes	—	—	—	,,
1832	,,	—	—	—	,,
1833	,,	Bourges	Dijon	—	,,
1834	,,	,,	Lyon	—	,,
1835	Douai	,,	Toulouse	Toulouse	,,
1836	,,	,,	,,	,,	,,
1837	Strasbourg	Besançon	,,	,,	,,
1838	,,	,,	,,	,,	,,
1839	,,	,,	,,	,,	,,
1840	,,	Lyon	,,	Valence	,,
1841	,,	,,	,,	,,	,,
1842	,,	,,	Rennes	,,	,,
1843	,,	,,	,,	,,	,,
1844	Valence	Toulouse	,,	Lyon	,,
1845	,,	,,	,,	,,	,,
1846	,,	,,	Metz	,,	,,
1847	,,	,,	,,	Strasbourg	,,
1848	Toulouse	Bourges	,,	,,	,,

Infantry garrisons

Regiment	1	5	13	24
1830	Boulogne	Soissons	Metz	Phalsbourg
1831	Paris	Givet	Besançon	Mâcon
1832	,,	Lille	Marseille	Aix
1833	Dijon	Calais	,,	Corsica
1834	Briançon	,,	,,	,,
1835	Lyon	Vannes	Africa	,,
1836	Versailles	,,	,,	,,
1837	Toulon	Africa	Corsica	Africa
1838	Antibes	,,	,,	,,
1839	Africa	Angers	Toulon	,,
1840	,,	Bayonne	Perpignan	,,
1841	,,	St Jean-pied-de-Port	Vannes	,,
1842	,,	Pau	Paris	,,
1843	,,	Bayonne	,,	,,
1844	Orléans	Toulouse	Ivry	Paris
1845	Paris	Perpignan	,,	,,
1846	,,	Africa	Mâcon	Saint-Omer
1847	Lorient	,,	Dijon	,,

Regiment	33	66	17 léger
1830	Thionville	—	Longwy
1831	Sedan	Lyon	Nancy
1832	Saint-Omer	Toulon	Bourbon-Vendée
1833	Lorient	Italy (Ancona)	Narbonne
1834	Vannes	Italy and Africa	Carcassonne
1835	Rennes	,,	Pyrénées-Orientales
1836	,,	,,	Africa
1837	Douai	,,	,,
1838	Valenciennes	,,	,,
1839	,,	Toulon	,,
1840	Paris	Lyon	,,
1841	Lyon	Paris	,,
1842	Africa	Metz	Courbevoie
1843	,,	,,	,,
1844	,,	,,	Paris
1845	,,	Belfort	Metz
1846	,,	Montbrison	Phalsbourg
1847	,,	,,	,,

Cavalry garrisons

Regiment	4 Cuir.	5 Cuir.	7 Cuir.	9 Cuir.
1830	—	—	—	—
1831	Cambrai	Verdun	Nancy	Chartres
1832	,,	Saint-Michel	,,	Melun
1833	Lunéville	Toul	Melun	Lunéville
1834	,,	,,	Paris	,,
1835	Aire	,,	Lille	Valenciennes
1836	,,	,,	,,	,,
1837	Vesoul	Lille	Stenay	,,
1838	Versailles	,,	Lunéville	Sedan
1839	,,	,,	,,	,,
1840	Lille	Versailles	Dôle	,,
1841	,,	,,	,,	Rambouillet
1842	,,	Paris	Vesoul	Versailles
1843	Vendôme	Le Mans	Epinal	,,
1844	,,	,,	,,	,,
1845	,,	Orléans	,,	Lunéville
1846	Amiens	Poitiers	,,	,,
1847	Chartres	,,	Meaux	Sarreguemines

Regiment	10 Cuir.	7 Dragoons	11 Dragoons
1830	—	Pont-à-Mousson	Belfort
1831	Meaux	Epinal	Vesoul
1832	,,	,,	Lyon
1833	Lunéville	Lyon	Epinal
1834	,,	,,	,,

1835	Vesoul	Belfort	Lunéville
1836	,,	Haguenau	Versailles
1837	Pont-à-Mousson	Versailles	Paris
1838	,,	Paris	Vesoul
1839	Lunéville	,,	Huningue
1840	Provins	Tours	,,
1841	Melun	Limoges	Compiègne
1842	,,	Vendôme	Thionville
1843	Chartres	Clermont	Lunéville
1844	,,	,,	Thionville
1845	,,	Versailles	Moulins
1846	Vesoul	,,	,,
1847	,,	,,	,,

Garrison towns, 1835*

20,000 man garrison:
    Paris
10,000 man garrison:
    Lyon
    Metz
    Strasbourg
8,000 man garrison:
    Perpignan
    Toulouse
4,000 man garrison:
    Belfort
    Besançon
    Douai
    Grenoble
    Rennes
3,000 man garrison:
    Bayonne
    Marseille
    Pau
    Tarbes
    Bourges
    La Fère
    Valence
    Laval
2,500 man garrison:
    Nantes
    Dijon
    Lille
    Nancy

Toulon
Tours
Thionville
Lunéville
Valenciennes
Bordeaux

1,600 man garrison:
    Mézières
    La Rochelle
    Vannes
    Saint-Brieuc
    Phalsbourg
    Avesnes
    Aix-en-Provence
    Briançon
    Saint-Omer
    Bastia
    Parthenay
    Montpellier
    Montbrison
    Caen
    Soissons
    Arras
    Cholet
    Orléans
    Brest
    Rouen
    Clermont-Ferrand
    Vendée
    Antibes
    Givet

* Because of quartering problems, battalions or companies were often stationed in smaller towns near the main garrison.

Dunkirk
Cherbourg
Lorient
Verdun
Romans
Nîmes
Amiens
Saumur
Périgueux

900 man garrison:
Gray
Aire
Toul
Vesoul
Joigny
Stenay
St-Michel
Epinal
Commercy

Moulins
Poitiers
Cambrai
Sarreguemines
Maubeuge
Vienne
Sedan
Meaux
Provins
Beauvais
Béziers
Carcassone
Haguenau
Libourne
Vendôme
Dôle
Niort
Auch
Auxonne

Military divisions, 1835

1st (Paris: HQ) Seine, Seine-et-Oise, Seine-et-Marne, Aisne, Oise, Eure-et-Loir, Loiret.
2nd (Châlons-sur-Marne) Marne, Meuse, Ardennes.
3rd (Metz) Moselle, Meurthe, Vosges.
4th (Tours) Indre-et-Loire, Loir-et-Cher, Vienne, Sarthe, Mayenne.
5th (Strasbourg) Bas-Rhin, Haut-Rhin.
6th (Besançon) Doubs, Haute-Saône, Jura.
7th (Lyon) Rhône, Ain, Isère, Hautes-Alpes, Drôme, Loire.
8th (Marseille) Vaucluse, Basses-Alpes, Bouches-du-Rhône, Var.
9th (Montpellier) Hérault, Aveyron, Gard, Ardèche, Lozère.
10th (Toulouse) Haute-Garonne, l'Ariège, Aude, Pyrénées-Orientales, Tarn, Tarn-et-Garonne, Gers, Hautes-Pyrénées.
11th (Bordeaux) Gironde, Basses-Pyrénées, Landes.
12th (Nantes) Loire-Inférieure, Vendée, Maine-et-Loire, Deux-Sèvres, Charente-Inférieure.
13th (Rennes) Ille-et-Vilaine, Morbihan, Finistère, Côtes-du-Nord.
14th (Rouen) Seine-Inférieure, Eure, Calvados, Orne, Manche.
15th (Bourges) Indre, Cher, Nièvre, Haute-Vienne, Creuse.
16th (Lille) Nord, Pas-de-Calais, Somme.
17th (Bastia) Corsica.
18th (Dijon) Côte-d'Or, Haute-Marne, Saône-et-Loire, Yonne, Aube.
19th (Clermont-Ferrand) Puy-de-Dôme, Allier, Haute-Loire, Cantal.
20th (Périgueux) Dordogne, Charente, Lot, Corrèze, Lot-et-Garonne.

Soldiers and NCOs arrested for republican activity, 1830–48

a. Condition of service			
Volunteer	236		
Replacement	38		
Conscript	94		
Récompensé national	10		
no information	122		

b. Civilian job		Saddler	4
		Butcher	4
		Printer	4
		Jeweller	4
Shop assistant	40	Watchmaker	3
Farmer	30	Gardener	3
Secondary student	28	Mason	3
Carpenter	24	Wigmaker	3
Labourer	18	Stonemason	3
Proprietor	13	Writer	3
Ex-soldier	9	Apprentice seaman	2
Weaver	9	Medical student	2
Clerk	9	Tinsmith	2
Smith	8	Hatter	2
Tailor	7	Dyer	2
Domestic servant	7	Primary teacher	2
Merchant	7	Lawyer	1
Cobbler	7	Actor	1
Baker	6	Confectioner	1
Soldiers' boy	6	Roofer	1
Practitioner	6	Draper	1
Commercial traveller	5	Plasterer	1
Law student	5	Glove maker	1
Musician	5	Cooper	1
Locksmith	5	Lace maker	1
Silk worker	5	Ribbon maker	1
Bookbinder	4	Ferryman	1
		Surveyor	1
		Polisher	1
		Engraver	1
		Miner	1
		Porcelain worker	1
		no information	174

c. Age

18–19	2
20–21	21
22–23	80
24–25	104
26–27	46
28–29	30
30–35	35
over 35	6
no information	176

d. Years of service

under 6 months	10
6 months to 2 years	12
2	37
3	78
4	84
5	42
6	41
7–10	38
over 10	34
no information	124

e. Time since last promotion

Years	Lunéville	July Monarchy
0–1	1	35
1	8	50
2	4	48
3	6	32
4	2	14
over 5	3	15

f. Last civilian residence

	Infantry	Cavalry	Artillery
Seine	62	12	5
Rhône	17	1	2
Côte-d'Or	13	—	—
Bas-Rhin	4	3	6
Basses-Pyrénées	10	2	—
Calvados	6	1	4
Isère	9	—	2
Aude	7	2	—
Drôme	6	2	—
Meurthe	5	1	2
Meuse	5	3	—
Moselle	7	1	—
Aisne	3	1	3
Vosges	6	1	—
Jura	1	5	—
Morbihan	3	3	—
Charente-Inférieure	4	1	—
Gard	5	—	—
Haute-Garonne	5	—	—
Hérault	4	1	—
Loire	4	1	—
Loire-Inférieure	4	1	—

Saône-et-Loire	3	1	1
Var	4	1	—
Vienne	5	—	—
Ardèche	3	—	1
Doubs	4	—	—
Eure	2	—	2
Finistère	3	1	—
Ille-et-Vilaine	—	1	3
Indre-et-Loire	2	2	—
Marne	2	1	1
Nord	3	—	1
Pyrénées-Orientales	4	—	—
Seine-Inférieure	2	1	1
Vendée	3	1	—
Ain	3	—	—
Bouches-du-Rhône	3	—	—
Charente	3	—	—
Corse	3	—	—
Gironde	1	1	1
Maine-et-Loire	1	1	1
Oise	1	1	1
Orne	1	2	—
Pas-de-Calais	2	—	1
Deux-Sèvres	3	—	—
Somme	3	—	—
Ariège	2	—	—
Côtes-du-Nord	1	—	1
Dordogne	1	—	1
Loir-et-Cher	2	—	—
Lot	2	—	—
Lot-et-Garonne	2	—	—
Manche	1	1	—
Hautes-Pyrénées	2	—	—
Haute-Saône	—	—	2
Sarthe	1	1	—
Seine-et-Marne	1	—	1
Vaucluse	—	1	1
Haute-Vienne	2	—	—
Allier	—	—	1
Ardennes	1	—	—
Corrèze	1	—	—
Eure-et-Loir	1	—	—
Landes	—	—	1
Mayenne	1	—	—
Haut-Rhin	—	—	1
Tarn-et-Garonne	—	1	—
no information	118		

Officers reported to the War Minister for republican activity, 1830–48

a. Promoted from

Ranks	69	
School	36	
Saint-Cyr		17
Ecole Polytechnique		19
Récompensé national	16	
no information	35	

b. Age

18–20	1
21–25	13
26–30	32
31–35	22
36–40	22
41–45	14
46–50	12
over 50	5
no information	35

c. Years of service

0–2	4
2–5	16
6–10	25
11–15	20
16–20	20
21–25	16
26–30	14
over 30	6
no information	35

d. Initial service under

Republic	5
Empire	32
Restoration	70
July Monarchy	16
no information	33

e. Rank

Sous-lieutenant	52
Lieutenant	57
Capitaine	29
Chef de bataillon	8
Lieut. colonel	5
Colonel	5

f. Time required to reach the rank of

Years	Sous-Lt.	Lt.	Cpt.	Chef de bn.	Lt.-Col.	Col.
0–2	—	—	—	—	—	—
3–5	10	14	—	—	—	—
6–10	11	18	2	—	—	—
11–15	5	11	4	—	—	—
16–20	—	5	10	—	—	1
over 20	2	2	5	2	1	1
over 30	—	—	—	—	2	—
no information 50						

g. Last civilian residence

	Infantry	Cavalry	Artillery
Seine	17	5	5
Corsica	6	—	1
Seine-et-Oise	3	1	1
Bouches-du-Rhône	3	—	1
Nord	1	2	1
Aisne	2	—	1
Haute-Garonne	3	—	—
Hérault	2	—	1
Ille-et-Vilaine	1	—	2
Meurthe	1	2	—
Morbihan	2	—	1
Bas-Rhin	1	—	2
Haute-Saône	2	—	1
Saône-et-Loire	—	1	2
Ariège	1	—	1
Aude	1	—	1
Charente	—	—	2
Charente-Inférieure	2	—	—
Côte-d'Or	—	—	2
Côtes-du-Nord	2	—	—
Doubs	—	2	—
Pas-de-Calais	2	—	—
Somme	1	—	1
Vosges	1	1	—
Ardèche	1	—	—
Cher	1	—	—
Dordogne	—	1	—
Drôme	1	—	—
Finistère	—	—	1
Gard	—	—	1
Gers	1	—	—
Gironde	1	—	—

Indre-et-Loire	1	—	—
Isère	1	—	—
Jura	—	—	1
Landes	1	—	—
Lot	1	—	—
Manche	—	—	1
Mayenne	—	—	1
Moselle	1	—	—
Puy-de-Dôme	—	—	1
Pyrénées-Orientales	—	—	1
Haut-Rhin	—	—	1
Rhône	1	—	—
Sarthe	—	1	—
Seine-et-Marne	1	—	—
Deux-Sèvres	1	—	—
Yonne	1	—	—

no information 38

By-laws of the Société Philanthropique des Francs Amis (discovered in the Ouvriers d'Artillerie and the 12th Infantry Regiment at Auxonne in the autumn of 1835)

Before God, eternal judge of human actions, the society declares:

1. The first and foremost goal of the association is to provide relaxation from life's trials while at the same time seeking to help our brothers in need.
2. Every religious belief is permitted, so long as it professes the existence of a creating and rewarding God.
3. No candidate may be admitted until he has proved beyond doubt that his whole life has been above reproach.
4. He must swear always to observe the laws of honour and to remain loyal to France, whatever form her government may take.
5. All politics are prohibited.
6. Any member guilty of a serious crime against the state will be immediately expelled.

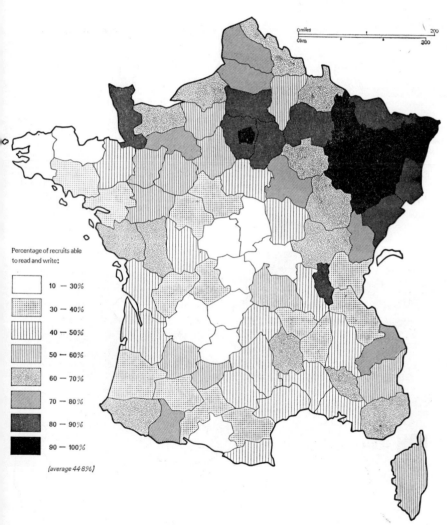

Percentage of recruits able
to read and write:

	10 — 30%
	30 — 40%
	40 — 50%
	50 — 60%
	60 — 70%
	70 — 80%
	80 — 90%
	90 — 100%

(average 44·8%)

Map 1   Conscript literacy, 1827–9

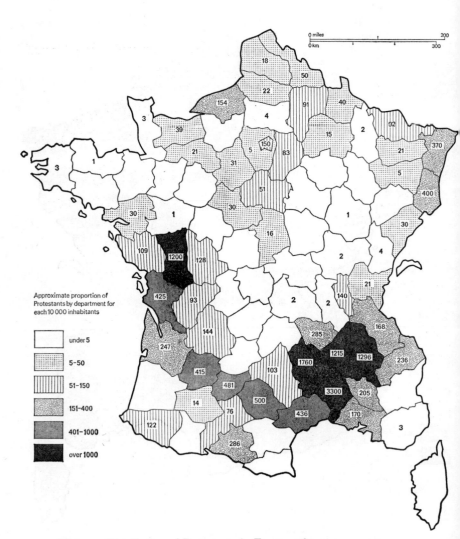

Map 2   Distribution of Protestants in France, 1824

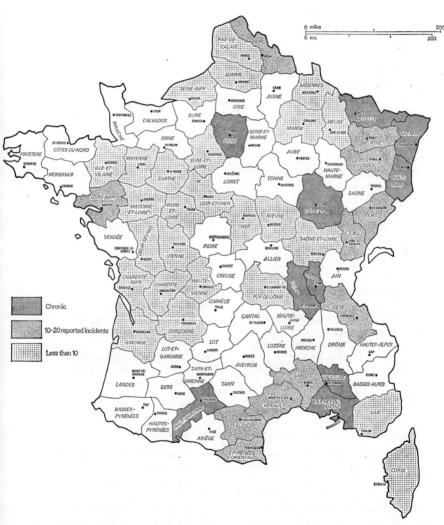

Map 3   Republican activity in the army, 1830–40

Notes

Preface and acknowledgments

1 Archives Historiques de la
   Guerre; H22, 27 September
   1833; and H27, 18 July 1834.

Introduction

1 E. Guillon, *Les Complots
   militaires sous la restauration*, p. 5.
2 Ibid., p. 16.
3 Ibid., p. 16.
4 G. de Bertier de Sauvigny, *La
   Restauration*, pp. 118–19.
5 J. Barrès, *Memoirs of a
   Napoleonic Officer*, pp. 214–19.
6 J. Vidalenc, *Les Demi-Soldes*,
   p. 34.
7 Bertier de Sauvigny, op. cit.,
   p. 158.
8 M. Lamarque, *Mémoires*, vol. 1,
   pp. 203–4.
9 F. P. G. Guizot, *Memoirs of
   my Time*, pp. 166–7.
10 J. Monteilhet, *Les Institutions
   militaires de la France*, p. 4.
11 Ibid., pp. 3–4.

12 Guillon, op. cit., p. 25.
13 Fantin des Odoards, *Journal*,
   p. 461.
14 A. Saint-Chamans, *Mémoires*,
   p. 354.
15 Barrès, op. cit., p. 224.
16 E. Harpaz, *L'Ecole libérale sous
   la restauration*, pp. 48–50.
17 Bertier de Sauvigny, op. cit.,
   p. 161.
18 Ibid., pp. 164–5.
19 Ibid., pp. 168–9.
20 G. Weill, *Histoire du parti
   républicain en France, 1814–1870*,
   p. 36.
21 G. Bourgin, *1848*, p. 152.
22 Guillon, op. cit., p. 215.
23 Ibid., p. 352.

Chapter 1   The 1823 reserve mobilization and the 1824 law

1 A. Carrel, 'De la guerre
   d'Espagne en 1823', *Revue
   Française*, p. 135.
2 E. Lavisse, *Histoire de la France
   contemporaine*, vol. 4, p. 178.
3 A. Saint-Chamans, *Mémoires*,
   p. 420.

4 P. de Pelleport, *Souvenirs*, vol.
   2, p. 153.
5 Carrel, op. cit., pp. 150–1.
6 Ibid., p. 151.
7 AHG, D³100, 15 June 1823.
8 AN, F⁷6703, dossier Rhône.
9 Ibid., F⁷6702, dossier Jura.

10 Ibid., F⁷6703, dossier Seine.
11 Ibid., F⁷6702, dossier Loire-Inférieure.
12 AHG, D³100, 10 June 1823.
13 AN, F⁷6702, dossier Basses-Alpes.
14 Ibid., F⁷6702, dossier Aube.
15 AHG, D³100, 10 June 1823.
16 AP, vol. 40, p. 656.

17 Ibid., vol. 41, p. 452.
18 Ibid., vol. 41, p. 455.
19 Ibid., vol. 42, p. 15.
20 AHG, D³100, 14 June 1823.
21 Ibid., 10 June 1823.
22 AP, vol. 42, p. 12.
23 Ibid., vol. 42, p. 101.
24 Ibid.
25 Carrel, op. cit., p. 145.

Chapter 2   The Restoration army, *1824–30*

1 G. de Bertier de Sauvigny, *La Restauration*, p. 300.
2 Ibid., pp. 311–12.
3 Ibid., p. 317.
4 Ibid., pp. 380–1.
5 Ibid., p. 380.
6 D. Bagge, *Les Idées politiques en France sous la restauration*, p. 144.
7 Ibid., p. 145.
8 G. Weill, *Histoire du parti républicain en France, 1814–1870*, p. 30.
9 Bagge, op. cit., p. 149.
10 Ibid., p. 148.
11 AHG, D³, 8 January 1824.
12 Ibid., D³, 5 October 1824.
13 Ibid., D³, 2 March 1825.
14 Ibid., D³, 20 May 1824.
15 Ibid., D³, 4 October 1824.
16 Ibid., D³, 21 March 1825.
17 Ibid., D³, 14 March 1826.
18 Ibid., D³, 9 April 1826. See also 4 and 11 August 1826.
19 Bertier de Sauvigny, op. cit., pp. 385–8.
20 AHG, D³, 1 February 1827.
21 Bertier de Sauvigny, op. cit., pp. 389–90.
22 AHG, D³, 28 April 1827.
23 Ibid., D³, 5 April 1827.
24 Ibid., D³, 9 May and 16 August 1827.
25 Ibid., D³, 23 August 1827.
26 Ibid., D³, 12 and 22 December 1827.

27 Bertier de Sauvigny, op. cit., p. 431.
28 AHG, D³, 24 January 1828.
29 Ibid., D³, 3 and 26 September 1828.
30 Ibid., D³, 17 and 8 September 1829.
31 Ibid., D³, 12 October 1829.
32 Ibid., D³, 6 December 1829 and 12 January 1830.
33 Parliamentary papers, *Estimates and accounts, Army Commissariat*, 1830, p. 90.
34 *La Solde des capitaines du Corps Royal d'Artillerie*, p. 10.
35 AHG, X^d344.
36 *La Solde . . .*, p. 5.
37 Sergent-Major Levé, *La Solde des sergents-majors d'infanterie*.
38 Ibid.
39 Ibid.
40 Maréchal de Camp Dejean, *Idées pour l'amélioration de la retraite des officiers*, p. 4.
41 Galisset, *Corps du droit français*, 28 fructidor, year VII.
42 AP, vol. 57, p. 690.
43 AN, F⁷6702, dossier Corse.
44 *Etat militaire en 1825*, p. 26.
45 Dejean, op. cit., p. 5.
46 Ibid., p. 4.
47 AHG, D³124, 27 March 1829.
48 *La Solde . . .*, p. 5.
49 L. Trochu, *L'Armée française en 1867*, p. 92.

50 P de. la Madelaine, *Le Malaise actuel dans le corps d'artillerie*, p. 22.
51 La Motte Rouge, *Souvenirs et campagnes*, vol. 1, p. 300.
52 P. Chalmin, *L'Officier français de 1815–1870*, p. 24.
53 AHG, D³128, 12 October 1829.
54 *Etat militaire en 1825*, pp. 18–20.
55 AHG, D³124, 27 March 1829.
56 C. A. Thoumas, *Les Transformations de l'armée française*, vol. 1, p. 422.
57 C. Rousset, *Un Ministre de la restauration*, p. 243.
58 Marmont, *Mémoires*, vol. 3, p. 8.
59 Madelaine, op. cit., p. 29.
60 *Le National*, 25 September 1830.
61 Contamine, 'La Révolution de 1830 à Metz', *Revue d'histoire moderne*, vol. 6, p. 117.
62 *Le Figaro*, 11 August 1829.

63 J. Barrès, *Memoirs of a Napoleonic Officer*, p. 248.
64 B. Castellane, *Journal*, vol. 1, pp. 358–9.
65 AP, vol. 71, p. 508.
66 Ibid., vol. 71, p. 509.
67 Ibid., vol. 71, p. 456.
68 Ibid., vol. 71, p. 411.
69 P. de Pelleport, *Souvenirs*, vol. 1, p. 188.
70 AHG, D³, 10 January 1827.
71 Ibid., D³, 24 August 1829.
72 Ibid., D³, 21 January and 2 February 1829.
73 Ibid., D³, 17 August 1829.
74 Ibid., Fonds Préval 2038.
75 Ibid., D³, 1 January 1825.
76 Ibid., D³, 23 July 1827 and 30 June 1828.
77 Ibid., D³, 8 November 1828.
78 Madelaine, op. cit., p. 30.
79 Barrès, op. cit., pp. 235–6.
80 E. de Barrey, *Petition à la chambre des députés*, p. 3.

Chapter 3 1830

1 G. de Bertier de Sauvigny, *La Restauration*, p. 424.
2 Ibid., p. 432.
3 Ibid., p. 441.
4 A. Marmont, *Mémoires*, p. 268.
5 Ibid., p. 241.
6 AN, F¹⁶I 159², dossier Esmangart.
7 AHG, D³, 3 August 1830.
8 Ibid., E⁵1, 10 August 1830.
9 Ibid., E⁵1, 7 August 1830.
10 Ibid., Fonds Préval, 1948.
11 Ibid., E⁵1, 8 August 1830.
12 Ibid., E⁵1, 10 August 1830.
13 La Motte Rouge, *Souvenirs*, vol. 1, p. 303.
14 B. Castellane, *Journal*, vol. 1, pp. 460–1.
15 Ibid.
16 C. de Rémusat, *Mémoires*, vol. 2, pp. 418–19.

17 AHG, E⁵1, 10 August 1830.
18 Ibid., E⁵1, 3 September 1830.
19 La Motte Rouge, op. cit., pp. 304–5.
20 G. Bapst, *Le Maréchal Canrobert*, vol. 1, p. 125.
21 Poncet de Bermond, *La Garde royale en 1830*, p. 85.
22 AN, F¹⁶I 159², dossier Esmangart.
23 J. Barrès, *Memoirs of a Napoleonic Officer*, p. 275.
24 Bapst, op. cit., vol. 1, p. 124.
25 Ibid., vol. 1, pp. 141–2.
26 Barrès, op. cit., p. 259.
27 La Motte Rouge, op. cit., vol. 1, p. 305.
28 Ibid., vol. 1, pp. 308–9.
29 AHG, E⁵1, 7 August 1830.
30 Ibid., E⁵4, 16 November 1830.
31 Ibid., E⁵2, 1 September 1830.

32 P. Thureau-Dangin, *Histoire de la monarchie de juillet*, vol. 1, p. 86.
33 P. Chalmin, *L'Officier français*, p. 82.
34 *Le National*, 14 September 1830.
35 L. Morand, *L'Armée selon la charte*, p. 36.
36 Rémusat, op. cit., vol. 2, p. 418.
37 AHG, $E^5 2$, 3 September 1830.
38 Ibid., $X^d 638$.
39 Ibid., Fonds Préval 1947.
40 Ibid., E^5, 15 April 1833.
41 AN, CC 619, 27 March 1834.
42 AHG, $E^5 50$, 14 April 1834.
43 Ibid., $E^5 55$, 31 May 1834.
44 Ibid., $E^5 57$, 5 June 1834.

45 A. Thiers, *La Monarchie de 1830*, p. 126.
46 AHG, $E^5 49$, 7 April 1834.
47 AN, CC 619, 24 March 1834.
48 AHG, $E^5 147$ and AN, BB^{18} 1360.
49 Ibid., $E^5 147$.
50 AN, CC 767, dossier Vaudrey.
51 AHG, $E^5 76$, 30 April 1837.
52 Ibid., $E^5 147$.
53 88 sergeant-majors, 258 sergeants, 70 corporals and 84 privates. This list, compiled mainly from the general correspondence of the War Ministry, series E^5, can be regarded as only a sample.

Chapter 4   Casimir Périer and the politics of stability

1 La Motte Rouge, *Souvenirs*, vol. 1, p. 312.
2 A. Carrel, *Œuvres*, vol. 1, p. 165.
3 G. Bapst, *Le Maréchal Canrobert*, vol. 1, p. 132.
4 A. Sers, *Souvenirs*, pp. 251–4.
5 Bapst, op. cit., vol. 1, p. 418.
6 AHG, $E^5 3$, 8 October 1830.
7 Ibid., $E^5 3$, 17 and 19 October 1830.
8 Ibid., $E^5 4$, 27 November 1830.
9 Ibid., $E^5 4$, 17 and 19 November 1830.
10 Ibid., $E^5 5$, 11 December 1830.
11 Ibid., $E^5 5$, 30 December 1830.
12 G. Weill, *Histoire du parti républicain en France, 1814–1870*, p. 31.
13 Ibid., p. 36.
14 Ibid., pp. 28–9.
15 Ibid., p. 80.
16 G. Perreux, *La Propagande républicaine au début de la monarchie de juillet*, pp. 143–7.
17 Weill, op. cit., pp. 76–7.
18 AHG, $E^5 6$, 18 and 19 January 1831; $E^5 8$, 21 March 1831.

19 Ibid., $E^5 7$, 15 and 19 February 1831.
20 Ibid., $E^5 6$, 13, 19 and 20 January 1831.
21 Ibid., $E^5 7$, 13 and 14 February 1831.
22 Ibid., $E^5 8$, 9 March 1831.
23 Ibid., $E^5 8$, 13 March 1831; $E^5 6$, 9 January 1831.
24 Ibid., $E^5 7$, 28 February 1831.
25 Ibid., $E^5 8$, 10 and 13 March 1831; $E^5 6$, 18 January 1831.
26 Ibid., $E^5 10$, 10 and 13 April 1831.
27 Ibid., $E^5 146$, 19 May 1831.
28 Ibid., $E^5 146$, 15 June 1831.
29 Ibid., Fonds Préval 2034.
30 Ibid.
31 Ibid.
32 Ibid., $E^5 10$, 30 April 1831.
33 Ibid., $E^5 11$, 8 and 9 May 1831.
34 Ibid., $E^5 11$, 5 and 10 May 1831.
35 Ibid., $E^5 146$, 17 May 1831.
36 Ibid., $E^5 12$, 11 June 1831.
37 Ibid., $E^5 12$, 12 and 20 June 1831.

38 AHG, E⁵12, 15 June 1831.
39 Ibid., E⁵12, 14 June 1831.
40 Ibid., E⁵146, 21 June 1831.
41 Ibid., E⁵12, 28 June 1831.
42 Ibid., E⁵13, 1 July 1831.
43 Ibid., E⁵13, 2 July 1831.
44 Ibid., E⁵13, 3 and 13 July 1831.
45 Ibid., E⁵13, 20 July 1831.
46 G. de Bertier de Sauvigny, *La Conspiration des légitimistes et la Duchesse de Berry*, p. 65.
47 G. de Bertier de Sauvigny, *Le Comte Ferdinand de Bertier et l'enigme de la congrégation*, p. 473.
48 G. de Bertier de Sauvigny, *La Conspiration des légitimistes*, p. 46.
49 AHG, E⁵13, 15 July 1831.
50 Ibid., E⁵14, 21 July 1831.
51 Ibid., E⁵14, 26, 27, 22 and 29 July 1831.
52 AN, BB¹⁸1322 and A⁷5678.
53 General Bachelu, *Opinion sur la situation en France.*
54 AHG, E⁵146, 22 October 1831.
55 Bouvier-Dumolard, *Compte rendu des événements qui ont eu lieu dans la ville de Lyon au mois de novembre 1831*, pp. 34–5.
56 Ibid., p. 32.
57 Ibid., p. 39.
58 Bouvier-Dumolard, op. cit., p. 30.
59 AHG, E⁵177, 20 November 1831.
60 Bouvier-Dumolard, op. cit., pp. 50–1.
61 AHG, E⁵177, 20 November 1831.
62 Ibid., E⁵177, 15 December 1831.
63 Bouvier-Dumolard, op. cit., p. 34.
64 P. Montagne, *Le Comportement politique de l'armée à Lyon*, p. 137.
65 AHG, E⁵178.

Chapter 5   The Soult law

1 J. Monteilhet, *Les Institutions militaires de la France*, p. 21.
2 G. de Bertier de Sauvigny, *La Restauration*, p. 459.
3 B. Schnapper, *Le Remplacement militaire en France*, p. 39.
4 AP, second series, vol. 69, p. 273.
5 Ibid.
6 Ibid.
7 Ibid., vol. 71, pp. 170–2.
8 Ibid.
9 AHG, X⁸67.
10 AP, vol. 71, p. 215.
11 Ibid., vol. 71, pp. 158–61.
12 Ibid., vol. 71, p. 284.
13 B. Castellane, *Journal*, vol. 2, p. 373.
14 R. Girardet, *La Société militaire*, p. 63.
15 Monteilhet, op. cit., p. 25.
16 M. Howard, *The Franco-Prussian War*, pp. 29–30.
17 C. A. Thoumas, *Les Transformations de l'armée française*, p. 378.
18 Ibid., p. 18.
19 R. D. Challener, *The French Theory of the Nation in Arms*, p. 78.
20 AP, vol. 69, p. 275.
21 G. Vallée, *La Conscription dans le département de la Charente*, p. 55.
22 AHG, Fonds Préval supplement 2038.
23 Ibid., X⁸67.
24 Thoumas, op. cit., pp. 21–2.
25 AP, vol. 69, p. 538.
26 Ibid., vol. 71, pp. 310–11.
27 Ibid., vol. 71, p. 325.
28 Ibid., vol. 71, pp. 317–18.

29 AHG, X⁸67, Commission report 53.
30 Ibid.
31 AP, vol. 71, p. 320.
32 AHG, Fonds Préval supplement 2036.
33 AP, vol. 71, p. 325.
34 AHG, D³, 17 October 1825.
35 Ibid., E⁵12, 11 June 1831.
36 *Situation du département de la guerre* (1831), p. 28.
37 Ibid. (1833), p. 30.
38 AHG, E⁵147, 1834.
39 'Du logement des militaires chez l'habitant', *Spectateur Militaire*, vol. 14, 15 March 1834.
40 AP, vol. 71, p. 311.
41 Ibid., vol. 73, p. 522.
42 Ibid., vol. 73, p. 523.
43 Ibid., vol. 65, pp. 474–5.
44 Ibid., vol. 67, p. 143.
45 AHG, X⁸67.

46 Howard, op. cit., p. 32.
47 L. Girard, *La Garde Nationale*, p. 215.
48 Monteilhet, op. cit., p. 80.
49 *Journal des Débats*, 5 November 1831.
50 AP, vol. 71, p. 320.
51 Ibid., vol. 71, p. 331.
52 Ibid., vol. 74, p. 563.
53 Ibid., vol. 71, p. 359.
54 AHG, X⁸67.
55 Ibid.
56 AHG, E⁵147, 1841.
57 F. P. G. Guizot, *Mémoires pour servir à l'histoire de mon temps*, pp. 166–9.
58 Thoumas, op. cit., p. 32.
59 A. Kovacs, 'French military institutions before the Franco-Prussian War', *American Historical Review*, January 1964, p. 221.
60 Monteilhet, op. cit., pp. 25–6.

Chapter 6 L'Arme Savante: Republicanism in the artillery

1 AHG, E⁵90, 22 October 1840.
2 Ibid., D³, 8 June 1824.
3 Ibid., D³, 2 July 1825.
4 Ibid., D³, 23 August 1827.
5 Ibid., D³, 10 March 1828.
6 Ibid., D³, 22 March 1829.
7 Ibid., E⁵, 31 August 1830.
8 Ibid., E⁵18, 1 November 1831.
9 Ibid., E⁵18, 28 June 1833.
10 AN, CC 619, 23 March 1834.
11 Ibid., 4 April 1834.
12 AHG, E⁵64, 25 February 1835.
13 Ibid., E⁵79, 8 January and E⁵81, 17 September 1838.
14 Ibid., E⁵81, 2 June 1833.
15 Ibid., E⁵81, 26 January 1834.
16 Ibid., E⁵81, 22 May 1835.
17 Ibid., E⁵75, 16 March 1837.
18 F. Ponteil, *L'Opposition politique à Strasbourg*, p. 676.
19 AN, CC 767–8.
20 AHG, D³, 17 April 1830.

21 Ibid., E⁵52, 24 April 1834.
22 Ibid., E⁵147, 1836.
23 Ibid., E⁵147, 1 November 1831; AN, CC 619, 23 March 1834; CC 767–8.
24 AHG, C¹⁸47, 1837.
25 See AHG, E⁵, 20 March 1833; 7 March, 22 and 28 April 1834; 26 January 1835; 13 June 1838; 26 January and 12 February 1842; E⁵147 and 148.
26 AEP, 21 September 1831. Black armbands were worn in memory of those killed in the July revolution.
27 J. Callot, *Histoire de l'Ecole Polytechnique*, p. 72.
28 AEP, 31 May 1832.
29 Ibid., 15 May 1833.
30 Ibid., July–October 1833.
31 AHG, E⁵92, 29 January 1841.

32 Ibid., X^d 344.
33 A. Vagts, *A History of Militarism*, p. 45.
34 L. Susane, *Histoire de l'artillerie française*, p. 237.
35 B. Castellane, *Journal*, vol. 2, p. 373.
36 AHG, X^{d}344.
37 Ibid.
38 AN, CC 767.
39 AHG, E^{5}146.
40 Ibid., E^{5}65, 25 June 1835.
41 Devalez de Caffol, *Statistique militaire*, Paris, 1843, 21^e tableaux A^{21}.
42 Ibid., tableaux 17 and 18.
43 AHG, X^{d}638.
44 AN, CC 619.
45 See appendix III.
46 AHG, E^{5}36, 1 June 1833.
47 Ibid., X^{d}368.
48 Ibid., E^{5}147.
49 Ibid., X^{d}368.
50 Ibid., C^{18}47.
51 Ibid., E^{5}90, 23 October 1840.
52 Ibid., C^{18}47.

53 Ibid., E^{5}146.
54 Ibid., X^{d}368.
55 Ibid., X^{s}95.
56 *Sentinelle de l'armée*, 20 March 1835.
57 236 volunteers, 38 replacements, 94 conscripts and 10 who had been given their stripes as *récompensé national*. This list, compiled principally from the general correspondence of the War Ministry, AHG series E^5, represents only a sample. See appendix IV.
58 AHG, X^{d}368.
59 Ibid.
60 Ibid.
61 J. B. Boichot, *La Révolution dans l'armée française*, pp. 5–6.
62 AHG, X^{d}368.
63 See, for example, AHG, E^{5}87, 21 January; E^{5}78, 8 September; E^{5}49, 8 April; C^{18}47.
64 Ibid., X^{d}344.

Chapter 7   The Droits de l'Homme

1 AHG, E^{5}25, 15 May 1832.
2 Ibid., E^{5}25, 5, 14 and 15 June 1832.
3 14 and 16 August 1832.
4 13 August 1832.
5 AHG, E^5, 2 October, 14 November and 15 December 1832.
6 Ibid., E^{5}146.
7 Ibid., E^{5}38, 8 July 1833.
8 G. Weill, *Histoire du parti républicain en France, 1814–1870*, p. 87.
9 Ibid., p. 91.
10 Ibid.
11 Ibid., pp. 94–7.
12 AN, CC 619, 17 May 1834.
13 AHG, E^5, 27 April 1833.
14 *Le National*, 17 May 1834.

15 AHG, E^5, 16 April 1833.
16 Ibid., E^5, 24 and 27 November 1833.
17 Ibid., E^5, 27 November 1833.
18 Ibid., E^{5}62, 27 October 1834.
19 Ibid., E^5, 7 and 8 April, 22 and 28 May 1833.
20 Ibid., E^{5}36, 4 June 1833.
21 Ibid., E^{5}36, 5 June 1833.
22 Ibid., E^{5}36, 6 June 1833.
23 Ibid., E^{5}40, 13 August 1833.
24 Ibid., E^{5}36, 7 June 1833.
25 Ibid., E^{5}36, 13 June 1833.
26 AN, CC 619, 16 April 1833.
27 AHG, E^{5}35, 18 May 1833.
28 Ibid., E^5, 4 April 1833.
29 Ibid., E^5, 26 April 1833.
30 Ibid., E^{5}34, 9 and 15 May 1833.

31 Ibid., E⁵, 18 April 1833.
32 Ibid., E⁵45, 21 and 24 January 1834; E⁵55, 1 May 1834.
33 Ibid., E⁵147.
34 Ibid., E⁵36, 13 June 1833.

35 Ibid., E⁵, 18 March 1833.
36 Ibid., E⁵38, 10 July 1833.
37 Ibid., E⁵39, 17 July 1833.
38 Ibid., E⁵39, 27 July 1833.

Chapter 8   Lunéville, 1834

1 AHG, E⁵45, 23 January 1834.
2 Ibid., E⁵46, 25 and 26 February 1834; E⁵47, 2, 7 and 10 March 1834.
3 Ibid., E⁵49, 8 April 1834.
4 *Le National*, 30 April 1834.
5 AHG, E⁵47, 8 March 1834; E⁵51, 1 May 1834.
6 Ibid., E⁵50, 15 April 1834.
7 Ibid., E⁵47, 12 March 1834; E⁵45, 26 January 1834.
8 AN, CC 619, 2, 4 and 27 March 1834.
9 AHG, E⁵49, 8 April 1834. Marshal Canrobert reported that, as late as the Franco-Prussian War, the 13th refused to enter Nîmes. Bapst, op. cit., p. 143.
10 Ibid., E⁵49, 5 April 1834.
11 Ibid., E⁵49, 7 April 1834.
12 *Le National*, 18 April 1834.
13 AHG, E⁵50, 15th April 1834.
14 Ibid., E⁵49, 3 April 1834.
15 Ibid., E⁵147.
16 AN, CC 574.
17 Ibid.
18 AHG, C¹⁸46.
19 AN, CC 574.
20 AHG, E⁵46.
21 AN, CC 574.
22 AHG, E⁵50, 13 April 1834.
23 Ibid., E⁵52, 21 April 1834.
24 Ibid., E⁵50, Prefect of the Vosges report, 13 April 1834.
25 Ibid., E⁵57, 6 June 1834.
26 Ibid., E⁵55, 18 May 1834.
27 Ibid., C¹⁸46, 20 April 1834.
28 Ibid., E⁵57, 7 June 1834.

29 AN, CC 574.
30 See AHG, E⁵54, 10 May 1834 and E⁵59, 4 July 1834 for Noel's testimony and AN, CC 575 for Bernard's.
31 AHG E⁵52, 25 April 1934.
32 AN, CC 575, dossier Thomas.
33 AHG, E⁵49, 1 April 1834.
34 *Le National*, 3 May 1834.
35 AHG, E⁵49, 7 April 1834.
36 Ibid., E⁵49, 5 April 1834.
37 Ibid., Fonds Préval 1948.
38 Ibid., E⁵49, 1 April 1834.
39 Ibid., E⁵48, 21 March 1834.
40 AN, CC 619.
41 AHG, E⁵49, 8 April 1834.
42 Ibid., E⁵59, 4 July 1834.
43 AN, CC 574.
44 Ibid., CC 575.
45 AHG, E⁵54, 6 May 1834.
46 AN, CC 574.
47 132 artisans, 52 merchants or shop assistants, 35 students, 33 farmers, 26 day labourers, 18 ex-soldiers or seamen, 17 professional men, 13 property owners. This list is taken from series E⁵ of the War Archives and can be regarded as only a sample. See appendix IVb.
48 AHG, Xᵇ626 and 627.
49 AN, CC 575.
50 Ibid.
51 AHG, E⁵52, 21 April 1834.
52 Ibid., E⁵46, 23 February 1834.
53 Commissaire, *Mémoires et souvenirs*, vol. 1, p. 140.
54 AHG, C¹⁸46.
55 Ibid.

Notes

56 Ibid.
57 Ibid.
58 Ibid.

59 Ibid.
60 Ibid., E⁵147.

Chapter 9   Professional revolutionaries and secret societies, 1835–7

1 AHG, E⁵54, 5, 6 and 8 May 1834.
2 Ibid., E⁵54, 3 May 1834.
3 Ibid., 10 and 5 May 1834; E⁵59, 5 and 29 July 1834.
4 Ibid., E⁵54, 12 May 1834.
5 Ibid., 9 May 1834.
6 Ibid., E⁵55, 15 May 1834.
7 Ibid., E⁵54, 1 May 1834.
8 Ibid., E⁵55, 21 May 1834.
9 Ibid., E⁵64, 7 and 10 June 1835.
10 Ibid., E⁵66, 25 June 1835.
11 Ibid., E⁵67, 15 September 1835.
12 Ibid., E⁵68, 19 December 1835.
13 Ibid., E⁵68, 9 October 1835.
14 Ibid., E⁵64, 25 February 1835, 17 March 1835.
15 Ibid., E⁵65, 22 May 1835.
16 Ibid., E⁵65, 20 May 1835; E⁵68, 20 October 1835.
17 Ibid., 20 May 1835.
18 Ibid., E⁵67, 22 August 1835.
19 Ibid., E⁵51, 17 August 1830.
20 Ibid., E⁵147.
21 G. Perreux, La Propagande

républicaine au début de la monarchie de juillet, p. 364.
22 136 of 381 soldiers and NCOs arrested for republican activity during the July Monarchy had enlisted after July 1830. Ten of fifty-six NCOs arrested at Lunéville also joined the army after the revolution. These lists, compiled principally from AHG series E⁵ and AN, CC 574–5, can be regarded as only samples.
23 See appendix IVf.
24 AN, BB¹⁸1361.
25 See appendix VI.
26 AHG, E⁵147.
27 Ibid.
28 Ibid.
29 Ibid.
30 Ibid., E⁵148.
31 Ibid.
32 Ibid., E⁵75, 23 January and 6 February 1837.
33 Ibid., E⁵75, 3 and 14 February 1837; E⁵76, 28 April 1837.
34 Ibid., E⁵76, 16 May 1837.
35 Ibid., E⁵78, 8 September 1837.

Chapter 10   Strasbourg, 1836

1 J. P. T. Bury, Napoleon III and the Second Empire, p. 5.
2 F. Ponteil, L'Opposition politique à Strasbourg, 1830–1848, p. 431.
3 F. A. Simpson, The Rise of Louis Napoleon, pp. 90–1.
4 J.-J. Coulmann, Réminiscences, vol. 3, p. 406.
5 AN, CC 767.
6 Ibid.

7 Ibid., F⁷6780, dossiers Loir-et-Cher and Indre-et-Loire.
8 Ibid., CC 768.
9 Ponteil, op. cit., p. 480.
10 AN, CC 767.
11 Ibid.
12 Ibid.
13 Appendix Vg.
14 Ponteil, op. cit., p. 509.

15 AN, CC 768.

16 A. Sers, *Souvenirs 1786–1862*, p. 294.

17 Ponteil, op. cit., p. 524.

18 Ibid., p. 509.

19 AHG, F⁷6782, 18 January 1837.

20 Ibid., E⁵75, 21 February 1837.

21 Ibid., E⁵75, 16 March 1837.

Chapter 11   Conclusion

1   8 September 1841.

Unpublished sources

ARCHIVES HISTORIQUES DE GUERRE

General correspondence, D³ series for Restoration and E⁵ for July
 Monarchy.
Xᵇ Infantry.
Xᶜ Cavalry.
Xᵈ Artillery.
Xˢ Organization and administration of the army.
C¹⁸ cartons 45, 46 and 47 concern Strasbourg and Lunéville.
Fonds Préval, correspondence and official reports.
Regimental rosters.

ARCHIVES NATIONALES

CC 574, 575 & 619 Lunéville, 767 & 768 Strasbourg 1836.
F⁷ 6702 & 6703 on 1823 reserve call-up.
 6780 on Vendôme conspiracy, 1836.
BB¹⁸ Ministry of Justice.

ARCHIVES DE L'ECOLE POLYTECHNIQUE

General correspondence.
Student rosters.

General works

Annuaire de l'armée.
Archives parlementaires, 1888.
Galisset, *Corps du droit français*, 1833.
Cour des Pairs, *Affaire du mois d'avril, 1834*, 15 vols, 1834–6.
Ministère de l'Instruction Publique, *Statistique de enseignement primaire,
 1829–1877*, vol. 3, 1880.

Journals

Le Moniteur de l'Armée.
Le Moniteur Universelle.

Le National.
Le Spectateur Militaire.

Memoirs and contemporary works*

AMBERT, J., *L'Armée française en 1836.*
——*Soldat*, 1854.
——'Essais en faveur de l'armée', *Sentinelle de l'armée*, vol. 1, 1837.
ANNÉE, A., *Le Livre noir de la police politique*, 1829.
ARAGO, F., *Lettre sur les forts détachés*, 1833.
——*Histoire de ma jeunesse*, Brussels, 1854.
BACHELU GENERAL: *Opinion sur la situation en France*, 1831.
BARRÈS, J., *Memoirs of a Napoleonic Officer*, London, 1925.
BARREY, BARON E. DE, *Pétition à la chambre des députés sur l'armée et ses besoins*, 1828–9.
BARROT, O., *Mémoires*, vols 1 and 2, 1875–6.
BOICHOT, J. B., *La Révolution dans l'armée française*, Brussels, 1849.
——*Aux électeurs de l'armée*, 1850.
BOSQUET, P. F. J., *Lettres de Maréchal Bosquet à sa mère, 1829–1858*, Pau, 1877–9.
——*Lettres de Maréchal Bosquet à ses amis, 1837–1860*, Pau, 1879.
——*Lettres inédites*, Pau, 1895.
BOUVIER-DUMOLARD, *Compte rendu des événements qui ont eu lieu dans la ville de Lyon au mois de novembre 1831*, 1832.
BUGEAUD, MARÉCHAL T. R., *Lettres inédites*, 1922.
CABET, E., *La Justice d'avril, lettre à Guizot*, 1834.
——*Biographie populaire de l'armée*, 1840.
CARREL, A., 'De la guerre d'Espagne en 1823', *Revue française*, May 1828.
——*Oeuvres*, 4 vols, 1857.
CASTELLANE, GÉNÉRAL B., *Journal*, 5 vols, 1895.
CASTILLE, H., *Les Hommes et les moeurs en France sous la règne de Louis-Philippe*, 1853.
CAVAIGNAC, GÉNÉRAL E., *Les Deux Généraux Cavaignac, souvenirs et correspondance, 1808–1848.*
CAVAIGNAC, G. (ed.), *Paris révolutionnaire*, 4 vols, 1833–4.
CHAMBRAY, GÉNÉRAL G. DE, *L'Ecole polytechnique*, 1836.
CHARTON, E., *Guide pour le choix d'un état*, 1851.
CHENU, A., *Les Conspirateurs, les sociétés secrètes*, 1850.
CLAUZEL, MARÉCHAL B., *Observations*, 1831.
COMMISSAIRE, S., *Mémoires et souvenirs*, vol. 1, 1888.
CONSTANT, B. *Cour de politique constitutionelle*, 1818–20.
COULMANN, J.-J., *Réminiscences*, 3 vols, 1862–9.
COURCELLE, F., *Documents pour servir à l'histoire des conspirations de partis et de sectes*, 1831.
DEJEAN, MARÉCHAL DE CAMP, *Idées pour l'amélioration de la retraite des officiers*, 1828.
DELAHODDE, L., *Histoire des sociétés secrètes*, 1850.

* All books published in Paris, unless otherwise stated.

DELARUE, D., *Mes Réflexions sur le procès d'avril*, 1835.

DEVALEZ DE CAFFOL, *Statistique Militaire*, 1843.

DROUET D'ERLON, *La Vie militaire*, 1844.

DU BARAIL, F. C., *Mes Souvenirs*, vol. 1, 1894.

DUBARET, N. B. J., *Retraites*, Montpellier, 1843.

DU CASSE, A., *Scènes militaires*, 1857.

—— *Le Maréchal Marmont*, 1857.

—— *Souvenirs de Saint-Cyr et l'école d'état major*, 1886.

DURAND, F., *Des Tendances pacifiques de la société Européenne et la rôle des armées dans l'avenir*, 1841.

FANTIN DES ODOARDS, *Journal*, 1895.

GIRARDIN, E. DE, *Vue nouvelle sur l'application de l'armée aux grands travaux de l'utilité publique*, 1938.

—— *Des Révolutions et des reformes*, 1842.

GISQUET, H., *Mémoires d'un préfet de police*, 1840.

GRASILIER, V., *Simon Duplay et son mémoire sur les sociétés secrètes et conspirations sous la restauration*, 1913.

GRESSIER, M., *De l'organisation de l'armée*, 1830.

GUILLEMOT, J., *Lettres à mes neveux sur la chouannerie*, Nantes, 1858.

GUIZOT, F. P. G., *Mémoires pour servir à l'histoire de mon temps*, 8 vols, 1858–67.

D'HAUTPOUL, A., *Souvenirs*, 1904.

JANIN, GÉNÉRAL E. F., 'Coup d'œil impartial sur l'armée française', *Spectateur Militaire*, vol. 8, 1829, p. 471.

LA MOTTE ROUGE, *Souvenirs et campagnes*, vol. 1, 1889.

LAITY, A., *Le Prince Napoléon à Strasbourg*, 1838.

LAMARQUE, M., *Nécessité d'une armée permanente*, 1820.

—— *Esprit militaire*, 1826.

—— *Mémoires*, 2 vols, Brussels, 1835.

LARRÉGUY, F., *De la constitution de l'armée sous la monarchie de 1830*, 1840.

LEDRU-ROLLIN, *Discours politique et escrits divers*, 1879.

LEVÉ, SERGENT-MAJOR, *La Solde des sergents-majors d'infanterie*, 1827.

LOCMARIA, N., *Etat militaire en France*, 1831.

MADELAINE, P. DE LA, *Le Malaise actuel dans le corps d'artillerie*, 1829.

—— *De l'admission à l'école polytechnique*, 1833.

MARMONT, A., *Mémoires*, 9 vols, 1857.

—— *Esprit des institutions militaires*, 1863.

MORAND, GÉNÉRAL L., *L'Armée selon la charte*, 1829.

OUDINOT, MARÉCHAL C. N., *De l'armée selon son application aux travaux d'utilité publique*, 1845.

PAGNERRE, L. A., *Dictionnaire politique*, 1842.

PECQUEUR, C., *Des Armées dans leurs rapports avec l'industrie, la morale, et la liberté*, 1842.

PELLEPORT, P. DE, *Souvenirs*, 1857.

PONCET DE BERMOND, *La Garde royale en 1830*, 1830.

PRÉVAL, GÉNÉRAL C. DE, *Sur les retraites*, 1842.

—— *Du Droit au commandement*, 1844.

RÉMUSAT, C. DE, *Mémoires de ma vie*, 4 vols, 1858–62.

SAINT-CHAMANS, A., *Mémoires*, 1896.

SCUDO, P., *Les Partis politiques en Province*, 1838.
SERS, A., *Souvenirs, 1786–1862*, 1906.
SÈVE, A., *Souvenir d'un aumonier militaire, 1826–50*, Lyon, 1851.
THIERS, A., *La Monarchie de 1830*, 1831.
TOCQUEVILLE, A. DE, *De la democratie en Amérique*, 1835.
VALLEY, *L'Inégalité de donner l'école polytechnique à la ministère de la guerre*, 1832.
VIGNY, A. DE, *Servitude et grandeur militaires*, 1960.

Anonymous pamphlets

ARTILLERY

Observations relatives au personnel du Corps Royal d'Artillerie, 1825.
Position des officiers de génie, 1832.
Outrages contre les officiers d'artillerie, 1834.

HOUSING

'Du logement des militaires chez l'habitant', *Spectateur Militaire*, vol. 14, 1834, p. 176.
Situation du département de la guerre, 1831 and 1833.

PAY – PENSIONS

Etat militaire en 1825 (official report).
La Solde des capitaines de génie, 1829.
La Solde des capitaines du Corps Royal d'Artillerie, 1829.
Retraites, 1829.

SCHOOL

Saint-Cyr en 1834.

Secondary sources

AGUET, J. P., *Les Grèves sous la monarchie de juillet*, Geneva, 1954.
BAGGE, D., *Les Idées politiques en France sous la restauration*, 1952.
BAPST, G., *Les Premières Années du Maréchal de Mac-Mahon*, 1894.
—— *Le Maréchal Canrobert*, 4 vols, 1898.
BAUMONT, H., *Histoire de Lunéville*, 1900.
BEAU DE LOMÉNIE, E., *La Responsabilité des dynasties bourgeoises*, 4 vols, 1943–63.
BELHOMME, V., *Histoire de l'infanterie en France*, vol. 5, 1893–9.
BENOIT, A., 'Colmar en 1832–1833', *Revue d'Alsace*, 1896, p. 459.
BERTIER DE SAUVIGNY, G. DE, *Le Comte Ferdinand de Bertier et l'énigme de la congrégation*, 1948.
—— *La Conspiration des légitimistes et la Duchesse de Berry*, 1950.
—— *La Restauration*, 1955.

BERTIER DE SAUVIGNY, G. DE, 'Popular movements and political changes in nineteenth-century France', *Review of Politics*, no. 19, January 1957.

BLANC, L., *Histoire de dix ans*, 1841.

BONNAL, E., *Les Royalistes contre l'armée, 1815–1820*, 1906.

BOURGIN, G., *1848*, 1948.

BUCHEZ, P., *De la Carbonari au Saint-Simonisme*, 1966.

BURY, J. P. T., *Napoleon III and the Second Empire*, London, 1964.

CALLOT, J., *Histoire de l'Ecole Polytechnique*, 1960.

CARRIAS, E., *La Pensée militaire française*, 1960.

CASEVITZ, J., *La Loi Niel, une loi manquée*, Rennes, 1959.

CAUVIÈRE, J., *Discipline militaire et obéissance passive*, 1907.

CHALLENER, R. D., *The French Theory of the Nation in Arms, 1866–1939*, New York, 1955.

CHALMIN, P., *L'Armée de la IIe république*, La Roche sur Yonne, 1955.

—— *L'Officier français de 1815–1870*, 1957.

CHARLÉTY, S., *Histoire du Saint-Simonisme*, 1931.

CHARNAY, P., *La Société militaire et suffrage politique en France depuis 1789*, 1964.

CHOPPIN, H., *Pajol*, 1890.

COLLINET, M., 'Le Saint-Simonisme et l'armée', *Revue française de sociologie*, April–June 1961.

CONTAMINE, A., 'La Révolution de 1830 à Metz', *Revue d'histoire moderne*, vol. 6, 1931, p. 117.

—— *Metz et la Moselle de 1814 à 1870*, 2 vols, Nancy, 1932.

DAUMARD, A., *La Bourgeoisie parisienne de 1815 à 1848*, 1963.

DESLANDRES, M., *Histoire constitutionnelle de la France*, vol. 2, 1833.

DUVERGIER DE HAURANNE, *Histoire du gouvernement parlementaire en France*, 10 vols, 1857–72.

FERMÉ, A., *Procès de Strasbourg*, 1868.

FINER, S. E., *Man on Horseback*, London, 1962.

GAUTHEROT, G., *La Vendée de 1832*, 1926.

GIRARD, L., *Le Libéralisme en France, 1814–1848*, Cour de la Sorbonne, 1962.

—— *La Garde Nationale*, 1964.

GIRARDET, R., *La Société militaire, 1815–1839*, 1953.

GODECHOT, J., *Les Institutions de la France sous la révolution et l'empire*, 1951.

GONNET, P., 'Esquisse de la crise économique en France, 1827–1832', *Revue d'histoire économique et sociale*, vol. 33, 1955, pp. 249–92.

GOOCH, B. D., *The New Generals in the Crimean War*, The Hague, 1959.

GRISOT, GÉNÉRAL P. A., *La Légion Etrangère de 1831 à 1887*, 1888.

GUICHEN, E., *La Révolution de juillet 1830 et l'Europe*, 1917.

GUILLON, E., *Nos Ecrivains militaires*, 1898.

—— *Les Complots militaires sous la restauration*, 1905.

HARPAZ, E., *L'Ecole libérale sous la restauration*, Geneva, 1968.

HOWARD, M., *The Franco-Prussian War*, London, 1961.

HUEBER, E., *Du rôle de l'armée dans l'état*, 1872.

IBOS, P., *Le Général Cavaignac*, 1930.

IRVINE, D., 'The Prussian and French staff systems before 1870', *Journal of the American Historical Foundation*, no. 10, 1938, pp. 169–79.

ISAMBERT, G., *Les Idées socialistes en France, 1815–1848*, 1907.

JOHNSON, D., *Guizot*, London, 1963.

KELLER, E., *Général Lamoricière*, 1874.

KOVACS, A., 'French military institutions before the Franco-Prussian War', *American Historical Review*, January 1946, p. 217.

LABROUSSE, E., 'Comment naissent les révolutions', *Actes du congrès historique du centenaire de la révolution de 1848*, 1948.

LAVISSE, E., *Histoire de la France contemporaine*, 1926, vol. 4.

LEBEY, A., *Les Trois Coups d'état de Louis-Napoléon*, vol. 1, 1906.

LIDDELL HART, B. H., 'Armed forces and the art of war', *The New Cambridge Modern History*, vol. 10, chapter 12, Cambridge, 1960.

LUCAS-DUBRETON, J., *Le Culte de Napoléon*, 1960.

MATHIEZ, A., 'Prince Louis-Napoléon à Strasbourg', *Revue de Paris*, 1899, p. 305.

MONTAGNE, P., *Le Comportement politique de l'armée à Lyon*, 1966.

MONTEILHET, J., *Histoire des diverses lois sur le recrutement depuis la révolution jusqu'à nos jours*, 1902.

—— *Les Institutions militaires de la France*, 1936.

MORANGE, G., *Les Idées communistes dans les sociétés secrètes et dans la presse sous la monarchie de juillet*, 1906.

ORNANO, R., *Gouvernement et haut commandement en régime parlementaire français, 1814–1914*, Aix-Marseille, 1958.

PERREUX, G., *La Propagande républicaine au début de la monarchie de juillet*, 1931.

PHILBEAM, P., 'The emergence of opposition to the Orléanist Monarchy, August 1830–April 1831', *English Historical Review*, January 1970.

PINET, G., *Histoire de l'Ecole Polytechnique*, 3 vols, 1887.

—— 'Le Saint-Simonisme dans l'Ecole Polytechnique', *Revue de Paris*, 1894.

PINKNEY, D., 'The Revolution of 1830 as seen by a combatant', *French Historical Studies*, vol. 2, no. 2, autumn 1961.

—— 'A new look at the French Revolution of 1830', *Review of Politics*, 1961.

—— 'The crowd in the French Revolution of 1830', *American Historical Review*, 1964.

PONTEIL, F., *L'Opposition politique à Strasbourg, 1830–1848*, 1932.

POUTHAS, C., *Guizot pendant la restauration*, 1923.

—— 'Les Ministres de Louis-Philippe', *Revue d'histoire moderne et contemporaine*, vol. 1, April–June 1954, pp. 102–30.

—— *La Population française pendant la première moitié du XIXe siècle*, 1956.

RAISSON, H., *Histoire de la police*, 1844.

REDIER, A., *Aumoniers militaires français*, 1940.

REINHART, M., *Le Grand Carnot*, 1955.

REVOL, J., *Histoire de l'armée française*, 1929.

ROBERT-PIMIENTA, *La Propagande bonapartiste en 1848*, 1911.

ROUBAUD, A., 'Les Troubles de recensement sous la monarchie de juillet', *Bulletin mensuel de la société d'histoire moderne*, June 1914.

ROUSSET, C., *Le Marquis de Clermont-Tonnerre*, 1885.

RUDÉ, F., *Le Mouvement ouvrier à Lyon de 1827 à 1832*, 1945.

SCHLUMBERGER, J., *La Bourgeoisie alsacienne*, Strasbourg, 1967.

SCHNAPPER, B., *Le Remplacement militaire en France*, 1968.

sée, h., *La Vie économique sous la monarchie censitaire, 1815–1848*, 1927.
sencier, g., *Le Babouvisme après Babeuf*, 1912.
simpson, f. a., *The Rise of Louis Napoleon*, London, 1960.
six, g., *Les Généraux de la révolution et de l'empire*, 1947.
spitzer, a., *The Revolutionary Theories of Blanqui*, New York, 1957.
susane, l., *Histoire de l'artillerie française*, 1874.
tchernoff, i., *Le Parti républicain sous la monarchie de juillet*, 1901.
thirria, h., *Napoléon III avant l'empire*, 1895.
thoreau-dangin, p., *Royalistes et républicains sous la restauration*, 1874.
—— *Le Parti libéral sous la restauration*, 1876.
—— *Histoire de la monarchie de juillet*, 8 vols, 1888.
thoumas, c. a., *Les Transformations de l'armée française*, 2 vols, 1887.
titeux, e., *Histoire de la maison militaire du roi de 1814 à 1830*, 1889.
—— *Saint-Cyr et l'école spéciale militaire*, 1898.
trochu, l., *L'Armée française en 1867*, 1867.
tudesq, a. j., *Les Grands Notables sous la monarchie de juillet*, 1965.
tulard, j., *La Préfecture de police sous la monarchie de juillet*, 1964.
vagts, a., *A History of Militarism, Civil and Military*, New York, 1959.
vallée, g., *La Conscription dans le département de la Charente, 1798–1807*, 1936.
valynselle, j., *Les Maréchaux de la restauration et la monarchie de juillet*, 1962.
vidalenc, j., *Les Demi-Soldes*, 1955.
——'Hohenlohe', *Revue d'histoire moderne et contemporaine*, 1964.
weill, g., *Histoire du parti républicain en France, 1815–1870*, 1900.

Aide-Toi, 18, 34
Algeria, vii, 35, 52
Amis du Peuple, 50–1, 95
artillery, 37, 79–92 *passim*
associations nationales, 52–4, 81

barracks, 28–9, 60, 74
Barrès, 1, 4, 30, 33, 41–2
Béranger, 9, 18, 120
Berry, Duchess de, 56–7, 94
Bonaparte, Louis Napoleon, 80–1, 84, 114, 127–37 *passim*, 138
Bourmont, 30, 32, 34–5, 56–7
Bugeaud, 54, 86

Canrobert, 40–2, 49
Carbonari, 101–2
Carlists, 39, 42–3, 54–8, 93–6
Carrel, 2, 9–11, 16, 18, 34, 47, 49, 53, 93, 95, 116
Castellane, 7, 30, 39, 41, 47, 66
Chateaubriand, 3, 5, 17, 56
Clermont-Tonnerre, 30, 58, 82
conscription, 3, 13, 61–78 *passim*
conseil supérieur de la guerre, 31–2
Constant, 4–5, 20–1

Decazes, 5
demi-soldes, 48–9
Droits de l'Homme, 51, 95–7, 100–2, 105, 120–1, 124

engineers, 24–5, 85–6

Fieschi, 120
four sergeants of la Rochelle, 6, 10–11

Foy, 5, 14–15, 30, 82
Franchet-Despérey, 10–11, 21

Gérard, 28, 40, 47–8, 77
Gouvion-Saint-Cyr, 2–5, 14, 61–2, 82
Guizot, 2–3, 18, 63, 78, 136

Jourdan, 28, 62, 68–9

Lafayette, 5, 18–20, 50, 81, 116
Laffitte, 47, 52, 94, 116
Lamarque, 63, 70, 72, 75, 94, 128, 135
La Motte Rouge, 28, 39–40, 42, 48
Latour-Maubourg, 4
literacy, 91–2
Louis-Philippe, 47, 50, 52, 78, 96, 128, 133

Marmont, 1, 20, 30, 35–6, 65, 82
masonic lodges, 17–18, 99
Metz, Ecole d'Application d'Artillerie, 21, 24, 54, 80–6, 91

Napoleon II, 9, 11, 94, 128
National Guard, 18, 20, 37–8, 40, 52, 55, 57–9, 73–8, 95, 99, 104, 108
NCOs, 29, 37–9, 42–6, 86–7, 108–9, 112–13, 123, 133–5

pay, officers', 22–5, 31, 108–9; NCOs' and soldiers', 25–6, 31
pensions, 26–8, 53, 109, 116, 135
Périer, 18, 35, 51–3, 93–4, 97, 120
Polish officers, 51, 81, 99, 118

Polytechnique, Ecole, 24, 80–6, 91, 95, 98, 131
prévenus d'avril, 121
promotion, 4, 7–8, 27–8, 43–4, 108–13, 131, 133–4
Protestants, 89

'récompensé national', 121–2, 124, 126
recruitment, 87–9
regimental schools, 29–30
Rémusat, 37–9, 44
replacement, 3, 15, 65–6, 69, 90, 112
reserve, 3–4, 6–7, 11–16, 61–78 *passim*
Richelieu, 2, 5
Rouget, 48, 52, 55, 58–60
Royal Guard, 3, 6, 21, 30–3, 35–6, 49, 57–8

Saint-Chamans, 4, 10
Saint-Cyr, Ecole de, 81, 85–6, 96, 98
Saint-Simonists, 80, 98
Saumur, Ecole de cavalerie, 110
Separation law (*loi de disjonction*), 136
Société des Familles, 120
Soult, 28, 39, 47, 53–4, 60, 61–78 *passim*, 98, 122
Spanish War (1823), 6–7, 9–16 *passim*
Swiss Guard, 31–3, 35–6, 58, 64

Thiers, 34, 78, 136

Vaudrey, 129–30
de Villèle, 9, 20
volunteers, 62, 69, 90, 111–12, 126